GARDENS AND GARDEN CENTRES IN BRITAIN

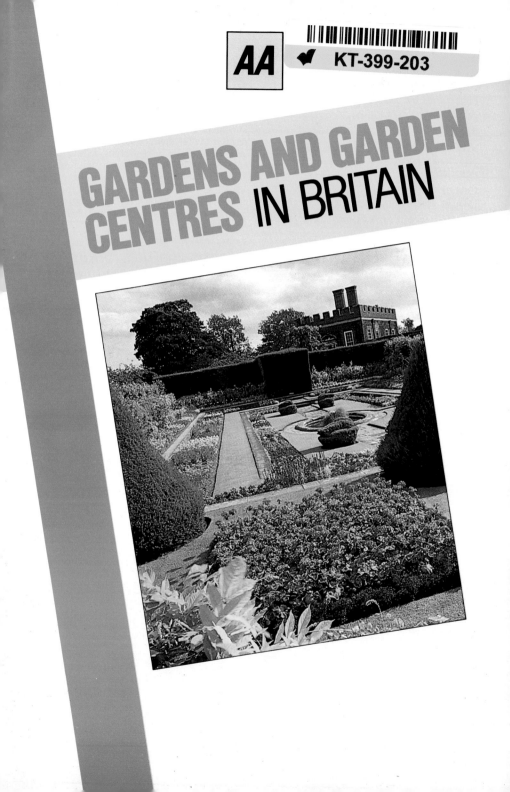

Editors: Penny Hicks & Jackie Rathband

Designer: Gerry McElroy

Illustrations by: Alan Roe

Directory compiled by: Pam Stagg and Karin Fancett

Maps: Prepared by the Cartographic Services Department of the Automobile Association

Cover Picture: Hampton Court Gardens (Martin Trelawny)

The Dark Secrets of the Labyrinth p.14 © Lindsay Heyes

Head of Advertisement Sales: Christopher Heard ☎ (0256) 20123 (ext 2020)

Advertisement Production: Karen Weeks ☎ (0256) 20123 (ext 3525)

Advertisement Sales Representatives: London, East Anglia, East Midlands, Central Southern and South East England: Edward May ☎ (0256) 20123 (ext 3524) or (0256) 467568
South West, West, West Midlands: Bryan Thompson ☎ (0272) 393296
Wales, North of England, Scotland: Arthur Williams ☎ (0222) 620267

Typeset by: Blackmore Press, Shaftesbury, Dorset.

Printed and bound in Great Britain by: Kingsdale Press, Reading, Berkshire.

Published by the Automobile Association, Fanum House, Basingstoke, Hampshire RG21 2EA.

ISBN 0 86145 506 1
AA Reference: 51965

CONTENTS

W hether you wish to explore the quiet tranquility of a garden or are looking for a particular plant for your garden, this new AA Guide to Gardens and Garden Centres will fit the bill.

The gardens featured in the book vary from beautiful and extensive landscapes to small cottage-style gardens; botanical collections, herbs, historic gardens and demonstration gardens. Some occupy the grounds of other attractions such as a stately home or museum.

Many of the gardens have special seasonal displays, they may be particularly renowned for their show of flowering shrubs in the spring; the arboretums in particular are ablaze with colour in the autumn.

If tending your own garden holds a greater appeal, you may be looking for a specific plant or garden accessories. In which case, refer to our directory of garden centres. Each entry will give all the information that you need, whether the garden centre specialises in a particular plant, or offers a wider range.

An A–Z index at the back of the book will help you to find the garden or garden centre you are looking for, and there is also a useful location atlas.

A display of old roses at Mottisfont Abbey.

A GARDEN OF OLD ROSES

By David Austin

The past twenty years has seen a great increase in Old Roses. Their soft colours, rich fragrance and more natural growth, have a strong appeal in an age that tends to be all too slick, mechanical and ordered. If we are lucky enough to have room to form a garden devoted to these roses, it should be possible to make something of great beauty.

Roses, even the Old Roses, are very much a man-made plant. Man has evolved them over the centuries to provide something quite different to their ancestors. The Old Roses, in spite of their rather haphazard and informal growth, are really best suited to a formal garden, or at least to the more formal areas of the garden.

Ideally, such a garden would be surrounded by a wall or hedge. Yew hedges are very suitable, as they provide the strict formality we require, and a dark background that shows off the flowers to perfection. Walls have the advantage that we can grow Climbing Roses upon them. They also provide protection for more tender roses like Noisettes, Teas and Banksian Roses. Failing this, trellis-work can be very effective and also provide support for Climbers.

Within this setting, it is possible to devise formal beds with paths. A border might run around the edges. The beds will take the small roses, while the border would be more suitable for the larger kinds. At the centre there should be a focal point. This might take the form of a piece of sculpture or a small pool with a fountain, or perhaps some form of structure to carry a Climbing Rose. Stone troughs, sun dials and numerous other objects can also be used.

Pathways may be of grass, gravel, paving stones, bricks; or perhaps paving or bricks with cobble-stones. If the beds can be edged with a small Box hedge, the picture will be complete.

If, surrounding this garden there are trees, of such a size and positioning that they do not shade it, then we shall have an added bonus. Such is the ideal formula; the centre point, surrounded by formal beds, filled with the informality of roses, surrounded by a formal hedge or wall or other structure, with this again surrounded by the billowing informality of trees. It is this contrast of the formal and the informal, that provides such a satisfactory effect.

Rosa Mundi — one of the oldest roses with a rich fragrance.

As to the varieties we should plant, there is no shortage of these. A great variety of Old Roses are obtainable from Old Rose specialists. All the following are pink except where otherwise stated. In the beds we might use Gallica Roses, with their short growth. Belle de Crecy, Belle Isis, Camaieux, Duchesse de Montebello, Empress Josephine, Jenny Duval, (*purple*), Officinalis, Rosa mundi (*striped*), Tuscany (*crimson*), are all good. Many Centifolias and Moss Roses are also not excessively large.

Three pretty little miniature flowered varieties spring immediately to mind; Burgundy Rose, De Meaux, Petite de Hollande. Amongst the larger flowered kinds; Centifolia itself, Chapeau de Napoleon, Ipsilante, could be used. Moss Roses include, General Kleber, Little Gem (*crimson*) Mme. de la Roche Lambert (*crimson*), Mousseline, Old Pink Moss, Shailer's White Moss.

For the surrounding borders we might plant the delicately coloured Alba Roses, with their grey-green foliage. Nearly all of these are first class; Alba Semi-Plena, Celestial, Felicite et Parmentier, Mme. Legras de St. Germain, Maidens Blush, and Queen of Denmark, particularly so. We then have the taller Centifolias, like Tour de Malakoff, in a mixture of parma-violet, lavender and grey, Fantin-Latour and Blanchfleur; while amongst the Moss Roses, Gloire des Mousseux, Comtesse du Murinais and William Lobb (*crimson purple*), are suitable.

Having gone this far with our selection, we are faced with a problem, the fact that Old Roses flower only in late June and early July. It is only the more recent roses that repeat flower throughout the summer. We should, I think, not be too strict in our interpretation of 'old'. While it would be inappropriate to mix these with Hybrid Tea and Floribundas, with their rather stiff, short growth, and often brilliant colours, it

The free-flowering Rosa Raubritter forms a low-sprawling bush.

would be entirely suitable to use more recent Shrub Roses like the Hybrid Musks, Rugosas and certain Modern Shrub Roses. The Hybrid Musks might include, Buff Beauty (*apricot*), Penelope (*blush-pink*), and Vanity (*deep pink*). Rugosas should include, Blanc Double de Coubert (*white*) Roseraie de l'Hay (*crimson purple*), and Fimbriata, with its small pink, fringed flowers. There are also some Bourbon Roses which are in fact old, and have some ability to repeat flower. Mme. Isaac Periere, with huge mader-crimson flowers, Gloire de Ducher (*rich purple*), and Honorine de Brabant (*a striped rose*). All these are larger shrubs suitable for the outer border.

When we come to look for smaller roses suitable for mixing in the beds, we are more restricted in our choice. Little White Pet is an excellent low growing pompom rose, The Fairy, with its salmon-pink flowers like those of a Rambler, continuing well into the autumn. Then we have some small Bourbons; Louise Odier (*pink*), Souvenir de la Malmaison (*blush*), La Reine Victoria (*rose-pink*) and its sport Mme. Pierre Oger, which is paler, Reine des Violettes in violet and purple, and Boule des Neige, of an exquisite silky white.

In recent years, I myself have been engaged in hybridising Old Roses with modern varieties. The object has been to combine the charm, form and fragrance of the Old Rose, with the repeat flowering habit of the Modern Hybrid Tea. I have called these 'English Roses'. They are in fact new versions of Old Roses, or to put it another way, new roses in the old style. All are very fragrant and have much of the charm of the true Old Rose.

An old rose garden need not consist entirely of roses, indeed I would go as far as to say it should not. Other plants, however, should never be allowed to dominate the roses, they should be selected to complement and enhance them.

I should like to close by saying that we do not have to have a garden for Old Roses, we can of course have Old Roses in the garden. Old Roses fit happily into the general garden scheme. Their gentle colours and informal growth rarely clash with other flowers, and they usually look entirely at home. Even here they are perhaps best suited to the more formal areas of the garden, particularly those nearest to the house.

Gardens open to the public, that contain good displays of Old Roses, are now quite numerous. Outstanding amongst these are Mottisfont Abbey, Sissinghurst Castle, Hidcote Manor, Castle Howard and Mannington Hall Gardens. There are also good collections at the R.H.S. Gardens at Wisley and the R.N.R.S. at St Albans. Amongst the nurseries, Peter Beales Roses have a display garden containing numerous varieties, as do my own nursery — David Austin Roses at Bowling Green Lane, Albrighton, Wolverhampton.

David Austin is Proprietor of David Austin Roses, specialising in Old and Shrub Roses, as well as Climbers. His book, '**The Rose**', will be published by The Antique Collector's Club, in 1987.

CREATING A BOG GARDEN

By Mary Stiller

A small patch of moisture loving plants can make a charming feature in the garden, but the vagaries of our British weather — we do sometimes have a hot dry summer — can spell disaster unless the bog garden is properly made. It is tempting if you have a waterlogged spot to fill it with marsh plants, but often such places though wet in winter dry out and bake hard in summer, just when the plants need water most. The soil of a natural bog is deep, rich and supplied with water all the year, but there is some drainage too so that it does not become stagnant. If you are lucky enough to have such a spot there is a wealth of beautiful plants which you can grow. If not you must create just those conditions — permanent moisture, some drainage and good rich soil.

The ideal place for a bog garden is beside a stream or pond, so if you are making a pool, include a boggy bit in your plan, or just make a bog on its own. It will look more natural in the lowest part of the garden but should not be too far from a water supply as it is bound to need filling up sometimes. A good way is to bury a length of hose or alkathene pipe, running from near a tap to the bog. Choose a spot which gets some sun, although most of the plants will tolerate part shade, the flowers look prettier in dappled light. Don't be too ambitious, large areas of waterlogged soil are difficult to weed, so plan the shape so that you can reach the centre easily.

Now the great work can begin. Mark out the shape on the ground and dig out the soil to a depth of 12 ". If you are digging it out of the lawn, skim off the grass with about 2 " of soil, these turves will come in handy later. Slope the sides of the hole and line it with a sheet of 500 gauge polythene. Unless you want to grow plants which need to stand in water, the polythene can stop a few inches below soil level so that it will be hidden. In areas of high rainfall it is advisable to jab a few holes in the lining to get some drainage. Cover the bottom with a 3 " layer of pebbles, then a similar layer of peat or manure, or those grass turves upside down. Enrich the soil you dug out by mixing some manure, peat or garden compost with it. Failing that add some hoof-and-horn and bonemeal, 2–4oz to a barrowload.

After the hard work of excavation comes the fun of choosing the plants. There are so many which like to have their toes in moisture so here is just a small selection. Perhaps the best known is marsh-marigold, like a large golden buttercup. Choose the neater double-flowered form Caltha palustris plena for a small garden, it grows well in water or wet soil. Astilbes are not for the boggiest spot but flourish in rich moist soil. They flower in July/August, fluffy red, pink or white blooms with fern like leaves. The tallest and easiest of the Iris family is Iris pseudacorus, yellow flag. Too big for the small garden but the striped leaf of Iris pseudacorus 'Variegata' is useful in a large area. Iris sibirica is not so rampageous, it can be grown in ordinary soil but loves moisture. The clusters of blue flowers sit like butterflies on top of a 2½' stem. Iris laevigatus has beautiful blue or purple flowers. It is happiest standing in water or very moist soil unlike Iris kaempferi which must be dry in winter and hates lime in the soil, a difficult plant. Hemerocallis are very easy. The large lily-like flowers come in a range of colours and stand out well

Above left: the Bog Garden at Oxford Botanic Gardens, below: Astilbes and Hostas at Savill Gardens.

against the grassy leaves in July and August. Very different are the striking yellow sheaths of Lysichtum americanum which appear suddenly in the spring. They are followed by large coarse leaves which make it unsuitable where space is restricted, though the white flowered Lysichitum camschatense is smaller. Lysimachia nummularia 'Aureum' on the other hand is little and good, a bright carpet of golden leaves. The yellow saucer shaped flowers, which are strung along the creeping stems, show up better on the green leaved form but it is rather invasive. Lysimachia vulgaris, spikes of yellow flowers and Lysimachia clethroides, white, are both taller plants 2–3' high which flower in July/August. In late summer the banks of many rivers are lined with purple loosestrife, the variety 'Robert' is smaller and neater with clear pink spikes, an excellent plant for a small bog. So too are the members of the musk family; Mimulus guttatus is a charming little plant with yellow flowers but the red and orange varieties such as

The curious Skunk Cabbage.

Whitecrofts Scarlet are not so robust. There are several primulas which thrive in damp places. Primula denticulata flowers April/May, round ball heads in shades of pinky purple and white on stiff stalks. Primula japonica comes a little later, whorls of red purple or pink flowers 18" high, followed in June/July by the drooping yellow flowers of Primula florindae, all easy plants to grow. Equally accommodating is Trollius, the globe flower, in all its shades of yellow and orange, like many petalled buttercups. In colour contrast though later in the year, the blue flowers of Gentiana asclepiadea sway on 18" stems. Hostas are a must for any garden, the sculptured and patterned leaves are a feature all summer, the lily like flowers an added bonus, plant them at the drier edges of the bog as they don't like to be too wet in winter.

There are many places to visit which feature bog plants and water gardens, notably Longstock Gardens Hampshire. The Saville Gardens in Windsor Great Park, Wisley Gardens in Surrey, Oxford Botanic Gardens and Hidcote Gardens, Gloucestershire, to name but a few. To see a wide range of plants visit a water garden nursery such as Stapeley Water Gardens, Nantwich, Cheshire.

Mary Stiller is the Manager of Waterperrys Garden Centre at Waterperry. She co-presented the TV programme Gardeners' World for two years, and frequently lectures and runs short training courses for amateur gardeners.

Iris Pseudacorus (Yellow Flag).

A display of Primulas at Wakehurst Place.

10

CREATING A CULINARY HERB GARDEN

By Simon Hopkinson

Herbs can offer an infinite variety of colours, scents and uses. They cross all recognised plant boundaries, for example a herb can be a shrub, herbaceous, evergreen, annual, perennial or even a tree such as Bay or Juniper.

Today we think of a herb as a plant which has a use — culinary, scented, medicinal or dye, and it is amazing just how many plants in the average garden fall into one or some of these categories. However, when it is decided that a 'Herb Garden' is called for, most beginners will opt for a culinary herb garden as their introduction to these fascinating plants.

A specific garden to provide plants to cook with must be simple to use, and sensibly positioned — preferable a site near the kitchen door as herbs should, where possible, always be used fresh and are often needed at the last minute. Pathways, both to the garden, and within it should be of stone or brick, with smaller dissecting paths between the plants to allow for easy access to all the herbs, with-

out having to walk on the beds at all. Most culinary herbs need plenty of sun to enhance the essential oils that give the flavours, therefore a site which is south facing will give many of the Mediterranean herbs, such as rosemary and thyme,

Top: An attractive border of herbs, below: Variegated Lemon Balm.

summer warmth with winter protection and shelter from wind. If it is not possible to position the garden in a warm sheltered spot, some protection can be created by planting a hedge of yew or sweet briar or perhaps erecting a trellis on which to grow lovely scented climbing roses and honeysuckles.

Selecting the herbs to make up the garden is essentially a matter of personal choice, however there are a number of useful considerations to bear in mind;

1 Should there be provision made for filling more than one section with the same herb? Parsley for example should be used with abundance and perhaps should have extra space.

2 Some of the non-invasive, less frequently used herbs can be grown within the same section.

3 Many of the common herbs have ornamental forms which can all be used to great effect within the garden, to give colour and added interest to a fairly green garden, and these can all be used in cooking to replace the green cousins. Examples of these are Red Sage, Bronxe fennel or Variegated Lemon Balm.

4 Space should be left for the annual herbs which should be available for the summer months. Seeds of herbs such as Dill, Chervil, Coriander and Basil can all be sown direct in the garden at intervals to give a continuous crop throughout the season.

The Plan

Our garden plan is based on our own design using simple formal shapes and readily available materials. The success of this design was rewarded by a gold medal at the Chelsea Flower Show in 1986, where we exhibited it for the first time. One of the great features of this garden is that it allows the planner to use the whole scheme or if space is tight the garden could be cut in half or down to a quarter. Having selected the site the ground should be levelled and cleared of weeds, and the appropriate size marked out. A suitable paving stone must be found — any finish will do but the size should be 18″ × 18″, and these should then be laid around the garden to make a perimeter path. The garden should then be dissected using paving bricks. These

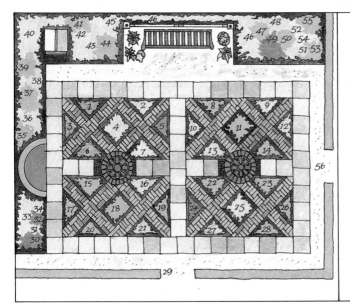

KEY TO PLANTING

1 Alpine Strawberries 2 Sweet Cicely 3 Coriander 4 Bay
5 Rocket 6 Fennel 7 Borage
8 Applemint 9 French Parsley
10 Bronze Fennel 11 Bay
12 Red Sage 13 French
Tarragon 14 Spearmint
15 Rosemary 16 Red Orach
17 Lemon Thyme 18 Bay
19 Sage 20 Sorrel 21 Parsley
22 Dill 23 Chervil 24 Tansy
25 Bay 26 Thyme 27 Golden
Marjoram 28 Chives 29 Box
hedging 30 *Salvia grahamii*
31 Southernwood 32 Borage
33 Lovage 34 *Rosa gallica*
35 Variegated Meadowsweet
36 Lemon Verbena 37 Poppies
38 Red Sage 39 Sweet Rocket
40 Comfrey 41 Verbascum
42 Nasturtium 43 Curry Plant
44 *Geranium macrorrhizum*
45 Soloman's Seal 46 Ladies
Mantle 47 Rosemary 48 Rose
'Mme. Caroline Testout'
49 Jacob's Ladder 50 Bronze
Bugle 51 Cowslips and Pasque
Flowers 52 Angelica
53 Variegated Lemon Balm
54 *Salvia elegans* 55 Juniper
56 Thymes and Heartsease

Hollington's award-winning Chelsea Garden.

are similar to a house brick, but thicker and stronger and made to cope with heavy frosts. Both brick and stone should be laid on a sand and cement base to prevent them moving when walked on.

A possible option, to be sited on the places where the paths intersect would be to place a birds bath and sundial, both traditional accessories in a herb garden, which would give structural effect and complement the stonework. Colours for the brick and paving are a matter of personal choice and finance, however a stone with a very pale pink tinge really sets off the green foliage of the herbs.

The basic culinary herbs that no garden should be without, make the backbone of the planting scheme. We think you must include the following: **Perennials:** (herbs which once planted will live from year to year) Rosemary, Sage, Bay, Thyme, Mint, Tarragon, Chives and Marjoram.
Annuals: (*Herbs which need sowing each spring*) Basil, Coriander, Borage, Dill, Parsley and Chervil.

If half the plan were used, these 14 herbs would exactly fill the places in the garden. The drawing shows the full scheme with 28 sections with a suggested planting plan that includes other useful herbs.

Once the herb garden is established, it should be relatively easy to look after — two major tidy-ups a year are all that are really needed. The Spring is the time to prune and cut back tatty plants, and to split any over grown herbaceous herbs. Annual seeds can be sown once the soil has started to warm up and the beds have been raked and levelled. The late autumn is best for cutting down the herbaceous plants, tidying and clearing the annual beds and weeding as needed. A mulch of well-rotted manure could be spread over the beds in the spring or Autumn, to suppress weeds and conserve moisture.

Simon Hopkinson and his wife Judith are the owners of Hollington Nurseries near Newbury in Berkshire. The nursery, which specialises in herbs, has in recent years won several medals at the Chelsea Flower Show.

13

THE DARK SECRETS OF THE LABYRINTH

By Lindsay Heyes

I have often heard it said that one should tread *"reverently"* around a maze, which is surprising in such special gardens — surely the only formal gardens designed for fun! Yet a Dorset witch was hanged for dancing on one, a hint of a secret past for mazes which can only really be appreciated by visiting them.

Mazes are not just fun, they can be very beautiful and many form an outstanding feature of country gardens. Those at Hever Castle, Kent and Somerleyton Hall, Suffolk are wonderful examples of a style which could so easily have fallen to the landscape schemes of 'Capability' Brown. They are perhaps typical of everyman's concept of a maze, but I would like to give you more of an idea of their rich variety. For example, they don't always have hedges (*there are over 300 mazes in Sweden alone without a hedge between them!*), and not all are part of a formal arrangement.

Our Victorian ancestors had the wrong idea about mazes altogether, thinking that they should get lost, an ungratifying experience indeed! We can blame the Earl of Stanhope for this, a mathematics buff whose maze at Chevening was in fact two, one inside the other. For such enthusiasts I recommend a visit to Longleat House, where the maze is just about the limit (*Margam Park near Swansea is another*). These are solved best by the Algorithm of Tremeaux, devised by a French mathematician and more commonly used to determine routing of silicon chip micro-conductors.

Kentwell Hall Maze inspired by the Tudor Rose.

A recent fashion in maze design gives the pattern significance, perhaps taking a coat of arms as a motif. A good example at Kentwell Hall in Suffolk has the theme of the Tudor Rose as the source of its inspiration. At the Beazer gardens in Bath there is a new maze without hedging — in this way then you can enjoy a complicated maze without the frustration of being confined.

Such mazes are more complicated than the "Labrynths of Love" which were popular in the 16th and 17th centuries. The oldest remaining example in Britain is at Hampton Court Palace, dating from 1690. Whilst you are there stroll around the Queen's art collection, and you'll see a painting of a maze showing a style of maze popular around 1600, with hedges only hip high, of simple design.

Low hedges have led many to think mazes developed from knot gardens, but they have a far more interesting past related to the way Christian missions dealt with heathenism. England provides the best examples to show how fertility rites involving human sacrifice evolved into part of Christian divine service and later, with the dark past forgotten, became the garden curiosity we see today.

Federigo II used a medieval Christian pattern of a maze to symbolise discretion and the pitfalls of romantic love, and the first garden maze filled a courtyard of his Palazzo de Te in Mantua in 1530, setting the modern fashion. Puzzle mazes were invented less than a century before, by misinterpretation of a description of the labyrinth of Theseus. Prior to that there were only three types: Christian; Roman; and Cretan types — none were puzzles (nor were they buildings), all were hedgeless dance floors or talismans.

At Hereford Cathedral *Mappa mundi* is one of the oldest maps of the world. On the island of Crete its Norman cartographer drew a labyrinth,

The Famous turf Maze at Wing.

which a guidebook says is a series of concentric circles, but look closely — the pattern is the same as the turf maze at Wing in Leicestershire, or another set in the stone floor at Chartres Cathedral, and others at Alkborough, Humberside, and Breamore, Hampshire. There are dozens in the turf of England and the floors of French churches. Norman invaders brought the pattern to England, bringing with them an Easter Dance which involved handing a globe between the Chapter and his novices, to the tune of *"Victimae paschali laudes"*, a sequence rooted in folk dances, still part of the liturgy. It survived the Inquisition, and was performed until 1690 in spite of episcopal protests about its heathen origin.

Pope Gregory the Great instructed missionaries to adapt heathen practices instead of destroying them. The Sacred Spring Wedding, which we know from the sagas was connected with maze dances, fertility and human sacrifice, became Christian Easter, named after the fertility goddess Eostre. The Maze dances took place on Cretan patterned mazes which can be traced back to the dawn of Indo-European agriculture.

15

Rock carvings of mazes at Rock Valley in Cornwall dating from 1800 to 1400 B.C., demonstrate that mazes came here with Bronze Age prospectors from the Mediterranean. They are thus older than the oldest Cretan mazes, and possibly as old as the origins of the tale of Theseus. This original pattern survives as a turf maze at Brandsby, North Yorkshire; laid out with pebbles in India; and carved on rocks in Arizona.

Names for mazes like *"City of Troy"* and *"Julian's Bower"* indicate that they existed during the Roman occupation, and their location outside churches shows that Christian pattern mazes were only Norman replacements for earlier ones in a country with a tradition of outdoor worship. The Romans brought a different type of maze with them, that of the mosaic at Caerleon, Gwent, connected with magically guaranteeing imperial security (although the Romans also carried out maze dances, on horseback, until well into Christian times).

Not surprisingly, the Roman pattern never displaced the Cretan original in England, but why did Christians invent a new pattern when they had been happy to use the older type? The answer lies in events like this: In 911 A.D. the Viking Eric Bloodaxe led a raid on the minor kingdom of Archenfield — he kidnapped a Bishop, ransomed him for £40, camped at Symonds Yat (now in Herefordshire) and was driven off after a battle at a place still called The Slaughter. Christendom felt gravely threatened.

Embarrassingly, both Christians and heathens used spring maze dances. It was too easy for heathens to convert Christians, so Christians designed a new maze to replace the Cretan one and so distance the religions. Within a century of Eric's raid it was a Viking, King Cnut, who outlawed heathenism in England, missionaries having converted their enemies, replacing human sacrifice with the *'sacrifice'* of the Son of God, who was made man, for all men.

So remember, when you play with your children in a maze in an English Country Garden, or walk around arm in arm with romance on your mind enjoying the illuminations at my own maze at Symonds Yat one summer's eve — you are never far from the history of these islands, which have seen mazes of different types for nearly 3,000 years.

Lindsay Heyes and his brother, Edward, designed and built the award-winning Jubilee Maze at Symonds Yat in the Wye Valley in 1977. Their maze and Museum of Mazes have become popular tourist attractions.

The Beazer Gardens Maze at Bath.

Bressingham.
The Plant Centre for the discerning gardener.

If you want to make the very most of your garden, take a trip to Bressingham Plant Centre.

The centre that can offer you a superb range of finest quality plants, combined with the expertise and friendly service of skilled horticulturalists.

Our recently extended development now includes a superb modern 'Garden Pavilion' which has its very own houseplant section, a comfortable refreshments area with facilities for the disabled and a gardening shop specialising in plant- associated gifts.

Within the spacious and imaginative layout, you'll also find a wide selection of rare, unusual and specimen garden plants from all over the world.

So make a visit to Bressingham Plant Centre soon. And just watch how your garden grows.

| EASY ACCESS | ALL DAY REFRESHMENTS | TOILETS |

Bressingham
PLANT CENTRE

Bressingham Plant Centre is open every day from 10.00 am to 5.30 pm. Situated on the A1066 Thetford to Diss road. Bressingham, Diss, Norfolk, IP22 2AB. Tel Bressingham (037 988) 8133.

ABOUT THE BOOK

In this book we list hundreds of gardens and garden centres to visit and try to provide as much information as possible for the intending visitor.

The directory is listed in alphabetical order of town or location. The only exception to this rule is when the establishment is on an island, eg Arreton, Isle of Wight would be under Wight, Isle of. As far as possible, gardens and garden centres situated within a short distance of a town or village are placed under the nearest town or village heading. However, some are too remote for this to be done, and such places are listed under their own name. Should you be in any doubt about a particular place, the comprehensive index at the back of the book will indicate where it can be found.

Atlas
If you are planning to visit a garden or garden centre in a particular area, you might find it useful to refer in the first instance to the atlas at the back of the book, which pinpoints all of the establishments that we list. A useful key at the front of the atlas section will help you to find the area you require. Each entry in the directory also gives a map reference which includes the atlas page number and grid code (see page 176). An open circle on the atlas indicates that the establishment indicated is a garden centre. A solid dot indicates that the establishment is a garden.

Opening dates
The dates quoted in the gazetteer are inclusive, so that Apr–Oct indicates that the establishment is open from the beginning of April to the end of October.

Telephone
Unless otherwise stated the telephone exchange given in the directory is that of the town under which the establishment is listed. Where the exchange for a particular establishment is not that of the town under which it appears the name of the exchange is given after the telephone symbol ☎ and before the dialling code and number.
In some areas telephone numbers are likely to be changed by British Telecom during the currency of this publication. If you have any difficulty it is advisable to check with the operator.

Disabled persons
If the wheelchair symbol ﹠ is shown in the entry it means that the property has suitable access for wheelchair-bound visitors. If the wheelchair symbol is followed by (wc) this means that the establishment has suitable purpose-built toilets.

Garden centres
Our directory of garden centres includes only those which belong to the British Group of International Garden Centre Ltd, acknowledged as the yardstick for quality in this field of business. Certain basic requirements must be met by any centre wishing to join the group, and these are explained by the British Group Director, David Nichol, on page 126. We would also like to clarify a few of the facilities which we mention in the directory.

Landscaping
This means that a landscaping service is offered to customers.

Advisory service
Resident experts are on hand to answer any questions and give help with garden planning.

Mail order
Plants and/or goods are available by post.

Delivery
A delivery service is offered, but this may be confined to the local area and will usually only apply to large items.

Gift vouchers
Gift vouchers can be bought or redeemed against goods bought at the garden centre. These may be part of a national network offering gift vouchers which can be redeemed all over Britain.

Discounts
Some of the garden centres offer special discounts to members of gardening and/or horticultural clubs on production of their membership card.

Refreshments
We include the symbol ♖ where a garden centre offers refreshments, but this may mean anything from drinks and ice cream to a full restaurant.

_____Symbols and abbreviations_____

P	Parking (at establishment, unless otherwise stated)	ch 20p	Children 20p
♖	Refreshments and/or restaurant	ch15 20p	Children under 15 20p
⅂	Picnic area	NCCPG	National Council for the Conservation of Plants & Gardens
✘	No dogs	NGS	National Gardens Scheme
🚌	No coaches	NT	National Trust
☎	Telephone number	NTS	National Trust for Scotland
♿	Suitable for visitors in wheelchairs	Pen	Senior Citizens
♿ (wc)	Purpose-built toilets for wheelchair bound visitors	Party	Special or reduced rates for parties booked in advance
AM	Ancient Monument	Party 30+	Special or reduced rates for parties of 30 or more booked in advance
BH	Bank Holidays		
PH	Public holidays	reg unemp	Reduced rate on production of UB40
Etr	Easter		
ex	except	wc	Toilets
Free	Admission free	Wknds	Weekends
10p	Admission 10p	→	Entry continued overleaf

Aster novi-belgii

Abbey Dore

Hereford and Worcester   Map 3 SO33

ABBEY DORE COURT GARDEN
☎ *Golden Valley (0981) 240419*

A 4-acre garden, bordered by the River Dore, which is being extended to accommodate an increasing number of unusual plants and shrubs. The emphasis here is on herbaceous plants and ferns. Home of the N.C.C.P.G. National Sedum and Euphorbia Collections. Most plants are labelled.

Open mid-March–31 Oct 11–6, closed Wed.

£1 (ch 25p).
P ⚑ ✹ ♿ wc *Plants for sale*

Abbotsbury

Dorset   Map 3 SY58

ABBOTSBURY GARDENS
Beach Rd ☎ *(0305) 871387*

Many unusual trees and tender shrubs in 20 acres of sub-tropical gardens near Chesil beach. The mild climate encourages early spring displays of camellias, azaleas, rhododendrons and magnolias which are followed by shrub roses and hydrangeas in the summer. There are palms, eucalyptus and myrtle trees, and a stream and ponds with moisture-loving plants.

* Open 16 Mar–19 Oct, daily 10–6.

* £1.50 (ch 50p, pen £1) Party.
P

Aberdeen

Grampian *Aberdeenshire*   **Map 15 NJ90**

CRUICKSHANK BOTANIC GARDEN
University of Aberdeen
☎ *(0224) 40241 ext 5250 or 5247*

A University botanic garden with 11 acres of lawn, specimen trees and shrubs, and collections of plants for research and teaching. The oldest features of the garden are the long herbaceous border, and the sunken garden with conifers, rhododendrons and heathers. Recent additions include the rock garden and patio garden, with work under way on a new rose garden.

Open all year Mon–Fri 9–4.30, also Sat & Sun May–Sep 2–5.

Free.
P (100 yds) ♿

Aberfeldy

Tayside *Perthshire*   **Map 14 NN84**

CLUNY GARDENS
☎ *(0887) 20795*

A 30-year-old wild woodland garden facing NE with an outstanding collection of plants, mainly from the Himalayas. Some fine species of trees from a previous planting include a pair of Sequoia Gigantea, one of which has a girth of 34ft 3in (the widest in Britain). Guided tours for coach parties by arrangement.

Open Mar–Oct daily 10–6.

£1 (ch under 16 free).
P ✹ *No pushchairs. Plants for sale*

Albrighton

Shropshire   Map 7 SJ80

DAVID AUSTIN ROSES
Bowling Green Lane ☎ *(090722) 3931*

Plant centre famous for its very extensive range of old, modern and English roses. Also herbaceous perennials, irises and many unusual varieties of paeonies.
See special feature on page 5.

Open Feb–Nov Mon–Fri 9–5, Sat, Sun & BH 10–6; Dec & Jan Mon–Fri 9–5, Sat 10–dusk, Sun 12–dusk. Closed from mid-Dec to 2nd week in Jan.

P ⚑ wc

Campanula medium
'Canterbury Bell'

Alcester
Warwickshire   Map 4 SP05
RAGLEY HALL
(2m SW) ☎ *(0789) 762090*

The present garden of 17th-century Ragley Hall was laid out in 1874. The main rose garden occupies a series of shallow terraces to the west of the house and is a fine example of high Victorian gardening. Lawns, trees and shrubs make up the remainder of the garden which is surrounded by a large park. Some plants labelled. House also open.

Open 12 Apr–4 Oct: Gardens & Park Tue–Thu, Sat & Sun 12–5.30 (Jun–Aug 10–6); House Apr–Sep Tue–Thu, Sat & Sun 1.30–5.30 (ex Tue–Thu in Jun–Aug 12–5.30) also open BH Mon.

Garden and park £1.90 (ch 90p); Garden, park and house £2.90 (ch £1.90, pen £2.40) Party 30+.

P ⚐ *(licensed)* ⅋ ✖

Alresford
Hampshire   Map 4 SU53
HINTON AMPNER
entrance on A272 1m W of Bramdean
☎ *Bramdean (9279) 344*

This 1,640-acre estate was left to the NT in 1985 by the 8th and last Lord Sherborne, who was responsible for the design of the present garden. Set in the Hampshire countryside, it is a luxurious and colourful garden with a most unusual and imaginative layout. A Magnolia garden, a sunken garden, a yew garden, a kitchen garden and a 'Long Walk' are among the delights to be seen here. Part of house also open.

Open Apr–Sep, garden Wed–Sun 2–6; house Wed only 2–6 (last admission 5.30).

Garden £1 (ch 50p), house £1 (ch 50p) Party.

P ⚐ *(wknds only) (NT)*

Alton
Staffordshire   Map 7 SK04
ALTON TOWERS
☎ *Oakamoor (0538) 702200*

Famous leisure park (over 100 attractions) with magnificent gardens of specimen trees, lawns, shrubs, topiary and island beds. Important collection of early 19th century follies including Stonehenge, Pagoda Fountain, Chinese Temple and Corkscrew Fountain.

Open 28 Mar–1 Nov daily; grounds 9 to 1 hr after attractions close; attractions 10–5/6/7pm as indicated at gate.

* *Adults & children £5.99 (pen £1.99) ch 4 free. Party 12+.*

P ⚐ ⅋ ⅋ *(wc) wc*

Altrincham
Gt Manchester   Map 7 SJ78
DUNHAM MASSEY HALL
(2m SW of B5160) ☎ *061-941 1025*

A recently-restored Edwardian garden of 30 acres with many interesting features including a moat, canals and an Orangery. There are attractive Parterre beds, informal plantings of rhododendrons, waterside and herbaceous plants. Many specimen trees. 'Meet the Gardener' evening tours in May and June. Edwardian Extravaganza in July. Some plants labelled. House also open.

Open Apr–Oct daily (ex Fri): Garden 12–5.30 (Sun & BH Mon 11–5.30); House 1–5 (Sun & BH Mon 12–5) Last admission to house 4.30.

£2.50 (ch £1, family ticket £6). Car park £1 (refundable). Parties by prior arrangement Mon–Thu only. Party 15+.

P *(£1)* ⚐ *(licensed)* ✖ ⅋ *(ground floor & gardens, wheelchair available on request) (NT)*

Ambleside
Cumbria   Map 7 NY30
STAGSHAW GARDENS
☎ *(0966) 32109*

Hillside, woodland garden with superb views of lakes and fells. A fine collection of spring bulbs, rhododendrons, camellias, azaleas, magnolias and South American shrubs. Wonderful display of foliage and late-flowering shrubs in the autumn. Plants labelled.

Open Apr–Jun & Sep–Oct daily 10–6 (other times by appointment).

* *60p (ch 20p).*

P *(Coaches park at Waterhead)* ✖ *wc*
Plants for sale (NT)

Ampfield

Hampshire   Map 4 SU42

HILLIER ARBORETUM
Jermyn's Lane ☏ Braishfield (0794) 68787

The largest collection of hardy, woody plants in the country, started by Sir Harold Hillier in 1953. The rich variety of ornamental plants, from all five continents, are displayed in over 100 acres of countryside and create a wide range of floral and foliage effects throughout the year. The Arboretum also plays an important role in conservation and education. Plants labelled. Guided tours Wed & Sun in May & Oct, also for booked parties. Advisory service weekdays.

Open all year Mon–Fri 10–5, Mar–8 Nov, Sat, Sun & BH 1–6.

£1 (ch 15 free) Party 30+.
P ☍ ✻ & *(wc) wc Plants for sale*

Lathyrus odoratus
'Sweet Pea'

Amroth

Dyfed   Map 2 SN10

COLBY LODGE GARDEN
☏ Llandeilo (0558) 822800

Attractive garden in secluded valley. The walled garden (replanted in 1986) has a flower garden, and herbaceous and shrub borders with some unusual species. Woodland with rhododendron garden.

Open Etr–Oct Tue–Fri & Sun 2–6.

Free.

P *(400 yds, disabled may park closer to garden)* ✻ & *(NT)*

Ardingly

West Sussex   Map 4 TQ32

WAKEHURST PLACE
(1½m N) ☏ (0444) 892701

An important collection of exotic plants from many parts of the world, set in the grounds of an Elizabethan mansion in the Sussex Weald. Administered by the Royal Botanic Gardens, Kew, this is primarily an arboretum, with specialist collections of rhododendrons and plants from the Southern Hemisphere. There are walled gardens, rare trees and shrubs, streams and water features and a deep wooded ravine leading to a lake and rock walks. A 120-acre nature reserve is open by prior application. Plants labelled. House also open.

Open all year: Nov–Jan 10–4; Feb & Oct 10–5; Mar 10–6; Apr–Sep 10–7 (closed Xmas & New Years Day).

£1.50 (ch 60p) Party.
P *(nearby)*⊞ ✻ *(ex guide dogs) (NT)*

Ardwell

Dumfries and Galloway Map 10 NX14
Wigtownshire

ARDWELL HOUSE GARDENS
☏ (077686) 227

Country house (not open) with a delightful woodland garden. Rock plants, daffodils, flowering shrubs and rhododendrons. Pond walk with sea views. Small garden centre.

Open daily Mar–Oct 10–6.

50p (ch 25p).

Arran, Isle of

Strathclyde *Bute*   Map 10 NS03

BRODICK CASTLE, GARDEN AND COUNTRY PARK
☏ Brodick (0770) 2202

Former home of the Dukes of Hamilton. The gardens contain a remarkable collection of rhododendrons and many fine trees and shrubs. The walled garden has herbaceous borders and well-planted beds. Woodland garden.

Open Gardens, country park & Goatfell daily 9.30–sunset; House 17 Apr–Sep daily 1–5, last entry 4.40.

Gardens only £1.20 (ch 60p); House & gardens £2 (ch £1).
⬚ (17 Apr–Sep, Mon–Sat 10–5, Sun 12–5) (NTS)

Ashford
Kent **Map 5 TR04**
GODINTON PARK
(2½m NW) ☎ *(0233) 20773*

Gabled house dating from 1628 with formal gardens laid out by Sir Reginald Blomfield in about 1900. Fine topiary work, herbaceous borders, an Italian Garden and an original 18th-century shrubbery from a previous planting are enclosed by a long yew hedge. Extensive lawns. House also open.

Open Etr Sat, Sun, Mon then Jun–Sep Suns & BH's 2–5, or by appointment.

Garden and House £1.20 (ch 16 60p) Party 20+.
P ✹ (in house) wc Plants for sale

Ashington
West Sussex **Map 4 TQ11**
HOLLY GATE CACTUS GARDEN
Billingshurst Lane (B2133)
☎ *Worthing (0903) 892930*

This unique collection of over 20,000 plants is attractively housed in over 10,000 sq ft of glasshouses. Many rare plants from the arid areas of the USA, Mexico, South America and Africa and the tropical jungles of Central and South America are featured. There are always many plants in flower. Plants labelled. Advisory service. Guided tours for parties on request.

Open all year daily, 9–5 (closed 25, 26 Dec).

75p (ch & pen 50p) Party.
P ✹ & wc Plants for sale

Ashton
Hereford and Worcester **Map 3 SO56**
BERRINGTON HALL
(3m N of Leominster)
☎ *Leominster (0568) 5721*

A 'Capability' Brown park of 455 acres with a more recent collection of interesting and unusual shrubs and plants. The grounds include a 14-acre lake, woodland gardens, and large lawns planted with cyclamen and orchids for autumn colour. Rare shrubs and climbers are planted in the sheltered walled gardens. The 18th-century house (also open) is by Henry Holland, 'Capability' Brown's son-in-law.

Open Apr & Oct Sat, Sun & Etr Mon 2–5; May–Sep Wed–Sun & BH Mon 2–6.

£1.60.
⬚ ✹ (NT)

Ashton under Hill
Hereford and Worcester **Map 3 SO93**
BREDON SPRINGS
☎ *Evesham (0386) 881328*

A 1½-acre garden with some interesting trees and shrubs and a large collection of hardy plants in 'natural style' planting. Special attention is paid to wildlife (no insecticides are used) and more than 20 species of birds normally nest here. Guided tours for parties on request. Some plants labelled.

Open Apr–Oct Sat, Sun, Wed, Thu, BH Mon & Tue following 10–dusk.

50p (ch free).
P wc Plants for sale (NGS)

Athelhampton
Dorset **Map 3 SY79**
ATHELHAMPTON
(on A35 1m E of Puddletown)
☎ *Puddletown (030584) 363*

Athelhampton, a fine Tudor mansion, is surrounded by 20 acres of formal and landscaped gardens. Nine walled gardens are planted with many rare shrubs, roses and mature topiary. Pavillions, terraces, fountains and a 15th-century dovecote are also important features of these gardens. River gardens with mature trees and waterfall. Craft Fair 11–12 Jul.

Open 15 Apr–11 Oct Wed, Thu, Sun & BH also Mon & Tue in Aug 2–6.

Garden £1 (ch free); House & Garden £2 (ch £1).
P ⬚ ✹ & (gardens & ground floor of house; wc) wc Plants for sale

Audley End

Essex   Map 5 TL53
AUDLEY END HOUSE
☏ *Saffron Waldon (0799) 22399*

A 17th-century mansion built by Sir Thomas Howard, treasurer to James I. The grounds, landscaped by 'Capability' Brown in 1763, have large expanses of lawns, a river and a lake. The follies are by Robert Adam, whose work can also be seen in the house. There are also many fine trees and a small rose garden. House also open.

Open Etr Sat–last Sun in Oct (House closes 1st Sun in Oct); Park and gardens 12–6.30, house 1–5. Closed Mon ex BH.

£2.
P ⬚ ⬚ (gardens and ground floor only)
(AM)

Avebury

Wiltshire   Map 4 SU06
AVEBURY MANOR
☏ *(06723) 203*

Early Elizabethan manor house surrounded by traditional English gardens and parkland. Walled gardens, herb borders, old yew and box topiary. Wishing well and 17th century dovecote. Jacobs sheep and fallow deer in the parkland. House also open.

Open all year: Apr–Sep Mon–Sat 11.30–6, Sun 12.30–6; Oct–Mar Sat & Sun 1.30–5. The above times are often extended in fine weather.

£2 (ch £1, pen £1.75) Party 25+.
P ⬚ ⬚ ⬚ (gardens & ground floor)

Bakewell

Derbyshire   Map 8 SK26
HADDON HALL
(2m SE) ☏ *(062981) 2855*

The 17th-century terraced gardens have a notable collection of standard, bush and climbing roses, with many old, highly scented species. The Fountain garden has a central pool and lawns flanked by rose beds and herbaceous and delphinium borders. The Hall is also open. There are special events most weekends.

Open Apr, May, Jun & Sep Tue–Sun; Jul & Aug Tue–Sat & BH 11–6.

* *£2.20 (ch 5–16 £1.10; pen £1.60) Party.*
P ⬚ (licensed) ⬚ ⬚ (gardens only) wc

Balerno

Lothian *Midlothian*   Map 11 NT16
MALLENY GARDEN
off Bavelaw Road ☏ *031-449 2283*

A delightful garden with a good collection of shrub roses and clipped yews.

Open all year 10–sunset.

£1 (ch 50p) Charge box.
P *(NTS)*

Galanthus elwesii
'Snowdrop'

Balmacara

Highland   Map 14 NG82
Ross and Cromarty
BALMACARA (LOCHALSH HOUSE & GARDEN)
☏ *(059986) 207*

Large estate with woodland garden. Self-guided and guided walks from Balmacara on the Kyle to Plockton Peninsula. Magnificent scenery.

Open woodland and garden daily 9.30–sunset; Coach house open Etr–Oct, daily 10–6.

60p (ch 30p).
(NTS)

Bamford

Derbyshire   Map 8 SK28

HIGH PEAK GARDEN CENTRE

☎ *Hope Valley (0433) 51484*

An exhibition garden in the Peak National Park with shrub borders, rock, rose and heather gardens and trees. Plants labelled. Advisory service.

Open all year daily from 10.

Free.

P ♘ ✗ ᕹ *wc*

Barnard Castle

Co Durham   Map 12 NZ01

BOWES MUSEUM

☎ *Teesdale (0833) 37139*

Impressive French-style château, housing an important collection of fine and decorative arts, standing in its own landscaped gardens. The formal garden (also in the French style) has yew trees, box hedges, bedding plants and fountains. A walk round the perimeter reveals extensive lawns and informally planted trees and shrubs. Museum also open.

Open all year: May–Sep Mon–Sat 10–5.30, Sun 2–5, Nov–Feb closes 4pm; Mar, Apr & Oct closes 5pm (Closed 21–27 Dec & New Years day).

* *Garden free; Garden & Museum £1.35 (ch, pen & reg unemp 45p).*
P ♘ *(Apr–Sep)* ⛲ ✗ *(ex in gardens)* ᕹ *(wc) wc*

Barnsley

Gloucestershire   Map 4 SP00

BARNSLEY HOUSE GARDEN

(on A433) ☎ *Bibury (028574) 281*

The original garden, dating from 1770, has been completely redesigned since 1962. The 4 acres include two 18th-century summer-houses, a knot garden, a small herb garden and a Laburnum Walk which flowers in early June. Herbaceous borders planted with shrubs and bulbs provide interest throughout most of the year. Plants labelled. House not open. Guided tours by arrangement.

Open Mon–Fri 10–6 & 1st Sun in May, Jun & Jul 2–6 other days by appointment.

£1.50 (pen £1).
P ⛲ ✗ ᕹ *wc Plants for sale*

Barnstaple

Devon   Map 2 SS53

MARWOOD HILL GARDENS

☎ *(0271) 42528*

Situated in a valley where the stream has been dammed to make three small lakes, with waterside planting, and an extensive bog garden. Many rare trees and shrubs, a scree bed for alpines and a formal rose garden. Plants labelled.

Open daily dawn–dusk.

50p.
P ♘ *(Sun & BH also parties by arrangement) wc Plants for sale*

Basildon

Berkshire   Map 4 SU67

BASILDON PARK

(2½m NW of Pangbourne on W side of A329) ☎ *Pangbourne (07357) 3040*

Six acres of landscaped gardens including trees, shrubs and lawns, one formal border and some informal planting. Beautiful views across parkland and the Thames Valley. Classical 18th-century house also open.

Open Apr–Oct, Wed–Sat 2–6; Sun & BH Mon 12–6. Last admission 5.30 (Closed Good Fri and Wed following BH).

House and grounds £1.80 (Thu and Fri £1.30).
P ♘ *(NT)*

Bath

Avon   Map 3 ST76

AMERICAN MUSEUM, CLAVERTON MANOR

(2½m E) ☎ *(0225) 60503*

Pleasant 'American' gardens, surrounding the museum, with arboretum, fernery, rose walk and apple orchard. Special events in summer include Folk Dancing (May), Indian Weekend (Jun), Independence Day Displays (Jul) American Civil War Weekend (Sep), dates to be announced.

Open 28 Mar–1 Nov daily (ex Mon) 2–5; BH Sun & Mon 11–5.

* *Grounds 50p*
Grounds & Museum £2.25 (ch & pen £1.75) Party 30 + .
P ♘ ✗ ᕹ *(gardens and ground floor only)*

BOTANICAL GARDENS
Royal Victoria Park ☎ *(0225) 314213*

Over 2,000 specimens of trees, shrubs and herbaceous plants, magnolias and rock garden both at their best in the spring. Maples, willows and bamboo planted on the banks of the pool. Award winner in the 'Britain in Bloom' competition. Plants labelled.

Open all year daily Mon–Sat 8–dusk, Sun 10–dusk.

Free.
P *(nearby)* &

Beaconsfield
Buckinghamshire   **Map 4 SU99**
BEKONSCOT MODEL VILLAGE
Warwick Road, New Town, (1m from A40)
☎ *(04946) 2919*

The oldest model village in the world, set in a magnificent garden of shrubberies, rock gardens and lawns. 4,000 conifers, 1,000 shrubs and many flowers (all miniatures).

Open Etr–Oct, daily 10–5; limited display in Mar, daily 10–5.

Gardens and Model Village: £1.20 (ch 70p, pen, students and reg unemp £1). Party.
P ⌷ ⩑ *wc No double buggies*

Beaminster
Dorset   **Map 3 ST40**
MAPPERTON
☎ *(0308) 862441*

Six acres of terraced and hillside gardens with formal borders, specimen shrubs and trees. The gardens also house 18th-century stone fish ponds, a summer house and a modern Orangery in the classical style.

Open 9 Mar–9 Oct Mon–Fri 2–6.

£1 (ch 5–18 60p, under 5 free).
P ⌷ ✗ *wc*

PARNHAM
☎ *(0308) 862204*

The 16th-century manor house is the home and workshop of John Makepeace, one of Britain's leading furniture designers. The 14 acres of gardens include formal Dutch and Italian Gardens, lawns, rose beds, shrubs and woodland with a newly established bog

garden. There are 2 terraces: the Ladies Terrace with topiary work and a gazebo; and the Yew Terrace, which has clipped yews and lawns bisected by water channels. House open. Exhibitions by living craftsmen.

Open Apr–Oct Wed, Sun & BH 10–5.

£2.20 (ch 10–15 £1, under 10 free).
P ⌷ *(licensed)* & *(gardens & ground floor only, wc)* wc

Bedale
North Yorkshire   **Map 8 SE28**
THORP PERROW ARBORETUM

A collection of over 2,000 different species of trees and shrubs in 70 acres of landscaped grounds. Plants labelled.

Open all year daily dawn–dusk.

£1 (ch & pen 50p).
P ⍭ & *wc*

Belsay
Northumberland   **Map 12 NZ17**
BELSAY HALL, CASTLE AND GARDENS
☎ *(066181) 636*

A 19th-century neo-classical mansion and a 14th-century castle lie at opposite ends of the 30-acre gardens. The formal gardens overlook the rhododendron valley and lead on to a large heather garden. The sheltered Quarry Garden (a rock garden on a huge scale) houses many tender and exotic trees not normally found in the north-east. Mansion and castle also open. Plants labelled.

Open Apr–Sep daily 9.30–6.30 (winter opening times not yet confirmed).

* *£1 (ch 50p, pen & reg unemp 75p).*
P ⍭ & *(wc) wc*

Belton
Lincolnshire   **Map 8 SK93**
BELTON HOUSE, PARK AND GARDENS
on A607 ☎ *Grantham (0476) 66116*

Splendid 17th-century house with formal Dutch and Italian gardens and an Orangery, built by Sir Jeffrey Wyatville, which contains specimen shrubs and camellias. The large pleasure ground area is planted with shrubberies and specimen trees and is noted for its spring colour. House also open.

Open Apr–Oct Wed–Sun & BH Mon (closed Good Fri); Garden 11–5.30, House 1–5.30 (last admission 5pm). Park closed occasionally for special events.

House and Garden £2.40 (ch £1) Party 15+. Park free.
P (250 yds) 🍴 ✠ ♿ *(wc) wc (NT)*

Belvoir

Leicestershire   **Map 8 SK83**
BELVOIR CASTLE
Between A52 & A607
☎ *Grantham (0476) 870262*

Beautiful 19th-century castle with magnificent views over the Vale of Belvoir. The 22 acres of terraced gardens house a collection of 17th-century sculpture by Caius Cibber, royal sculptor to Charles II. The gardens are planted with roses, shrubs and herbaceous borders. Many special events on Sundays at no extra charge. Plants labelled. Castle also open.

Open 21 Mar–4 Oct, Tue–Thu & Sat 12–6, Sun 12–7, BH Mon only 11–7; Oct Sun only 2–6 (last admission ¼ hr before closing time).

£2.40 (ch £1.30) Party 30+.
P 🍴 ⛲ ✠ ♿ *(wc; ground floor & garden only) wc Plants for sale*

Beningbrough

North Yorkshire   **Map 8 SE55**
BENINGBROUGH HALL
off A19, entrance at Newton Lodge
☎ *York (0904) 470715/470666*

Baroque house, completely restored, set in 356 acres of wooded park and garden. The gardens include double herbaceous borders, a 19th-century American garden, and a Victorian conservatory. House with exhibition of pictures from National Portrait Gallery also open. Adventure playground.

Open Apr Sat & Sun only & Etr wk 12–6; May–Oct Tue–Sun & BH Mon 12–6; Nov Sat & Sun 12–5.

Garden & Exhibition £1.50 (ch 70p). House & garden £2 (ch £1) Party.
P (nearby) 🍴 *(12–5.30) (NT)*

Benmore

Strathclyde *Argyll*   **Map 10 NS18**
YOUNGER BOTANIC GARDEN
☎ *Dunoon (0369) 6261*

Famous collection of mature conifers, many over 100 years old and including some of the largest in Britain. Formal, walled garden containing garden conifers and heathers. Extensive collection of rhododendrons and other flowering shrubs from the Himalayas. Attractively landscaped in a Highland setting. Plants labelled. Part of the Royal Botanic Garden, Edinburgh.

Open Apr–Oct, daily 10–6.

* *20p (ch & pen 10p) Party 11+.*
P 🍴 ♿ *(wc) wc*

Hibbertia scandens
'Snake vine'

Benthall

Shropshire   Map 7 SJ60

BENTHALL HALL
(on B4375) ☎ *Telford (0952) 882159*

Elizabethan house with interesting, small garden. Raised terraced gardens to the west of the house with many unusual shrubs and plants. Topiary. House also open.

Open Etr Sun–Sep, Tue, Wed & Sun; BH gardens and ground-floor rooms only 2–6.

Gardens 80p, House and Gardens £1.60. (NT)

Berkeley

Gloucestershire   Map 3 ST69

BERKELEY CASTLE
on B4509 (1½ W of A38)
☎ *Dursley (0453) 810332*

Splendid 12th-century and later castle with terraced gardens and a large lower lawn which extends round much of the castle. Choice shrubs, roses and climbers with a superb wisteria down the full depth of the castle wall. The terraced gardens include an Elizabethan Bowling Green and a large lily pond. Butterfly house with hundreds of exotic and British butterflies.

Open Apr–Oct: Apr and Sep daily 2–5; May–Aug weekdays 11–5, Sun 2–5; Oct Sun only 2–4.30; BH Mon 11–5 (Closed Mon ex BH).

* Garden, castle and Butterfly House £2 (ch £1, pen £1.80) Party 25+.
P ⬚ 🐎 ✘ *wc*

Bexley

Gt London   Map 5 TQ47

HALL PLACE
(Near junction of A2 & A233)
☎ *Crayford (0322) 526574*

Extensive gardens and parkland around a 15th-16th century mansion. There are rose, water, rock, herb and peat gardens, seasonal bedding displays and topiary in the form of the 'Queen's Beasts'. House also open.

Open Gardens all year daily Mon–Fri 7.30–dusk, Sat & Sun 9–dusk; House Mon–Sat 10–5, Sun 2–6 (closed Sun in winter)

Free.

P ⬚ *(weather permitting)* ✘ ⅙ *(gardens only)*

Bickleigh

Devon   Map 3 SS90

BICKLEIGH CASTLE
off A396. Take A3072 from Bickleigh Bridge and follow signs. ☎ *(08845) 363*

Beautiful medieval castle with attractive gardens, including rare shrubs and trees. The moat has been transformed into a delightful water garden with water lilies, irises and bulrushes. A huge grass mound behind the castle has been planted with a great variety of rhododendrons and a walk to the summit is well rewarded. Some plants labelled. Castle also open. Flower festival 18–20 Sep.

Open Etr wk, then Wed, Sun & BH Mon to Spring BH, then daily (ex Sat) to early Oct 2–5.
* Garden, House, Museum & Exhibition £1.80 (ch 5–16 90p, pen & students £1.50) Party 20+ by arrangement.
P ⬚ 🐎 ✘ ⅙ *wc*

Bicton

Devon   Map 3 SYO8

BICTON PARK
☎ *Colaton Raleigh (0395) 68465*

Fifty acres of beautiful grounds, including a pinetum and individual gardens. The historic Italian Garden was laid out in 1735 to a design by André le Nôtre who was famous for the gardens at the Palace of Versailles. Fuchsia and geranium houses. Plants labelled. Theme Halls, Woodland Railway and Countryside Museum are some of the many other attractions here.

Open Apr–end Oct daily 10–6; see local press for winter opening.

* £2.50 (ch £2.30, only one child in each family charged for, under 5 free; pen £2.30, Tue, Wed & Thu ex Aug £1.20).
P ⬚ 🐎 ⅙ *(wc) wc Plants for sale*

Birchington

Kent   Map 5 TR36

POWELL-COTTON MUSEUM
Quex Park (1m SE village off B2048)
☎ *Thanet (0843) 42168*

Regency mansion and adjoining museum set in 200 acres of gardens and wooded parkland. The gardens contain roses, spring bulbs, a sunken lawn and pool. There are extensive lawns and rare specimen trees and shrubs. Museum and part of house open.

Open Gardens, Museum & House: Apr–Sep Wed, Thu, Sun & BH; also Fri in Aug 2.15–6 (last entry 5pm). Museum: Oct–Mar Sun only 2.15–4.30.

Apr–Sep £1 (ch & pen 60p); Oct–Mar 60p (ch & pen 40p).
P ⬚ ✱ & *(ground floor & garden)*

Birmingham
West Midlands   Map 7 SP08

BIRMINGHAM BOTANICAL GARDENS
Westbourne Rd, Edgbaston ☏ 021-454 1860

Ornamental gardens, landscaped in 1830, with walks, rock pools, shrubs, herbaceous borders and a waterfowl enclosure. Tropical glasshouses with collections of lillies, orchids, cacti and succulents. Many mature and rare trees. Garden for the disabled. Plants labelled. Garden Centre, Events (folk dancing, bands etc) Sun afternoons in summer.

Open all year: Apr–Oct Mon–Sat 9–8, Sun 10–8; Nov–Mar Mon–Sat 9–4, Sun 10–4 (closed Xmas Day).

* £1.35 (ch 5, pen & students 65p). Party 10+.
P ⴕ ✱ & *(most parts; wc) wc*

SELLY MANOR & MINWORTH GREAVES
Sycamore Rd, Bournville off A38 ☏ 021-472 0199

Small garden surrounding two half-timbered houses, bordered on two sides by yew hedging and on a third by pleached limes. Re-

planted in the last four years with native and pre-1800 herbaceous plants and herbs. Plants labelled. Houses also open.

Open mid Jan–mid Dec Tue–Fri 10–5 (ex BH)
Free.
P *(nearby)* ✱

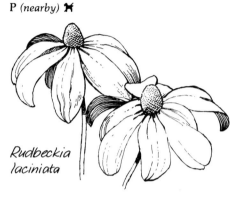

Rudbeckia laciniata

Bobbingworth
Essex   Map 5 TL50

BLAKE HALL GARDENS
☏ *Ongar (0277) 362502*

Attractive gardens with herbaceous borders, roses, flowering shrubs, woodlands and Japanese Garden. The Tropical House has a collection of exotic plants and cacti.

Open all year daily 10–6 (5 in winter)

Sat & Sun £1.50 (ch & pen 75p) weekdays half price.
P ⬚ *(weekdays)* ⴕ & wc

Bodmin

Cornwall   Map 2 SXO6
PENCARROW HOUSE
Washaway (4m N on unclass rd off A389)
☎ *St Mabyn (020884) 369*

Georgian mansion house dating from about 1770 with 35 acres of mainly woodland gardens laid out by Sir William Molesworth Bt in the 1830s and 1840s. The mile-long drive is flanked by massive rhododendrons, hydrangeas, camellias and a nationally recognised specimen conifer collection. Many plants labelled. House also open.

Open Gardens Etr–15 Oct daily; House Etr–15 Oct Mon–Thu & Sun 1.30–5; BH Mon & June–10 Sep 11–5 (last tour of house 5pm).

* *Gardens 50p (ch 25p).*
Garden House £1.90 (ch 95p) Parties 30+.
P ⌂ ⅏ ﺣ*(ground floor & gardens only) wc*
Plants for sale

Boldre

Hampshire   Map 4 SZ39
SPINNERS
School Lane ☎ *Lymington (0590) 73347*

A plantsman's garden situated on a wooded slope high above the Lymington River. Created by the owners over the past 25 years, there are many choice shrubs, rhododendrons, azaleas and camellias, with ground-cover plants, massed beds, ferns and fine specimen trees. Nursery with many rare and unusual plants open all year. Exhibition and sale of flower paintings.

Open 20 Apr–1 Sep daily 10–6. Other times by arrangement.

75p (ch under 5 free).
P ✖ *(NGS)*

Bookham, Great

Surrey   Map 4 TQ15
POLESDEN LACEY
(1m S) ☎ *Bookham (0372) 58203 or 52048*

The house, built in the early 1820s, is set at the end of long beech and lime avenues, amongst lawns and colourful flower beds. The enclosed gardens lie to the right of the house, and here the main feature is the rose garden with pergolas covered in rambling roses. There are fine views from Sheridan's Walk (a long grass promenade) named after Richard Sheridan, a former owner of the estate. A garden guide and plan produced by the NT details the main trees, shrubs, roses and garden features. House also open.

Open gardens daily 11–sunset; House Mar Sat & Sun 11–2.30 & 3–5; Apr–end Oct Wed–Sun & BH Mon 11–2.30 & 3–6; Nov–mid Dec Wed–Sun 11–2.30 & 3–5.

Gardens £1. House £1.20.
⌂ *(licensed, open as house)* ✖ *(NT)*

Borough Green

Kent   Map 5 TQ65
GREAT COMP GARDEN
(off B2016) ☎ *(0732) 882669*

A well designed garden with a wide variety of trees and shrubs planted since 1957 and now in the first stages of maturity. Perennials often planted in an informal 'cottage garden' style. Fine l⸱ ⸍ns and paths and many heathers.

Open Apr–Oct daily 11–6.

£1.50 (ch 70p).
P ✖ ﺣ *wc Plants for sale (NGS)*

Bowness-on-Windermere

Cumbria   Map 7 SD49
(see also Windermere)
BELLE ISLE
☎ *Windermere (09662) 3353*

Beautiful island (38 acres) in the middle of Lake Windermere with woodland and rhododendron walks, an arboretum and a small formal garden. Laid out by Thomas White in 1780. House also open. Trees labelled. Motor launch runs continuously from far end of Bowness promenade.

* *Open May–Sep Sun–Thu 10.15–5. Guided tour of house 3pm, browse around house 11.15, 12.30 & 2.15.*

* *£2.50 (ch £1.25) (includes return boat trip, garden and 'Below Stairs' museum); £1 (ch 50p) guided tour of house; 60p (ch 30p) browse around. Party.*
P *(on mainland)* ⌂ *(licensed)* ⅏

Bramham

West Yorkshire Map 8 SE44

BRAMHAM PARK
(on A1 4m S of Wetherby)
☎ *Boston Spa (0937) 844265*

Queen Anne mansion set in 66 acres of formal gardens laid out over 250 years ago with cascades, tall beech hedges, temples, ornamental ponds and loggias. The design (inspired by André le Nôtre, creator of the gardens at Versailles) features three long vistas which stretch into woodland. Nature trails. Horse trials 28–31 May.

Open Garden: Etr & Spring BH wknds 1.15–5.30; Gardens & House 7 Jun–27 Aug Tue, Wed & Thu including BH wknd.

Gardens only 80p (ch 5 40p, pen 70p); House and Gardens £1.40 (ch 5 60p, pen £1.20). Party 20+.
P ₺ *(gardens only)*

Bramhope

West Yorkshire Map 8 SE24

GOLDEN ACRE PARK
☎ *Leeds (0532) 610374*

The Park covers 137 acres of mature woodland and gardens, and incorporates an attractive lake, with wildfowl. There is a collection of trees and shrubs as well as herbaceous and aquatic plants. Created features include rock gardens, a large Alpine house, a demonstration garden for vegetables and flowers, old shrub roses, rhododendrons and azaleas, an arboretum and a pinetum. Some plants labelled. Guided tours by arrangement. Gardening demonstrations first Sun of Apr, May, Jul, Sep, Oct (2–4pm) and 'Heavyweight Challenge' for giant vegetables early Oct.

Open daily.

Free.
P ₺ ₮ ₺ *(wc) wc*

Bransgore

Hampshire Map 4 SZ19

MACPENNYS NURSERY
☎ *Bransgore (0425) 72348*

This 4-acre woodland garden and nursery was started in 1937 on the site of an old gravel pit. A wide variety of herbaceous plants and shrubs including old-fashioned rhododendrons and camellias are grown, and a number of winding paths criss-cross the garden. Most plants labelled. Guided tours for parties 25+. Some special events (50th anniversary).

Open daily Mon–Fri 8–5, Sat 9–5, Sun 2–5.

Admission by donation.
P ₮ ₺ *Plants for sale (NGS)*

Brasted

Kent Map 5 TQ45

EMMETT'S GARDEN

Four-acre hillside garden with a fine collection of trees and shrubs. Beautiful spring and autumn colours. Bluebell wood.

Open Apr–Oct, Sun & Tue–Fri 2–6 (last admission 5pm).

£1.30 (ch 60p).
P *(NT)*

Eryngium
'Sea Holly'

31

Brenchley

Kent   Map 5 TQ64

MARLE PLACE
☎ (089272) 2304

Many garden 'rooms' hedged with yew and beech. Unusual plants, topiary, ornamental ponds and a herb rockery. Good collections of shrub roses and trees, and colourful mixed shrub and herbaceous borders. Herb nursery. Plants labelled.

Open Apr–Sep Wed 10.30–5.

£1.
P � No children. Plants for sale

Bressingham

Norfolk   Map 5 TM07

BRESSINGHAM GARDENS & LIVE STEAM MUSEUM
(on A1066) ☎ (037988) 386

An informal 6-acre garden in the grounds of the Live Steam Museum, displaying over 5,000 varieties of alpines, conifers, heathers and perennials. Plants labelled. The large Plant Centre (open all year) incorporates display beds and has an extensive range of plants and many ideas for their uses and combinations. Advisory service.

Open 19 & 20 Apr; Suns 26 Apr–27 Sep & BH Mons 11.30–6; Thu 4 Jun–10 Sep; Weds in Aug 11.30–5.30.

£1.50 (ch 80p, pen £1.20) Party 12+.
P ⊟ & (gardens & ground floor) wc

Bridgwater

Somerset   Map 3 ST33

BARFORD PARK
☎ Spaxton (027 867) 269

The park and gardens at Barford Park occupy about 8 acres, 4 acres of which are woodland. There are many fine trees. The formal gardens are walled and both herbaceous plants and shrubs are grown. Candalabra primulas (best in June) are a speciality, and there is also a water garden.

Open May–Sep, Fri, Sat, Sun & BH 2–6.
Coach parties by appointment only.

Gardens only 50p (ch 14 free); gardens and house £1.50.
P ✘ wc (NGS)

Bridlington

Humberside   Map 8 TA16

SEWERBY HALL, PARK & ZOO
☎ (0262) 673769

Formal gardens of great botanical interest with some mature trees from South America. The Old English Walled Garden has flower beds laid out in geometric design and an ornamental pool. Aromatic herbs and plants in the Garden for the Blind. Some plants labelled. Other attractions include the Hall (with art gallery and museum), Zoo, parkland and recreation facilities. Special displays and exhibitions during the year.

Open Gardens, Park & Zoo all year daily 9–dusk. Games facilities Spring BH–mid Sep; Art Gallery & Museum Etr–last Sun in Sep.

* 70p (ch 30p) Spring BH–mid Sep; out of season Gardens and Park free, Zoo 10p. Art Gallery & Museum free. Concessions for school parties.
P ⊟ (Etr & weekends to Spring BH then daily to end Sep) 🎪 & (wc) wc Plants for sale Jun & Jul

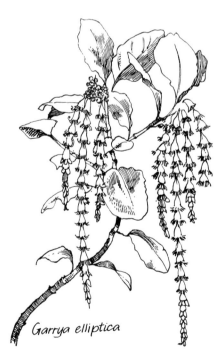

Garrya elliptica

32

Brighton

East Sussex **Map 4 TQ30**

PRESTON MANOR

Preston Park (off A23)
☎(0273) 603005 ext 59

Georgian manor in 4 acres of late Victorian/Edwardian grounds. The walled garden is a rare example of an 'old-fashioned' garden combining modest formal and informal styles of planting. Plants labelled. House also open.

Open Wed–Sat 10–5; Tue & Sun 10–1 & 2–5 (Closed Mon ex BH Mon, Good Fri & Xmas).

** Gardens free; House 90p (ch 55p, pen, students & reg unemp 75p); family ticket (2 + up to 4 ch) £2.15, (1+ up to 4 ch) £1.45.*
P 🐕

Gentiana acaulis

Bristol

Avon **Map 3 ST57**

UNIVERSITY OF BRISTOL BOTANIC GARDEN

Bracken Hill, North Road, Leigh Woods (3m W) ☎ (0272) 733682

The gardens have over 4,000 different kinds of plants and are used mainly for educational and research purposes. There are trees, shrubs, a rock garden, herbaceous borders, greenhouses and special displays of plants including some very rare local species. Plants labelled.

Open all year Mon–Fri 9–5 (ex Etr wk, Xmas wk & BH).

Free.
🐕

Broadway

Hereford and Worcester **Map 4 SP03**

SNOWSHILL MANOR

(3m S) ☎ (0386) 852410

Cotswold manor house with a small, formal garden which incorporates old farm buildings including a dovecote. The gardens are terraced with outdoor 'rooms' and are planted with a great variety of shrubs and hardy perennials. House also open.

Open Etr Sat–Mon, Apr & Oct Sat & Sun 11–1 & 2–5; May–Sep Wed–Sun & BH Mon 11–1 & 2–6 Parties by written appointment.

£2.50 (ch £1.25).
P *(nearby) wc (NT)*

Brobury

Hereford & Worcester **Map 3 SO34**

BROBURY HOUSE GALLERY & GARDENS

☎ Moccas (09817) 229

Mainly semi-formal gardens of 8 acres with sweeping lawns, mature trees and views over the River Wye to the Black Mountains. The gardens also feature herbaceous borders, sunken gardens and three ornamental pools. Art gallery also open.

Gardens open Jun–Sep, Mon–Sat 9–4.30. Gallery open all year, Mon–Sat 9–4.30 (4pm in winter).

Garden £1 (ch 16 50p). Gallery free.
P *wc*

Broomfield

Somerset **Map 3 ST23**

FYNE COURT

☎ Kingston St Mary (082345) 587

Ten acres of gardens planted with native trees and shrubs now a nature reserve for plants and animals. Numerous paths, some ponds and a small formal herb garden.

Open all year daily 9.30–5.30.

Free (car park 40p).
P ☕ 🐕 ♿ *wc Plants for sale*

Buckland Abbey

Devon   Map 2 SX46

BUCKLAND ABBEY
(3m W of Yelverton off A386)
☎ *Plymouth (0752) 668000*

Former home of Sir Francis Drake, now a naval and Devon folk museum. Gardens with flowering shrubs, herbs and a large medieval tithe barn.

Open Apr–Sep daily 11–6, last admission ½hr before closing time. (Closed from Sep 1987 until Summer 1988).

£1.50 (ch 75p) Party.
🚽 *(NT)*

Buckland Monachorum

Devon   Map 2 SX46

THE GARDEN HOUSE
☎ *Yelverton (0822) 854769*

Seven-acre garden, of interest throughout the year, with good collections of woody and herbaceous plants. Two-acre walled garden, one of the finest in the country. Plants labelled. Advisory service.

Open Apr–Sep daily 12–5.

£1 (ch 50p).
P ✗ *wc Plants for sale*

Burford

Shropshire   Map 7 SO56

BURFORD HOUSE GARDENS
(off A456) ☎ *Tenbury Wells (0584) 810777*

A well-designed, modern garden of 4 acres with a wide variety of plants including many rare and unusual species. Alpines, heathers, old-fashioned roses, herbaceous plants, shrubs, ornamental pools and stream gardens with moisture-loving plants. The adjoining nursery 'Treasures of Tenbury' (open all year) houses the National Collection of Clematis and many of these are featured in the garden growing through shrubs and trees and trained on walls. House not open.

Open 21 Mar–25 Oct Mon–Sat 11–5, Sun 2–5. Winter Mon–Fri by appointment only.

£1.75 (ch 75p) Party 25+.
P 🚽 ✗

Burgh-le-Marsh

Lincolnshire   Map 9 TF56

GUNBY HALL
(2½m NW off A158)
☎ *Scremby (075485) 691*

Sweeping lawns and long herbaceous borders surround the charming early 18th-century house, immortalised in Tennyson's 'Haunt of Ancient Peace'. The large walled gardens house a good collection of old roses, herbs and herbaceous plants. Some plants labelled.

Open Apr–Sep Thu 2–6 (other times by appointment).

Garden 80p, ground floor of House and Garden £1.20.
P & *wc Coaches by arrangement. Plants for sale (NT)*

Burton Agnes

Humberside   Map 8 TA16

BURTON AGNES HALL
on A166 ☎ *(026289) 324*

Magnificent Elizabethan house set in 4 acres of woodland gardens with lawns, herbaceous borders, statues and pools. House also open.

Open Apr–Oct daily 11–5.

£1.50 (ch & pen £1).
P *(nearby)* 🚽 ✗ *(in hall)* & *(wc; gardens & ground floor only) wc*

Burwash

East Sussex   Map 5 TQ62

BATEMAN'S
(1m SW) ☎ *(0435) 882302*

17th-century house with attractive garden which was partly laid out by the novelist Rudyard Kipling who bought the house in 1902. There are beautiful rose beds next to the pool, also lawns, yew hedges and many daffodils. Dudwell Stream flows through the garden and powered the watermill which has been recently restored. House also open, Kipling's designs for the pool and rose garden can be seen in his study.

Open Apr–Oct, Sat–Wed, 11–6 (last admission 5.30).

£2.20 (ch £1.10) weekdays; £2.50 (ch £1.20) BH & wknds.
P 🚽 ✗ *(NT)*

Buscot

Oxfordshire   **Map 4 SU29**

BUSCOT PARK
off A417 ☎ Faringdon (0367) 20786, Mon–Fri only

Landscaped gardens and parkland surround the 18-century house. Attractive garden walks lead through ornamental trees and woodland to a large lake. Formal water garden. House also open.

Open Apr–Sep, Wed–Fri, Etr, 2nd & 4th wknd in each month 2–6 (last admission to house 5.30).

Gardens £1, House and gardens £1.80.
✸ *(NT)*

Bute, Isle of

Strathclyde *Bute*   **Map 10 NS06**

ARDENCRAIG
Rothesay ☎ (0700) 4225

A most attractive and interesting garden, where particular attention has been paid to improving the layout and introducing rare plants. The greenhouse and walled garden produce plants for use in floral displays throughout the district. A variety of interesting fish are to be found in the ornamental ponds and the aviaries contain many foreign species of birds.

Open May–Sep, Mon–Fri 9–4.30, Sat & Sun 1–4.30.

Free.
P ⬚ ✸ &

Cadbury

Devon   **Map 3 SS90**

FURSDON HOUSE
☎ Exeter (0392) 860860

A Georgian-fronted manor house with 2 acres of gardens currently being restored. Lawns and shrubs in front of the house lead into parkland with specimen trees. Terraced and walled gardens and a small herb garden are found at the rear of the house. House also open.

Open Etr Sun & Mon; then 3 May–Sep Thu, Sun & BH also Wed in Jul & Aug 2–5.30.

Gardens 80p (ch 40p, under 10 free).

Gardens & House £1.75 (ch 85p, under 10 free). (Admission to house by guided tour only at 2.30, 3.30 & 4.30).
P ⬚ ✸ *wc*

Cairndow

Strathclyde *Argyll*   **Map 10 NN11**

STRONE HOUSE
☎ (04996) 284

Pinetum with rhododendrons, azaleas, conifers and daffodils, also the tallest tree in Britain measuring 200ft.

Open Apr–Sep, dawn–dusk.

Admission fee payable.
P ⚘

Calne

Wiltshire   **Map 3 ST96**

BOWOOD HOUSE & GARDENS
(2m W off A4) ☎ (0249) 812102

A Georgian house (c1745) with a splendid 90-acre Park landscaped by 'Capability' Brown from 1761 to 1767. The gardens around the house are carpeted with flowers during the spring and there are colourful displays of roses and geraniums on the formal terraces during the summer. The grounds lead down to a long, peaceful lake with cascades, caves and a Doric Temple at one end. Separate rhododendron and azalea gardens 2m from house on A342. Plants labelled. House also open. Garden centre.

Open Apr–Sep daily 11–6; Rhododendron Gardens mid May–mid Jun 11–6.

* £2.25 (ch £1.25, pen £1.50) Rhododendron Gardens £1.
P ⬚ ⚘ ✸ & *(gardens & ground floor only; wc) wc*

Viola odorata

Calstock

Cornwall   **Map 2 SX46**

COTEHELE HOUSE
(2m W on W bank of Tamar, 8m SW of Tavistock off A390)

Medieval manor house with 12 acres of formal and landscaped gardens. Formal terraces planted with roses, magnolias and climbers lead to the sheltered Valley Gardens where you'll find unusual shrubs, rhododendrons, azaleas and a medieval dovecote. Small acer plantation. Woodland walks to Calstock and Cotehele Mill. Plants labelled. Special events in summer.

Open Garden: all year daily 11–6 or dusk House: Apr–Oct daily (ex Fri) 11–6 or dusk, last admission 5.30.

Gardens, grounds & Mill £1.50 (ch 75p). House, garden & Mill £3 (ch £1.50).
🚻 wc (NT)

Cambo

Northumberland   **Map 12 NZ08**

HERTERTON HOUSE
Hartington ☎ *Scots Gap (067 074) 278*

Small, formal country garden laid out to 18th-century design with topiary, herbs, flower garden and nursery.

Open May–Sep daily (ex Tue & Thu) 1.30–5.30.

Free (guided tour and talk for pre-booked coach parties mornings or evenings £14).
P ✖ wc No pushchairs. Plants for sale

WALLINGTON HOUSE, WALLED GARDEN AND GROUNDS
☎ *Scots Gap (067074) 283*

A 17th- and 18th-century house set in attractive parkland with lawns, ponds and woodland walks. The Walled Garden has colourful borders, roses, ornamental trees and shrubs, and magnificent fuchsias which are housed in the conservatory. House also open.

Open Walled Garden; all year daily, Apr–Sep 10–7, Oct 10–6, Nov–Mar 10–4, Grounds: open all year; House: 1–16 Apr & Oct Wed, Sat & Sun 1–5; 17 Apr–Sep daily (ex Tue) 1–5.

* Walled garden & grounds £1; House, walled garden & grounds £2.40. Party.
P 🚻 ♿ ✖ (in house) & (gardens & ground floor only; wc) wc (NT)

Cambridge

Cambridgeshire   **Map 5 TL45**

Many of the colleges have nice gardens to which the public may sometimes have access.

UNIVERSITY BOTANIC GARDEN
Cory Lodge, Bateman St ☎ *(0223) 336265*

Fine botanical collections covering 40 acres including wild flowers, roses, herbaceous borders and Chronological bed. Attractive winter garden where flowers, bark, berries and evergreens provide interest and colour. Glasshouses, rock garden.

Open all year Mon–Sat 8–6.30 (dusk in winter) Sun May–Sep 2.30–6.30. Glasshouses 11–12.30 & 2–4 (other times by arrangement).

Free.
P (nearby) 🚻 ✖ (ex guide dogs) &

UNWINS SEEDS TRIAL GARDENS
Impington Lane, Histon (3m NW off A45 and A604) ☎ *Histon (022023) 2270*

Four acres of seed trials create a colourful display with 2,000 varieties of flowers and over 1,000 varieties of vegetables. Plants labelled.

Open 19 Jul–13 Sep daily dawn–dusk.

* 25p (proceeds to charity).
P 🚻 ♿ & wc

Canford Cliffs

Dorset   **Map 4 SZ08**

COMPTON ACRES GARDENS
Canford Cliffs Rd (on B3065)
☎ *(0202) 708036*

A spectacular series of individual gardens including woodland and semi-tropical glen, rock and heather gardens, Japanese, Roman, English and Italian gardens and a Palm Court. The gardens, which were started in 1914, cover about 15 acres and have fine views over Poole Harbour and the Purbeck Hills.

Open daily Apr–Oct 10.30–6.30 or dusk.

* £1.50 (ch 75p, pen £1) Party 30+.
P 🚻 ✖ & (wc) wc Garden centre

Capesthorne

Cheshire   Map 7 SJ87

CAPESTHORNE HALL
(on A34 between Congleton and Wimslow)
☎ *Chelford (0625) 861221 or 861439*

Colourful gardens with rhododendrons, azaleas, spring flowers and woodlands. The chain of ornamental pools is flanked by lawns and double herbaceous and shrub borders. 18th-century Hall also open. Numerous events throughout the year.

Open Apr–Sep. Apr Sun only; May & Sep Wed, Sat & Sun; Jun–Aug Tue, Wed, Thu, Sat & Sun; also open all BH. Park & Garden 12–6; Hall 2–5.

* Park, Garden & Chapel £1 (ch 50p); Hall, Park & Garden £1.95 (ch 95p) Party 20+.

P ⏣ ✠ ᵴ *(ground floor & gardens only)*

Lavatera trimestris

Carradale

Strathclyde *Argyll*   Map 10 NR83

CARRADALE HOUSE
(off B879) ☎ *(05833) 234*

Beautiful gardens, overlooking Kilbrennan Sound, with flowering shrubs, mainly rhododendrons. Best visited between Apr and Jun.

Open Apr–Sep 10–5.30.

20p (ch free).
P

Castle Ashby

Northamptonshire   Map 4 SP85

CASTLE ASHBY GARDENS
☎ *Yardley Hastings (060129) 234*

Elizabethan mansion with 18th- and 19th-century gardens and grounds which are being restored. Formal Victorian terraces overlook parkland landscaped by 'Capability' Brown. Italian Gardens with large conservatory; arboretum and woodland gardens with wild flowers and bulbs. Two guided walks around Parkland — dates to be announced. Some plants labelled.

Open all year daily 10–6.

50p (ch 25p).
P *(100 yds)* ⏣ ᵴ *wc*

Castle Cary

Somerset   Map 3 ST63

HADSPEN HOUSE GARDENS
(2m SE off A371) ☎ *(0963) 50200*

A sheltered, south-facing garden with a walled garden, a sunken garden and herbaceous borders. Many rare and unusual plants. Garden centre.

Open all year (ex Jan) Tue–Sat 10–5, also Apr–Oct Sun & BH 2–5.

£1 (ch 50p) Party 15+.
P ✠ ᵴ *Plants for sale*

Castle Douglas

Dumfries and Galloway   Map 11 NX76
Kirkcudbrightshire

THREAVE GARDEN
(1m W of Castle Douglas)
☎ *Castle Douglas (0556) 2575*

This fine garden of roughly 80 acres has a wide and varied collection of plants. There are water, woodland, rock, rose and peat gardens, glasshouses and a walled garden with mixed vegetable plots and flower beds. Over 200 varieties of daffodil are grown and provide a splendid springtime display. The house is the NTS School of Gardening.

Open daily 9–sunset; walled garden and glasshouses 9–5.

£1.80 (ch 90p) Party.
⏣ *(Etr–Sep)* ⌁ ᵴ *wc (NTS)*

Castle Kennedy
Dumfries and Galloway Map 10 NX15
Wigtownshire
CASTLE KENNEDY GARDENS
(3m E of Stranraer on A75)
☎ *Stranraer (0776) 2524*

The gardens are situated on a peninsula between two locks and are nationally famous for their rhododendrons, azaleas, magnolias and embothriums. The extensive grounds (89 acres) offer interesting and varied walks. Some plants labelled. Plant centre.

Open Apr–Sep daily 10-5.

£1 (ch 16 25p, pen 80p) Party.
P ⏣ ⅋ *wc*

Cawdor
Highland *Nairn* **Map 14 NH84**
CAWDOR CASTLE
☎ *(06677) 615*

The ancestral home of the Thanes of Cawdor, standing in attractive grounds. Superb collection of Spring and Autumn flowering bulbs, rhododendrons and azaleas in the Wild Garden. Large herbaceous borders. Nature trails. 'Cawdor Castle Entertains' — living crafts in flower garden Jul & Sep. Guided tours of gardens, by arrangement, for parties. Castle also open.

Open May–4 Oct daily 10-5.30.

Gardens, Grounds and Nature Trails £1.20. Castle, Garden, Grounds and Nature Trails £2.20 (ch 5-15 £1.20, pen/disabled £1.80). Party 20+.
P ⏣ *(licensed)* ⅋ ✖ ⅋ *(gardens & ground floor) wc*

Chalfont St Giles
Buckinghamshire **Map 4 SU99**
MILTON'S COTTAGE
Dean Way ☎ *(02407) 2313*

John Milton's 16th-century half timbered cottage with a charming cottage garden. Many roses, including miniatures and old fashioned shrub varieties, fruit trees, herbs and well kept lawns. Plants labelled. House also open.

Open Mar–Oct Tue–Sat 10-1, 2-6; Sun 2-6. Also open Spring & Summer BH.

£1 (ch 15 40p) Party 20+.
P *(50 yds)* ✖

Chard
Somerset **Map 3 ST30**
FORDE ABBEY
☎ *South Chard (0460) 20231*

Informal gardens (30 acres) with beautiful spring displays of bulbs and early flowering shrubs. There are five lakes, joined by cascades, and a bog garden with asiatic primulas and other moisture-loving plants. The arboretum contains many rare trees and shrubs. House also open.

Open Apr–mid Oct Gardens: Mon–Fri 10.30-4.30; House & gardens: Sun, Wed & BH 2-6.

Gardens £1.50 (ch 14 free); House & gardens £2.50 (ch 14 free) Party.
P ⏣ ⅋ *(ground floor & gardens only) garden centre*

Charlecote
Warwickshire **Map 4 SP25**
CHARLECOTE PARK
(on B4086)

Restored Elizabethan house in a peaceful setting. There are shrub borders, a terrace rose garden and a selection of flowers mentioned in Shakespeare's plays. Deer park where Shakespeare is said to have been caught poaching. House also open.

Open Apr–Oct Sun, Tue, Wed, Fri, Sat & BH Mon 11-6, last admission 5pm. Closed Good Fri. Evening parties by prior arrangement on 2nd Wed in month.

£2.40 (family ticket £6.50).
⏣ *(NT)*

Charsfield
Suffolk **Map 5 TM25**
AKENFIELD
1 Park Lane ☎ *(047337) 402*

Small cottage garden (former council house garden) featured on BBC2's Gardeners' World. Beautiful displays from over 800 varieties of shrubs and flowers, some in tubs and hanging baskets. Many fuchsias, 2 small pools, 2 greenhouses. Vegetable garden. Plants labelled.

Open Spring BH Sun–Sep, daily 10.30-7.30.

50p (all money given to charity).
P *(near petrol station)* ✖ ⅋ *Plants for sale*

38

Chatsworth

Derbyshire　　　　　Map 8 SK27

CHATSWORTH HOUSE AND PARK
(3½m E of Bakewell)
☎ Baslow (024688) 2204

This large garden, extending to 105 acres, is particularly famous for its elaborate cascade and fountains. 'Capability' Brown was responsible for much of the planting and landscaping of the Park, but the present gardens owe a great deal to Joseph Paxton's work. As well as the extensive woodlands, the park includes water and bog gardens, an azalea dell, herbaceous borders, rose garden, lawns and statuary. House also open.

Open Apr–Oct 11.30–5.

Garden £1.50 (ch 75p); House and garden £3.20 (ch £1.50, students & pen £2.25, family ticket £8) Party.
P ⬚ (licensed) ⅋ (wc) wc Garden centre

Chester

Cheshire　　　　　Map 7 SJ46

ZOO AND GARDENS
☎ (0244) 380280

Animal enclosures set in 110 acres of landscaped gardens with formal flower beds, shrubberies and a magnificent Rose Garden. Many tropical plants inside animal houses.

Open all year daily 10–dusk (closed Xmas Day).

£3 (ch £1.50) Party 16+.
P ⬚ (licensed) ⅋ ✕ ⅋(wc) wc

Chichester

West Sussex　　　　　Map 4 SU80

PALLANT HOUSE GALLERY
9 North Pallant ☎ (0243) 774557

A very small formal garden planted in authentic 18-century style. The design is by Claude Phillimore and only plants known before the year 1800 are used. Herbaceous plants and shrubs and a few small trees are grown. Queen Anne House also open, affording fine views of the garden. Occasional lectures on garden design and history. Some plants labelled.

Open daily Tue–Sat 10–5.30 (closed BH).

£1.00 (ch 16, pen and students 60p).
✕ ⅋ wc

Chiddingstone

Kent　　　　　Map 5 TQ54

CHIDDINGSTONE CASTLE
(off B2027) ☎ Penshurst (0892) 870347

17th-century house, remodelled in the 'castle style', set in 30 acres of landscaped grounds. The park, laid out in 1770 is being restored and contains a Gothic well house, gazebo and a lake. Fine views over the Weald.

Open Mar 29–Sep Wed–Sat 2–5.30, Sun 11.30–5.30; Tue also mid Jun–mid Sep 2–5.30; Oct wknds only (advisable to check Sat opening as sometimes closed for functions).

£2 (ch 5–15 £1, under 5 free) Party 20+.
P ⬚ ✕ wc

Chilham

Kent　　　　　Map 5 TR05

CHILHAM CASTLE GARDENS
☎ Canterbury (0227) 730319

Hexagonal Jacobean manor house (not open) and medieval castle keep set in beautiful gardens and grounds with views over the Stour Valley. Magnificent formal terraces lead down to a lawn bordered by topiaries. The 3½-acre lake has its own informal gardens of lawns, shrubs and specimen trees. The landscaped Park is separated from the gardens by a ha-ha and features an avenue of ancient Spanish chestnuts. Medieval jousting on Suns and BH in Park.

Open 5 Apr–18 Oct daily 11–6 (last admission 5pm).

Tue–Thu £1.80 (ch 90p); Mon & Fri £1.60 (ch 80p); Sun (with jousting) £2.40 (ch £1.20); BH Sun & Mon £3.50 (ch £1)
P ⬚ (licensed) ⅋ wc

Begonia
semperflorens

39

Chippenham
Wiltshire   Map 3 ST97

SHELDON MANOR
☏ (0249) 653120

Part 13th-, 15th- and 17th-century manor house with 12 acres of gardens which descend in informal terraces to the south. The former orchard is now planted with old fashioned roses, rare shrubs, climbers and trees. Ancient yew trees, hedges and water garden. Plants labelled. "Shakespeare at Sheldon" 7–11 July. House also open.

Open 22 Mar–Oct, Sun, Thu & BHs 12.30–6 (House opens 2pm).

* Garden £1 (ch 50p); House and Garden £2 (ch 50p).
P ⚲ (licensed) ⚲ & (gardens & ground floor) wc

Chirk
Clwyd   Map 7 SJ23

CHIRK CASTLE
(off the A5, ½m W Chirk Village, 1½m driveway) ☏ (0691) 777701

13th-century castle in 5 acres of landscaped gardens with many fine trees and shrubs. The New Garden has beds of shrubs, conifers, herbaceous and rock plants. There are also rhododendrons, topiary yews and hedges, and a rose garden. 18th-century parkland. Castle also open.

Open 17 Apr–Sep Sun, Tue–Fri & BH Mon; 3–25 Oct Sat & Sun 12–5 (last admission 4.30).

£1.80 (ch 65p), Family ticket £4.50 Party 20 +.
P ⚲ (licensed) ⚲ (ex guide dogs) & (ground floor and gardens only) (NT)

Claydon
Suffolk   Map 5 TM15

THE ROSARIUM
☏ Ipswich (0473) 830334

At this world-famous garden, over 500 varieties of old roses can be seen, many of which are very rare and others which were thought to be extinct. Other plants are interspersed with the roses and the grounds also feature an 18th-century lime-kiln. The owners are often on hand and are willing to answer questions about the roses.

Open daily 15 May–Jul 2–7. Other times by appointment.

* 75p.
P (nearby)

Clearwell
Gloucestershire   Map 3 SO50

CLEARWELL CASTLE
☏ Dean (0594) 32320

Eight acres of formal gardens on five different levels are being restored to their former Edwardian glory. The grounds belong to a country house hotel and include shrubs, herbaceous borders and large trees can be seen, and there is also a lake with wild duck, and bird gardens. Some plants labelled.

Open daily. Coaches by prior arrangement.

Free.
P ⚲ No picnics ⚲ & (wc) wc

Clevedon
Avon   Map 3 ST47

CLEVEDON COURT
(off B3130) ☏ (0272) 872257

The terraces of this attractive garden are thought to date from the 18th century. There are informal plantings of rare shrubs and herbaceous plants. Chusan palms, magnolias and a large Himalayan musk rose are amongst the plants which can be seen. House also open.

Open Apr–Sep, Wed, Thu, Sun & BH Mon 2.30–5.30 (last admission 5). Coach parties by prior arrangement.

£1.50.
P ⚲ ⚲ wc (NT)

Cliveden
Buckinghamshire   Map 4 SU98

CLIVEDEN
(3m NE of Maidenhead)
☏ Burnham (06286) 5069

Landscaped gardens and grounds covering 180 acres set high above the River Thames.

There are fine lawns with box hedges, herbaceous borders, topiary, a rose garden and a grassed amphitheatre. The oriental-style water gardens have spring and autumn flowering shrubs, trees and ground cover. Garden pavillions, statues and vantage points are found throughout the gardens. The wooded slopes lead down to riverside walks. The 19th-century mansion, is now an hotel. Open-Air Theatre 24-28 Jun & 1-5 Jul.

Open Grounds Mar-Dec daily 11-6 or sunset if earlier.

Grounds £2 (Mon-Wed (ex BH) £1.50).
P ⌷ *(Apr-Oct)* ✘ *(NT)*

Cockermouth

Cumbria   **Map 11 NY13**

WORDSWORTH HOUSE

The birthplace of William Wordsworth in 1770. Very pleasant walled garden planted with old-fashioned perennials and annuals. Large lawn with steps leading to terrace walk overlooking the River Derwent.

Open Apr-Oct daily (ex Thu) 11-5, Sun 2-5 (last admission 4.30).

£1.30 (ch 65p).
⌷ *wc No pushchairs (NT)*

Colchester

Essex   **Map 5 TL92**

BETH CHATTO GARDENS, WHITE BARN HOUSE
(4m E on A133 at Elmstead Market)
☎ *Wivenhoe (020622) 2007*

Six acres of attractively landscaped gardens showing many unusual plants thriving under varying conditions. The Water Garden has five large pools surrounded by exotic bog plants. There is also a Shade Garden and a Mediterranean Garden. Some plants labelled. Adjoining nursery.

Open all year: Mar-Oct Mon-Sat 9-5; Nov-Feb Mon-Fri 9-4 (closed BH & 2 weeks Xmas).

50p.
P ✘ ふ *(NGS)*

Colonsay, Isle of

Strathclyde   **Map 10 NR39**
Argyll

KILORAN GARDENS
2m N of Scalasaig ☎ *(09512) 301*

Set close to Colonsay House, these peaceful gardens and woodlands, occupying about 30 acres, are a riot of colour during the Spring, and are noted for their fine display of rhododendrons and shrubs, including embothriums and magnolias. The Gulf Stream encourages plants not normally found at this latitude. Some plants labelled.

Open daily dawn to dusk.

Free.
P

Coniston

Cumbria   **Map 7 SD39**

BRANTWOOD
(2½m SE off B5285, on unclass rd east side of Coniston Water) ☎ *(0966) 41396*

Former home of John Ruskin, beautifully situated with views over Coniston Water. The 15-acre woodland garden, with rhododendrons and azaleas, was originally laid out by Ruskin and is now undergoing restoration. Nature trails. House also open.

Open all year mid Mar-mid Nov 11-5.30, then Wed-Sun 11-4.30.
Gardens, grounds and nature trails 50p (ch 35p); House & gardens £1.50 (ch 75p).
P ⌷ *(licensed)* ✘ *wc*

Corsham

Wiltshire   **Map 3 ST86**

CORSHAM COURT
☎ *(0249) 712214*

Elizabethan manor with 12 acres of grounds by 'Capability' Brown and Humphrey Repton. The secluded gardens and lawns contain specimen trees, herbaceous borders, rose gardens and a lily pond. The arboretum (commenced in 1983) has many rare species of trees and shrubs. Some plants labelled.

Open 15 Jan-15 Dec Tue-Thu, Sat & Sun 2-4, Jun-Sep & BH 2-6.

Gardens £1.20 (ch 60p); House & Gardens £2.50 (ch £1.20) Party 20+.
P ✘ *wc*

Coton

Northamptonshire   Map 4 SP67

COTON MANOR GARDENS
☎ Northampton (0604) 740219

Beautiful gardens, full of charm and character, with trees, shrubs, herbaceous plants, roses etc., displayed on different levels. Water gardens. Extensive collection of waterfowl and other birds. Some plants labelled.

Open Apr–Oct Thu, Sun, BH Mon & Tue following; also Wed in Jul & Aug; Oct Sun only 2–6.

£1.50 (ch 50p).
P ⌂ ㄙ wc *Unusual plants for sale*

Cranborne

Dorset   Map 4 SU01

CRANBORNE MANOR PRIVATE GARDENS AND GARDEN CENTRE
☎ (07254) 248

Beautiful 17th-century gardens originally laid out by John Tradescant with many interesting plants, trees and avenues. The Walled Garden includes herbs, old roses, a Jacobean mount garden and a knot garden planted with 16th- and 17th-century flowers. River garden with daffodils and flowering cherries. Garden centre with old roses, and unusual and rare plants.

Open Gardens: Mar–Oct Wed only 9–5. Garden Centre open all year Mon–Sat 9–5, Sun 2–5.

£1 (ch 10p).
P ⋔ ✕ ㄙ

Crathes

Grampian   Map 15 NO79
Kincardineshire

CRATHES CASTLE AND GARDEN
(3m E of Banchory on A93) ☎ (033044) 525

A 16th-century baronial castle with interesting and colourful gardens divided into eight small specialised areas. There are old yew hedges, herbaceous borders and a great many trees and shrubs. Nature trails in the grounds. Castle also open.

Open Gardens & grounds daily 9.30–sunset; castle Etr–Sep daily, wknds in Oct (ex 31st Oct) 11–6.

Grounds and garden £1.80 (ch 90p); grounds 80p (ch 40p); grounds and castle £2 (ch £1); Castle, gardens and grounds £2.50 (ch £1.25).
⌂ *(Etr–Sep) (NTS)*

Crewkerne

Somerset   Map 3 ST40

CLAPTON COURT GARDENS
(3m S on B3165) ☎ (0460) 73220

Interesting and beautiful gardens, of over 10 acres, with formal terraces, lawns, rockery, rose and water gardens. Woodland garden with streams and glades. Many interesting plants and shrubs including 200-yr-old ash tree. Good spring and autumn colour. Plants labelled. Fuchsia and Pelargonium Festival 1 May–5 Jun. Garden Centre.

Open all year Mon–Fri 10.30–5, Sun 2–5, Etr Sat and all Sats in May only 2–5.

£1.50 (ch 14 30p, pen £1.20) Party 20+.
P ⌂ ✕ ㄙ wc

Culross

Fife   Map 11 NS98

CULROSS PALACE
☎ New Mills (0383) 880608

Three tiers of terraced gardens form the grounds to the palace (dating from 1597 and 1611 and also open to the public). These 'hanging gardens' are very sheltered and have many varieties of shrubs. Other features include a rose garden, fruit trees and a bed of Scottish thistles!

Open all year daily: Apr–Sep Mon–Sat 9.30–7, Sun 2–7; Oct–Mar Mon–Sat 9.30–4, Sun 2–4.

* *£1 (ch and pen, 50p) Party 11+ (Includes guided tour of house and garden).*
P *(nearby) (AM)*

Cusworth

South Yorkshire   Map 8 SE50

CUSWORTH HALL MUSEUM
(2m NW Doncaster)
☎ Doncaster (0302) 782342

18th-century house, now a museum, in parkland landscaped by Richard Woods in 1763.

There are lawns, ornamental trees and shrubs and lakes.

Open Park: all year daily until dusk. Museum all year Mon–Thu & Sat 11–5 (4pm Nov–Feb). Sun 1–5 (4pm Nov–Feb) (Closed Xmas).

Free.

P (ex coaches) ✻ ⴵ *(ground floor & gardens only) wc*

Dacre

Cumbria   Map 12 NY42

DALEMAIN

☎ *Pooley Bridge (08536) 450*

Beautiful and historic garden in parkland setting enjoying far-reaching views of the surrounding fells. Elizabethan in origin, with many walls remaining from that period. There is also an Elizabethan-style knot garden and a famous herbaceous border on the terrace walk. The Hasell family — all keen gardeners — have collected many rare and unusual plants including shrub and species roses. The wild garden lies alongside Dacre Beck and the deer park has many fine trees. Special guided tours and 'garden walks' by arrangement. Plants labelled. Craft Fair 25–26 Jul.

Open Etr Sun–mid Oct, Sun–Thu 11.15–5.

Gardens £1 (ch free); House & Gardens £2 (ch 5–16 £1, family ticket £5).

P 묘 *(licensed)* ⟱ ✻ ⴵ *(wc) wc Garden centre*

Dalwood

Devon   Map 3 ST20

BURROW FARM GARDEN

(4m NW Axminster off A35)

☎ *Wilmington (040483) 285*

A 5-acre landscaped garden in a beautiful secluded setting, with panoramic views over the Devon countryside. It has been planted for foliage effect and includes a large bog garden set in woodland with gunnera, astilbes, etc. Rhododendrons and azaleas are a feature of the woodland slopes. Rose and herbaceous garden with a pergola walk. Some plants labelled. Guided tours for parties by arrangement. Advisory service.

Open Apr–Sep daily 2–7.

£1 (ch 20p).

P ✻ ⴵ *wc Plants for sale*

Dartington

Devon   Map 3 SX76

DARTINGTON HALL

☎ *Totnes (0803) 862271 ext 285*

Gardens of 28½ acres dating back to the 14th-century and created alongside Great Hall. Careful plantings of trees and shrubs, taking account of natural landscape features, create vistas and views of hall and surrounding countryside. Spring-flowering bulbs, azaleas, rhododendrons and magnolias, and autumn colours are particular attractions. Advisory service.

Open daily (gardens occasionally closed for special events), dawn to dusk.

Admission by donation. Guided tours (by arrangement) £1.50 per person.

P 묘 *wc Plants for sale (NGS)*

Devizes

Wiltshire   Map 4 SU06

BROADLEAS GARDENS

☎ *(0380) 2035*

An 8-acre garden with an attractive 'Dell' which is planted with unusual trees and shrubs, azaleas and rhododendrons. Many rare plants can be found in the 'secret garden' and winter garden. New Woodland Walk. Plants labelled. Guided tours available for booked parties.

Open Sun, Wed and Thur Apr–29 Oct, 2–6.

£1 (ch 50p).

P 묘 *(by prior arrangement) wc Plants for sale*

Dinmore

Hereford and Worcester   Map 3 SO45

DINMORE MANOR

☎ *Canon Pyon (0432) 71322*

Small gardens of about one acre, mainly rock gardens with alpine plants, in the grounds of the Chapel of the Knights Hospitallers of St John of Jerusalem. Chapel also open.

Open all year (ex 25 Dec) 10–6.

60p (ch and pen 30p).

P ✻ ⴵ *(gardens & ground floor) wc*

Drewsteignton

Devon   Map 3 SX79

CASTLE DROGO
(2m NE of Chagford, turn off A382 at Sandy Park) ☏ *Chagford (06473) 3306*

A formal garden of 12 acres enclosed by yew hedges. Designed by Sir Edwin Lutyens with plantings advised by George Dillestone. Formal terraces with roses and herbaceous borders. Other features include aromatic herbs, rhododendron dell and large, round croquet lawn. Plants labelled. House also open. Guided tours by special arrangement.

Open Apr–Oct daily 11–6 (last admission 5.30).

Garden & grounds £1.20 (ch 60p); House & Garden £2.50 (ch £1.25) Party.
P 🚽 🕏 🍴 ⚰ *(wc) wc (NT)*

Dunbar

Lothian *East Lothian*   Map 12 NT67

TYNINGHAME GARDENS
(1m N of A1 between Dunbar & East Linton) ☏ *East Linton (0620) 860330*

Beautiful and varied gardens. 'Secret Garden' including large rose collection; 'Walled Garden' of nearly 4 acres including apple walk and miniature arboretum (some trees and shrubs labelled); 'The Wilderness' with woodland beds including maples, cherries and azaleas providing fine autumn colour and 'The Parterre'. Guided tours for parties by arrangement.

Open Jun–Sep, Mon–Fri, 10.30–4.30.

* *70p (ch 25p, pen 40p).*
P 🍴 ⚰ *wc*

Dunfermline

Fife   Map 11 NT08

PITTENCRIEFF HOUSE MUSEUM GARDENS
Pittencrieff Park ☏ *(0383) 722935 or 721814*

Gardens attached to the 17th-century mansion which is now a museum. Situated in a rugged glen with lawns, hothouses and borders, it is overlooked by the ruined 11th-century Malcolm Canmore's Tower.

Open 3 May–5 Sep daily (ex Tue) 11–5.

Free.
P 🍴 ⚰ *(gardens & ground floor)*

Dunoon

Strathclyde *Argyll*   Map 10 NS17

SCOTTISH WHITE HEATHER FARM
(5m SW of Dunoon) ☏ *Toward (036987) 237*

Extensive gardens including both white and coloured heathers and conifers.

Open all year Apr–Sep Tue–Sun, Oct–Mar Mon–Fri 9–6 (visitors advised to telephone in advance during winter months).

Free.
P ⚰ *Plants for sale*

Dunster

Somerset   Map 3 SS95

DUNSTER CASTLE
☏ *(0643) 821314*

Fourteen acres of subtropical terraced gardens with shrubs. Surrounded by parkland. Also 11th-century and later castle open to public. Plants labelled.

Open Apr–Oct, grounds daily; Castle Sat–Wed 11–5 (Oct 12–4).

Garden & Park £1 (ch 50p) Castle, Garden & Park £2.50 (ch £1.20).
P 🍴 🍴 *(NT)*

Durham

Co Durham   Map 12 NZ24

ST AIDAN'S COLLEGE GROUNDS
Windmill Hill ☏ *(091) 3865011*

The spacious and well-stocked grounds surround the college which was designed by Sir Basil Spence and was built in the early 1960s. Landscaped by Professor Brian Hackett, they are at their best during July when the shrub beds are in flower. Features include a laburnum walk and a reflecting pool with aquatic plants and fish. From the garden there are fine views of Durham Cathedral. Guided tours by prior arrangement.

Open all year daily from 9–dusk.

Free, but donations to NGS.
P 🚽 *(by prior arrangement)* 🍴 ⚰ *wc*

UNIVERSITY OF DURHAM BOTANIC GARDEN
Hollingside Lane, off South Road
☏ *64971 ext 657 or 743*

The Botanic Garden, which covers 18 acres, is set in mature woodland on a beautiful southwest-facing site. Major forest types from North America, Central Europe, and the Himalayas are represented and arranged in ecological groups to give an indication of how the plants would interact in the wild. Also heather garden, rose garden, herbaceous bed, cactus house and tropical houses. Plants labelled. Guided tours last Wed in month (10 a.m., free), other times for parties by arrangement.

Open daily 10–4.

Free.

P

Dursley

Gloucestershire   **Map 3 ST79**

HUNTS COURT GARDEN AND NURSERY

☎ *Dursley (0453) 47440*

Nearly 400 varieties of specie, climbing and old-fashioned roses can be seen in this 2½-acre garden. The roses are interspersed with interesting ground-cover plants and unusual shrubs. The garden holds part of the National Collection of pre-1900 paeony cultivars. Other attractions include heather and herbaceous borders and a recently planted area containing trees with interesting foliage. Plants labelled.

Open Gardens 5 May–Jul & Sep Tue–Sat, also Suns 14, 21, 28 Jun & 5, 12 Jul 2–6.

60p (ch 15 20p).

P ⌂ *(on request)* ✗ *wc Plants for sale*

East Grinstead

West Sussex   **Map 5 TQ33**

STANDEN

(1½m S, signposted from B2110)

☎ *East Grinstead (0342) 23029*

This beautiful hillside garden of 12 acres overlooks the Medway Valley. There are many mature trees, both exotic and native species, which provide good autumn colour. Heathers, magnolias, azaleas and rhododendrons are also grown. There is a wild garden, a quarry garden with pond, ferns etc., and a special woodland walk. Most plants labelled. House also open.

Open Apr–Oct Wed–Sun, 2–6 (last admission 5.30) Coach parties by prior arrangement only.

Gardens £1 (ch 50p) House & Garden £2 (ch £1). Party 15+.

P ⌂ ✗ *(ex woodland walk) wc (NT)*

East Lambrook

Somerset   **Map 3 ST41**

EAST LAMBROOK MANOR GARDEN & MARGERY FISH NURSERY

☎ *South Petherton (0460) 40328*

This Grade One 'Plantsman's' garden dates from the turn of the century, and is one of the earliest cottage-style gardens in Britain. Many rare plants are grown within the 2 acres and the nursery also has unusual stock. The garden is a memorial to its late owner, Margery Fish, and as well as a fine collection of hellebores there are also 'green' and 'silver' gardens. Guided tours by appointment. Some plants labelled. Advisory service available.

Open daily (ex Sun, other than BH) 9–1 & 2–5.

£1 (ch 10 free).

P *(nearby)* ✗ *wc Plants for sale*

Iris xiphioides

Chrysanthemum segetum
'Corn Marigold'

Eastnor

Hereford & Worcester   Map 3 SO73

EASTNOR CASTLE
☎ Ledbury (0531) 2304

The extensive grounds of this early 19th-century house contain some fine mature specimens of trees. Most of the trees to be seen are conifers and a leaflet is available with details of the individual trees. There is also a deer park of around 500 acres.

* Open 19 May–Sep Sun; also Wed & Thu in July & Aug, and BH Mons, 2.15–5.30 Coach parties by prior apointment only.

* £1.20 (ch & pen 60p).
P ⊒ wc

Eccleshall

Staffordshire   Map 7 SJ82

ECCLESHALL CASTLE
☎ Eccleshall (0785) 850250

Twenty acres in all, consisting of a formal garden which surrounds the William and Mary House and a woodland garden. The formal garden includes roses, herbaceous and other borders, climbing plants in the dry moat and a fine, old Wisteria sinensis. The woods include avenues of lime and hornbeam, as well as a wide variety of native and exotic trees and flowering shrubs. Plants labelled. House also open.

Open 19 Apr–11 Oct Sun and BH Mon & also Mon & Tue Jun–Sep, 2–5.30, Parties at other times by arrangement.

£2 (ch 80p, family £5).
P ⊒ ⊼ ⅙ (wc) wc

Edinburgh

Lothian *Midlothian*   Map 11 NT27

ROYAL BOTANIC GARDEN
Inverleith Row ☎ 031-552 7171 ext 260

Scotland's national botanic garden, covers 70 acres. Internationally famous rock garden with over 4000 alpine plants. Extensive arboretum, woodland garden and large collection of rhododendrons (over 400 species). Demonstration garden with botanical and horticultural displays. Ten landscaped plant houses with succulents, orchids, ferns, cycads and many other tropical plants. Plants labelled. Also Exhibition Hall and Inverleith House Gallery with museum-type exhibits, paintings, etc, relating to botany and horticulture. Specialist tours and courses by arrangement.

Open daily (ex 1 Jan & 25 Dec), Mar–Oct Mon–Sat 9–1 hr before sunset, Sun 11–1 hr before sunset; Oct–Mar Mon–Sat 9–sunset, Sun 11–sunset; Plant houses and Exhibition Hall, Mon–Sat 10–5, Sun 11–5.

Free.
P *(Arboretum Place)* ⊒ *(Apr–Sep)* ✖ *(ex guide dogs)* ⅙ *(wc)* wc

Ednaston

Derbyshire   Map 8 SK24

EDNASTON MANOR
☎ Ashbourne (0335) 60325

This 3-acre garden, the grounds of a Lutyens house (not open to the public), is of botanical interest. There is a large collection of shrubs, shrub roses, clematis and unusual plants. Most plants labelled.

Open Etr–Sep, Mon–Fri 1–4.30 & Sun 2–5.30.

Free.
P ⊒ *(Suns)* ✖ ⅙ Garden Centre

Edzell

Tayside *Angus*   Map 15 NO56

EDZELL CASTLE
☎ 031-244 301

The ruined castle of Edzell contains a spectacular walled garden dating from the 17th century. Lord Edzell and his master mason achieved triumph in the decorative treatment given to the garden wall. The garden also contains a summerhouse designed as a retreat from the main house, from which the garden can be seen.

Open Apr–Sep Mon–Sat 9.30–7, Sun 2–7; Oct–Mar Mon–Sat 9.30–4, Sun 2–4 (closed Tue & Thu throughout year).

50p (ch 16 & pen 25p).
P & wc (AM)

Elcot
Berkshire   **Map 4 SU36**
ELCOT PARK HOTEL
(5½m W Newbury off A4)
✆ *Kintbury (0488) 58100*

Sixteen-acre garden with superb views across the Kennet Valley. Mainly lawns and lovely mature woodland, laid out by Sir William Paxton in 1848. There is also a magnificent display of daffodils, rhododendrons and other shrubs in spring.

Open all year daily 10–6.

Free (ex on NGS Suns).
P ⚑ (licensed restaurant) & wc (NGS)

Elsham
Humberside   **Map 8 TA01**
ELSHAM HALL COUNTRY PARK
Brigg ✆ *Barnetby (0652) 688698*

Fifteen acres of wide lawns and lakes set in an area of mature trees. Arboretum planted in 1982 and containing 85 varieties of British native and forestry trees. Butterfly garden with over 80 butterfly and moth host plants grown. Good displays of spring flowers and snowdrops. Some plants labelled. Many other attractions at site including crafts, rare livestock breeds, bird garden, fishing, nature trails and quizzes and adventure playground. Guided tours by appointment.

Park open daily, Etr–Sep 11–8 (or dusk), last entrance 5.30 Mon–Sat, 6.30 Sun & BH. Oct–Etr open Sun only, 11–4 (or sometimes earlier). (Closed 17 Apr and 25 Dec).

£1.50 (ch 16 80p ch 3 free). Parties 20+. Reduced rates in winter.
P ⚑ (licensed) ✗ & (wc) wc Plants for sale

Enfield
Gt London   **Map 4 TQ39**
CAPEL MANOR
(2½m NE)
✆ *Lea Valley (0992) 763849*

There are many large trees in the 25–30 acres of grounds of the Horticultural College at Capel Manor. Herbaceous plants, old-fashioned roses and other shrubs are grown, as well as bedding plants. Other features include a 17th-century garden with herbs, a rock and water garden, extensive glasshouses and trials gardens. Guided tours by appointment. Some plants labelled. Special events include: 19 Apr 'Spring Colour' (NGS); 16–17 May Countryside Fayre & Cacti Show; 20–21 Jun Horticultural Show; 25–26 Jul Fuschia Show and 'Gardening Which' Open Day; 12–13 Sep Chrysanthemum Show and Craft Fayre.

Open daily 10–4.30 (5.30 on Sat & Sun from Apr–Oct).

£1.25 (ch 18 & pen 60p) Party Special rates for open weekends available on application. P ⚑ ⛽ & (wc) wc Plants for sale on open weekends (NGS)

Esher
Surrey   **Map 4 TQ16**
CLAREMONT LANDSCAPE GARDEN
(On S edge of Esher, E of A307)
✆ *Bookham (0372) 53402*

This is the earliest surviving example of an English landscape garden and has recently been restored. It has a lake with an island pavilion, grotto, turf amphitheatre, viewpoint and avenue, and covers about 50 acres. Guided tours are available for parties by arrangement. Claremont Fete 15–18 July.

Open daily (ex 25 Dec & 1 Jan): Apr–Oct 9–7 or sunset; Nov–Mar 9–4.

Mon–Sat 80p (ch 40p), Sun £1 (ch 50p).
P ⚑ wc (NT)

Exbury
Hampshire   **Map 4 SU40**
EXBURY GARDENS
✆ *Fawley (0703) 891203*

Woodland gardens on the east bank of the Beaulieu River, extending to 200 acres. →

Contains the Rothschild collection of rhodo-dendrons together with azaleas, magnolias, camelias and many fine trees. Two acres of rock garden. Most of plants labelled.

Open daily 7 Mar–Etr 1–5.30, Etr–19 Jul 10–5.30.

7th Mar–Good Fri £1.50 ch & pen 80p; Etr wknd & every Sun in May incl BH 24 & 25 May £2.50, ch & pen £2. May–June ex BH Mon & Sun £2, ch & pen £1.50; 1–19 Jul £1.50, ch & pen 80p. Party.
P 🚻 🛗 ♿ *(wc) wc Plants for sale*

Exeter

Devon   Map 3 SX99

UNIVERSITY OF EXETER GARDENS
The Queen's Drive ☎ (0392) 263263

Extensive landscaped grounds covering 250 acres. Includes Reed Hall Gardens (laid out in 1860s by the firm of Veitch) which formed the nucleus for the rest of the estate. Wide range of evergreen and deciduous trees and shrubs from many parts of the world. Diverse plant collection including roses, heathers, rhododendrons and magnolias. National Azara collection in the Old Botanical Gardens. Plants labelled.

Open daily (parties by arrangement only and during university vacations).

Free.
P 🚌

Exmouth

Devon   Map 3 SY08

A LA RONDE
Summer Lane (2m N on A376)
☎ (0395) 265514

Ten acres of parkland with wide views of coast and Dartmoor, surrounding unique 16-sided house with lawns and ha ha.

* *Open Etr–Oct Mon–Sat 10–6, Sun 2–7.*

*Free; guided tour of house * £1.50 (ch 7–16 50p) Party.*
P 🚻 🛗 ✗ wc

Falkland

Fife   Map 11 NO20

FALKLAND PALACE AND GARDEN
☎ (0337) 57397

A series of herbaceous beds with mixed planting surround a large lawn in this 3-acre garden. Around this colourful perimeter runs a circular walk with splendid views of the ruins of the East Range of the Palace. Plants labelled. Palace also open to public. Displays of archery, falconry, dancing and music in garden on 27/28 June & 25/26 July.

Open Apr–Sep Mon–Sat 10–6 & Sun 2–6, Oct Sat 10–6 & Sun 2–6.

Gardens £1.20 (ch & pen 60p); Palace & Garden £1.80 (ch & pen 90p).
P *(nearby)* 🛗 ✗ ♿ *(garden only) wc (NTS)*

Falmouth

Cornwall   Map 2 SW83

FOX-ROSEHILL GARDENS
Melvill Road ☎ Truro (0872) 78131 ext 353

This is a long-established, picturesque garden of 2 acres, owned and maintained by Carrick District Council. There are many mature, exotic trees and shrubs, and fine lawns and vistas. In recent years a number of rare and tender species have been planted in the shelter of the mature trees. Guided tours available by arrangement. Special open day as part of Cornwall Gardens Festival on 23 Apr.

Open daily; coach parties should arrange visits in advance.

Free.
P *(on road near garden)* ♿

Papaver rhoeas
'Poppy'

THE DISAPPEARING GARDEN
By Alan Titchmarsh

It happened to the dodo, the great auk and the Arabian oryx. All three became extinct in the wild. As far as the dodo and the auk were concerned that meant total extinction; the oryx was luckier. A bunch of conservationists ensured it's survival in captivity and it's now been returned to nature.

Animals and birds have one great advantage over plants: they're cuddly. Nobody seems to want to stroke a sunflower, tickle a tagetes or pat a petunia. Plants don't move much either, so you can't watch them flitting from flowerbed to flowerbed, or flying around looking for food, or playing with their seedlings. All they seem to do is bask in the sun, and it's much more fun to watch a fox do that.

But plants are living things, too, and just as likely to slip off the face of the earth as any mammal or bird.

As far as the gardener is concerned, conservation is usually a matter of putting in a pond to attract frogs and toads and newts, and having a patch of nettles to encourage butterflies to lay their eggs. It's vital and very enjoyable to take part in this kind of conservation.

But while gardeners are busy encouraging wildlife, the very things they've been growing and developing over three centuries are slipping quietly into extinction behind their backs.

Garden flowers are dying out. I'm not talking about the petunias and

'Clive Greaves' — one of the few surviving Scabiosa Caucasica.

French marigolds that are offered in ever-increasing numbers year after year, but the older varieties that grew in our grandfathers' gardens and which were often possessed of a grace, a fragrance, and a healthy vigour that would easily earn them a place in today's garden.

Take scabious for instance. My grandad grew it on his allotment as a cut flower. At one time there were several named varieties with different coloured flowers. They'd been raised by a west-country nurseryman called Isaac House.

Eight or ten of them there were, from the pale blue of 'Clive Greaves' to the rich iris purple of the one the raiser was proud enough to name after himself. 'Isaac House'. 'Clive Greaves' alone has survived, apart from a white and the odd insipid pink.

Why did the rest die out? Well, they were pricy when first offered by the nurseryman; one or two of them were a touch tricky to grow, but really the reason for their disappearance was that nobody cared. Sad.

50

Agrostemma Milas 'Corncockle' — near extinction in the wild.

So how can gardeners help to prevent plants from becoming extinct without the help of a crystal ball to see which varieties are likely to fall from favour?

The answer is to keep an eye on old gardens whose owners you know, and to encourage them to pass on cuttings to you of anything you don't recognise, or which you don't recall seeing in any other garden.

Occasionally this may lead you into embarrasing situations (they may have paid a fortune for the plant and hacking at it with a knife doesn't appeal one jot), or the plant may be brand new and equally valuable. But with older border plants there's less likely to be a problem. Gardeners are an incredibly generous lot and nearly always willing to do swaps.

But there is one area where all gardeners can act positively to prevent plants that are available right now from becoming extinct, and that is in the annual flower garden.

Flip through the pages of a seed catalogue under the heading of 'hardy annuals' and see how many names you don't recognise. Order a packet of each. There's a tremendous conservatism among gardeners which makes them stick to the same varieties year after year; that's why we end up with more and more varieties of fewer and fewer plants. Specialisation leads to extinction.

A seed catalogue in front of me at the moment lists 33 varieties of Petunia and 42 varieties of French and African marigolds. They're good plants, but so too are the far less trumpeted Anchusa 'Blue Angel', with rich blue forget-me-not flowers; Agrostemma 'Milas', the corncockle that's near extinct in the wild and which has graceful pink flowers pencilled with dusky purple. *Phacelia campanularia* is a dwarf annual with bell flowers of pure gentian blue and yet hardly anyone grows it, in spite of the fact that it's just 45p a packet.

Ten years ago the seed catalogues were bursting with far more varieties of annual flowers than they are now. In another ten years time will my beloved corncockle and phacelia have disappeared too?

The rich blue flowers of Phacelia Campanularia.

There's much talk of wild flower gardens today, but relatively little action on the part of gardeners. They may leave a corner of their garden 'fallow' as a gesture in the direction of a wild flower plot that attracts butterflies, but it's possible to do much more if a small chunk of grass can be properly managed and planted with wild flowers.

I say 'planted' rather than sown because it's easy to believe that wild flower seeds will thrive if you just scatter them on your lawn and refrain from mowing. In reality the grass smothers the germinating seeds and they will often fail to amount to much. Seeds sown in pots and trays in autumn and germinated outdoors where they can be sheltered from heavy rains but not from the low temperatures that are often necessary to break dormancy, will emerge the following spring (though some may take a couple of years to come through) and can then be pricked out and eventually transplanted to bare patches made in the existing lawn. That gives them a head start.

Now you can enjoy knapweed, field scabious, cowslips, primroses and foxgloves, where previously only grass and plantains grew. Autumn mowing, where the long growth is raked off is vital to keep the plants seeding themselves.

So if summer mowing has never appealed, settle instead for a flowery meadow. But above all, bring back some of the rarities into the flower border.

A nodding blue phacelia may not sound as romantic as an Arabian oryx, but it has just as much right to survival, and will give any kindly gardener just as much pleasure. It's cheaper, too.

Footnote Keen garden plant conservationists can join the National Council for the Conservation of Plants and Gardens (NCCPG). Details available from NCCPG, Wisley Gardens, Woking, Surrey GU23 6QB.

Alan Titchmarsh is a well-known gardening expert and author of several books on gardening. He appears regularly on television and radio. He also writes a weekly column for the Daily Mail.

Felbrigg

Norfolk · Map 9 TG23

FELBRIGG HALL

The grounds of this fine 17th-century house contain formal gardens and a walled garden with a restored dovecote. There is an impressive display of camellias in the orangery and the house and gardens are surrounded by mature landscaped park and woodland.

Open 11 Apr–1 Nov Mon, Wed, Thu, Sat, Sun & BH 1.30–5.30 (closed Good Fri).

£2 (ch £1) includes admission to principal rooms of house. Party 15+.

⌂ ✹ *(NT)*

Fishbourne

West Sussex · Map 4 SU80

FISHBOURNE ROMAN PALACE AND MUSEUM

Salthill Road ☏ Chichester (0243) 785859

The northern half of the formal garden of the Palace has been replanted to its original 1st century AD plan based on information recovered from excavation. This includes decorative box hedging, espalier fruit trees and beds of Acanthus and sweet briar. There is also a herb bed which contains labelled examples of more than 20 herbs known to have been grown in Roman times.

Open daily Mar, Apr & Oct 10–5, May–Sep 10–6, Nov 10–4, and on Sun only Dec–Feb 10–4.

* *£1.30 (ch 60p, pen and students £1) Party 20+.*

P ⌂ ⑂ ✹ ♿ *(wc) wc Plants for sale*

Flimwell

Kent · Map 5 TQ73

BEDGEBURY NATIONAL PINETUM

(1½ m N off A21)

☏ Goudhurst (0580) 211392

Established in 1925 by the Forestry Commission, this 160-acre site houses the National Collection of conifers. There is also a large collection of dwarf conifers, and various specie rhododendrons and rare broadleaved trees and shrubs, especially oaks and maples. Other features of the pinetum include streams and a lake, and wide grass avenues.

Plants labelled. Advisory service on request.

Open daily 10–8 or dusk.

* *60p (ch 5–18 30p).*

P ⑂ *(Sat & Sun Apr–Sep & BH) wc*

Fontwell

West Sussex · Map 4 SU90

DENMANS GARDENS

Clock House, Denmans

☏ Eastergate (024368) 2808

This garden, which covers just over 3½ acres, has been developed over the last 30 years. The emphasis is on shape, colour and texture, and individual plantings are allowed to self-seed and ramble — often in gravel. Many rare shrubby plants and climbers can be seen in this garden, which occupies a level sheltered setting at the foot of the South Downs, only 5 miles from the sea. Day courses are run at the garden, and guided tours are available by special arrangement.

Open Apr–1 Nov Wed–Sun and also BH, 1–6.

£1.50 (ch 75p, pen £1.40) Party 15+.

P ⑂ ✹ ♿ *wc Plants for sale*

Gawsworth

Cheshire · Map 7 SJ86

GAWSWORTH HALL

☏ North Rode (02603) 456

Peaceful English country garden with lawns sweeping down to large medieval fishponds. Courtyard and rose garden. The extensive grounds also have a unique tilting ground. Open-air theatre Jun & Jul. Tudor manor also open.

Open 25 Mar–Oct daily 2–6 & 26 Dec–2 Jan 2–5.

Gardens 95p (ch 50p) House and Gardens £1.90 (ch 95p) Party.

P ⑂ ⑂ ♿ *(garden only) wc*

Gigha, Isle of

Strathclyde *Argyll* · Map 10 NR64

ACHAMORE GARDENS

Ardminish ☏ Gigha (05835) 254

60 acres of mainly woodland gardens with wonderful displays of wild hyacinths, →

candelabra primulas, rhododendrons and azaleas.

Open all year 10–sunset.

£1 (ch & pen 50p).
P ⛁ (licensed) ⛩ & Garden centre

Glamis

Tayside *Angus*   **Map 15 NO34**

GLAMIS CASTLE

☏ *(030784) 242 and 243*

Family home of Her Majesty Queen Elizabeth the Queen Mother set in attractive grounds. The 2-acre Italian Garden on the east side of the castle has 2 gazebos, shrub and herbaceous borders, and is surrounded by high, neatly clipped yew hedges. The 17th-century sundial (21ft high) is the main feature of the grounds. Scotland's Garden Scheme Open Day 28 Jun; Transport Extravaganza 12 Jul. Castle also open.

Open Etr then May–Sep daily (ex Sat) 1–5.

Grounds 70p (pen 50p, ch & disabled free)
Castle & grounds £2 (ch £1, pen £1.50).
P ⛁ ⛩ ✠ & (ground floor & gardens; wc)
wc Plants for sale

Glasgow

Strathclyde *Lanarkshire*   **Map 11 NS56**

BOTANIC GARDEN

(off Great Western Road)
☏ *041-334 2422*

Established in 1817, this garden contains an outstanding collection of plants. The Kibble Palace is a unique glasshouse with, among others, a famous collection of tree ferns. The main glasshouse contains numerous tropical and exotic plants. The 40 acres of gardens include systematic and herb gardens, and a chronological border. The garden is also well known for its orchid collections and houses the National Begonia Collection. Guided tours for parties by prior arrangement. Plants labelled.

Gardens open daily 7–dusk. The main glasshouse open Mon–Sat 1–4.45 (4.15 in winter) Sun 12–4.45 (4.15 in winter). The Kibble Palace open 10–4.45 (4.15 in winter).

Free (coach parties only by prior arrangement).
P (in nearby streets) & (wc) wc

GREENBANK GARDEN

Clarkston (off B767 on southern outskirts of city) ☏ *041-639 3281*

The aim of this 16½-acre garden is to show what can be achieved in Britain's more northerly regions and is particularly relevant to the small garden. 3½ of the acres are cultivated to show a wide variety of plants which provide colour all through the year in herbaceous borders, demonstration beds, seed plots, fruit and conifers. Most plants labelled. Programme of special events Mar–Sep. Advisory service.

Open all year daily 9.30–sunset.

£1 (ch 16 50p, reduction for pen).
& (wc) wc Plants for sale (NTS)

PROVAN HALL

Auchinlea Rd ☏ *041-771 6372*

Formal and informal gardens occupy the grounds of this restored 15th-century house. There is also a scented garden for the blind.

Please telephone for opening hours.

Free.
P ⛼ &

ROSS HALL PARK

☏ *041-882 3554*

Beautiful and well-maintained gardens with artificial ponds containing a variety of aquatic plants and fish. There are extensive heather and rock gardens and woodland nature trails.

Open all year daily Apr–Sep 1–8; Oct–Mar 1–4.

Free.
P ⛼ &

Bouganvillea glabra

Gogar

Lothian *Midlothian* **Map 11 NT17**

SUNTRAP

Gogarbank (1m S off A8 Edinburgh to Glasgow Rd) ☎ *031-339 7283*

A 3-acre garden with facilities to instruct horticultural students and amateur gardeners. The many features of interest to owners of small gardens include a rock and scree garden, summer bedding, rose garden, shrub borders and patio areas. There is also a small area for fruit and vegetables. The Gardening Advice Centre has a lecture hall, glasshouses and demonstrations. Many plants labelled. Annual Open Day 6 Jun 10–5.

Garden open all year daily 9.30–dusk. Advice Centre all year Mon–Fri 9.30–1 & 2–4.30 (also Sat & Sun Apr–Sep 2.30–5).

50p (ch accompanying adult free).
P ♿ *(parts of ground floor and garden) wc (during office hours)*

Golspie

Highland *Sutherland* **Map 14 NH89**

DUNROBIN CASTLE

(1m NE) ☎ *(04083) 3177*

Ancient seat of the Earls and Dukes of Sutherland looking down on 7 acres of magnificent, formal gardens laid out in 1850. There are box hedges, rose beds, fountains, summer bedding and herbaceous borders with recent additions of flowering shrubs and Alpine plants. Some plants labelled. Castle also open.

Open Jun–15 Sep, Mon–Sat 10.30–5.30, Sun 1–5.30 (last admission 5pm).

£1.90 (ch 95p) Family Ticket £5 Party.
P ☕ 🐕 *(in house) wc*

Gordon

Borders *Berwickshire* **Map 12 NT64**

MELLERSTAIN HOUSE GARDENS

(3m S on unclass road) ☎ *(057381) 225*

The Georgian house at Mellerstain stands in beautiful parkland. It also has about 2 acres of formal terraced gardens in Italian style laid out by Sir Reginald Blomfield in 1909. Besides lawns and trees, the gardens include herbaceous borders, privet hedges cut into shapes, and a fishpond. Near the thatched cottage in the grounds there is a small rose garden. Some of the trees are labelled. House also open.

Open Etr then May–Sep Mon–Fri & Sun 12.30–5 (last admission 4.30).

** Gardens 80p (reductions for ch and pen). House & Gardens £1.80 (ch 80p, pen £1.30) Party 20+.*
P ☕ ♿ *(gardens & ground floor) wc*

Goudhurst

Kent **Map 5 TQ73**

FINCHCOCKS

(1½m SW on unclass rd off A262)
☎ *(0580) 211702*

A fine, early Georgian house set in attractive gardens and parkland. The gardens, extensively restored over the past 5 years, include a large lawn with a lime avenue, long borders of fine and rare shrubs, 18th- and 19th-century shrub roses, an Autumn Garden, and many unusual plants and flowers. Open Air Concert in Sep; musical and other events throughout the year. House also open.

Open 19 Apr–27 Sep Suns & BH Mon 2–6; Aug Wed–Sun 2–6. Details of group visits on application.

Gardens £1; House and gardens £2.80 (ch £1.80) Party.
P ☕ 🛒 🐕 *wc*

Grasmere

Cumbria **Map 11 NY30**

DOVE COTTAGE & THE GRASMERE & WORDSWORTH MUSEUM

☎ *(09665) 544*

William Wordsworth described his garden as 'The loveliest spot man hath ever found'. →

The half-wild garden, designed by the poet and his sister Dorothy, is filled with early 19th-century plants including ferns, mosses, primroses and wild daffodils. The well, steps and terrace he built are still intact. Cottage and museum also open.

Open Apr–Sep Mon–Sat 9.30–5.30, Sun 11–5.30; Oct & Dec–Mar Mon–Sat 10–4.30, Sun 11–4.30. Closed Nov.

* Garden, Cottage, Museum & Exhibition £2.50 (ch £1) Museum & Exhibition £1.25 (ch 60p). Family ticket. Party 15+.
P ✕ wc

Great Saling
Essex   Map 5 TL72
SALING HALL
☎ Great Dunmow (0371) 850141

Twelve acres of attractive formal and informal gardens with an interesting new collection of trees in the small park. The walled garden dates from 1698 and has colourful borders of shrubs, roses, plants and bulbs. There are also water gardens and a Japanese Garden. Plants labelled.

Open 13 May–Jul & 2 Sep–16 Oct Wed, Thu & Fri 2–5.

£1 (ch free).
P ✕ & wc

Phlox paniculata

Hailsham
East Sussex   Map 5 TQ50
MICHELHAM PRIORY
(2½m W) ☎ (0323) 844224

Six acres of gardens surround the Augustinian Priory and include fine mature trees, roses and herbaceous plants. There is also a 'physic' garden with the kind of plants which would have been used by medieval monks. There is a Garden Art and Science exhibition and a working watermill. Priory also open.

Open 25 Mar–Oct daily 11–5.30.

£1.50 (ch 5–16 70p, disabled & school parties 50p) Party 20+
P ⌺ (licensed) ⟠ ✕ &(gardens & ground floor; wc) wc Plants for sale

Ham
Gt London   Map 4 TQ17
HAM HOUSE
☎ 01-940 1950

An outstanding Stuart house with authentically restored formal gardens featuring a parterre and a walled rose garden. Plants labelled. House also open (Annexe of Victoria and Albert Museum).

Open Tue–Sun & BH Mons 11–5 (last admission 4.30) (Closed Good Fri, 4 May & 24–26 Dec & 1 Jan).

Grounds free; House £1.60 (ch & pen 80p) Children under 12 must be accompanied by an adult. Admission arrangements may be subject to change.
⌺ (Apr–Sep) ✕ wc (NT and Victoria & Albert Museum)

Hampton Court
Gt London   ·   Map 4 TQ16
HAMPTON COURT PALACE
☎ 01-977 2810

Henry VIII's palace with 60 acres of gardens and parkland which lead down to the River Thames. The most famous features are the maze, the Privy Garden with a colourful parterre, the pond gardens and knot garden, and the vine planted in 1768, which still flourishes. There are colourful herbaceous borders, spring and summer bedding displays, naturalised bulbs and a recently opened arboretum. Plants labelled. State apartments also open.

Open gardens all year daily; State apartments Apr–Sep, Mon–Sat 9.30–6, Sun 11–6; Oct–Mar Mon–Sat 9.30–5, Sun 2–5; (closed Good Fri, 24–26 Dec & 1 Jan).

Gardens free; admission fee payable for maze and State Apartments.
P *(30p)* ⬚ ⚶ & *(ground floor and gardens; wc) wc (Dept of Environment)*

Handcross

West Sussex   Map 4 TQ22

NYMANS GARDEN

A large garden with a world-wide collection of rare and beautiful trees, shrubs and plants. The many features here include a walled garden with an Italian fountain, and a hidden sunken garden. The picturesque ruins of the house overlook the lawns, topiary and fine old cedars. Plants labelled.

Open Apr–Oct Tue–Thu, Sat, Sun & BH Mon 11–7 (or dusk). Last admission 1 hr before closing.

Sun & BH Mon £1.80, other days £1.40.
⬚ ✖ *wc (NT)*

Hardwick

Derbyshire   Map 8 SK46

HARDWICK HALL

☎ *(0246) 850430*

Former home of Bess of Hardwick, built in 1597, with walled courtyard gardens. The South Court, divided by grass walks and high yew and hornbeam hedges, has orchards, flower borders, a herb garden and a lawn set with ornamental trees. The remaining Courts have fine trees, shrubs, and rose and herbaceous borders. Plants labelled. Hall also open.

Hall & garden open Apr–Oct Wed, Thu, Sat & Sun & BH Mon 1–5.30 (or dusk). Park open all year daily.

Garden £1.20 (ch 60p); Hall and garden £2.80 (ch £1.40).
P ⬚ *(Apr–Oct; licensed)* ⚶ ✖ & *(gardens only) wc (NT) (NGS)*

Harewood

West Yorkshire   Map 8 SE34

HAREWOOD HOUSE AND BIRD GARDEN

☎ *Leeds (0532) 886225*

Grounds landscaped by 'Capability' Brown surround the home of the Earl and Countess of Harewood. There are attractive terraces, a water garden and woodland and lakeside walks. The bird garden contains many exotic species and there is an adventure playground. House also open.

Open Apr–Oct daily, Gardens from 10am, House from 11am. Feb, Mar & Nov Sun only.

* *£3.50 (ch £1.50) Party.*   ·
P ⬚ *(licensed)* ⚶ & *Garden centre*

Harlow

Essex   Map 5 TL41

MARK HALL CYCLE MUSEUM & GARDENS

Muskham Rd, off First Av ☎ *(0279) 39680*

Three walled demonstration gardens showing a wide range of gardening techniques and plant species. There are three principal areas, the 'Unusual Fruits Garden', the '17th-century Garden', and the 'Peace Garden' which includes roses, a cottage garden, island beds, a model allotment and theme plantings. Plants labelled. Advisory Service. Museum also open.

Open all year daily 10–4.45 (or dusk) (closed Xmas).

Free.
P ✖ & *(wc) wc*

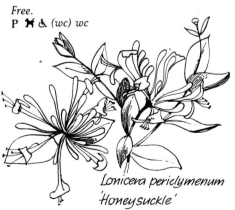

Lonicera periclymenum
'Honeysuckle'

Harrogate

North Yorkshire   Map 8 SE35

HARLOW CAR GARDENS
Crag Lane, Otley Rd ☎ (0423) 65418

Demonstration and trial gardens where many new varieties of trees, shrubs, bulbs and plants are grown by the Northern Horticultural Society. There are also many colourful ornamental gardens, an alpine house, woodlands, an arboretum and a conservation area. Plants labelled.

Open all year daily 9.30–7.30 (or dusk).

£2 (accompanied ch free, pen £1.50) Party 20+.
P ⚑ ⛩ ✗ (ex guide dogs) ⅋ Plants for sale Apr–Oct

RUDDING PARK
Follifoot (3½m S off A661) ☎ (0423) 870439

Beautiful park with wide lawns, magnificent beech trees and many rhododendrons and azaleas.

Open May & Jun daily 9–6.

£1 per car (occupants free).
P ⅋ (wc) wc

Hartley Wintney

Hampshire   Map 4 SU75

WEST GREEN HOUSE GARDEN
(1½m W on unclass road)

The charming gardens around this attractive 18th-century house are divided into separate areas. The walled, kitchen area is a mixture of vegetables, flowers, shrubs and climbers. Other parts include terraced lawns with an orangery and rustic garden house.

Open Apr–Sep. Garden Wed, Thu & Sun 2–6; House Wed 2–6 by appointment only. Apply Lord McAlpine of West Green, 40 Bernard St, London WC1N 1LG (last admission 5.30).

Garden £1 House & garden £1.40.
✗ (NT)

Hascombe

Surrey   Map 4 SU94

WINKWORTH ARBORETUM
(1m NW on B2130)

A wooded hillside overlooking two lakes with many rare trees and shrubs. The arbo-

retum is at its best in the spring and autumn when the slopes are ablaze with colour. Plants labelled.

Open all year daily, dawn–dusk.

£1.
wc (NT)

Hatfield

Hertfordshire   Map 4 TL20

HATFIELD HOUSE
☎ (07072) 62823

Jacobean house set in parkland and gardens. The beautiful parterre garden has roses, shrubs and herbaceous plants surrounding a formal pool and fountain. Below this lies the scented garden with aromatic herbs, scented shrubs and trees. The knot garden, a recent addition, displays 15th-, 16th- and 17th-century plants. There is also a maze and a wilderness garden. Some plants labelled. Festival of Gardening 20 & 21 June. House also open.

Open 25 Mar–12 Oct, Mon–Sat 12–5, Sun 2–5.30 BH Mon 11–5 (closed Good Fri).

Admission fee payable.
P ⅋ (licensed, in Old Palace Yard) ⛩ ✗ ⅋ (wc) wc Garden centre

Lunaria annua
'Honesty'

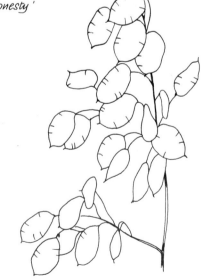

Hathern

Leicestershire   Map 8 SK42

WHATTON HOUSE GARDENS

*Long Whatton (4½m NW of Loughborough
on A6 between Hathern & Kegworth)*
☎ *Loughborough (0509) 842268*

The gardens extend to 25 acres, 15 of which
are devoted to trees and flowering shrubs.
There are also water gardens, Chinese and
Dutch gardens and a rose garden. A curious
feature of the garden is the Bogy Hole, a
garden ornament built in 1885, and there is a
dog cemetary.

Open Etr–Sep Sun & BH Mon 2–6.

Admission fee payable.
P ⏚ ⅊ *Garden centre*

Haywards Heath

West Sussex   Map 4 TQ32

BORDE HILL GARDEN

(1½m N on Balcombe Rd) ☎ *(0444) 450326*

This large (30 acre) garden with woods and
parkland, rare trees and shrubs is of great
botanical interest. It is renowned for its
rhododendrons, azaleas, camellias and magnolias. Most plants labelled. Guided tours by
prior arrangement.

* *Open Mar & Oct Sat & Sun only 10–6;
Apr–Sep Tue–Thu, Sat, Sun & BH's 10–6.*

* *£1.50 (ch 50p) Party 20+.*
P ⏚ *(licensed)* ⅊ ⅊ *(wc) wc Garden centre*

Heacham

Norfolk   Map 9 TF63

NORFOLK LAVENDER

Caley Mill (on A149) ☎ *(0485) 70384*

This garden holds the National Collection of
Lavenders, and a wide selection of lavenders,
including those grown commercially, can be
seen. These are complemented by a herb garden, laid out like an old monastry garden
with about 60 different herbs each in its own
plot. There is also a tranquil river garden.
Guided tours of the gardens, distillery and
lavender fields at appropriate times of year
for parties (by arrangement) and individuals.
Plants labelled. Main lavender harvest Jul–
mid Aug.

Gardens open all year (but tours only Spring
BH–Sep).

Free (charges for tours).
P ⏚ *(Summer only)* ⅊ ⅊ *(wc) wc Plants for
sale*

Helmingham

Suffolk   Map 5 TM15

HELMINGHAM HALL GARDENS
☎ *(047339) 363*

The 8 acres of gardens, dating from Elizabethan times, are separated from the surrounding deer park by a Saxon moat and a 1740
brick wall. There are magnificent herbaceous
borders and one of the finest kitchen gardens
still in perfect condition. Other features to be
seen include old English roses, espaliered
fruit trees, spring and autumn borders and a
conservation garden of 2 acres. Plants
labelled.

* *Open Sun May–Sep, 2–6.*

* *£1.20 (ch 70p, pen 90p) Party.*
P ⏚ ⅊ ⅊ *wc Garden centre*

Henley-on-Thames

Oxfordshire   Map 4 SU78

GREYS COURT

(3m W) ☎ *Rotherfield Greys (04917) 529*

Beautiful and varied gardens including a rose
garden, a white garden, a wisteria walk and
a recently-built 'Archbishop's' maze.

*Open Apr–Sep, garden Mon–Sat; house
Mon, Wed & Fri 2–6 (closed Good Fri).*

Garden £1.30, house & garden £1.80.
⏚ *(Wed & Sat) (NT)*

Hever

Kent   Map 5 TQ44

HEVER CASTLE AND GARDENS

(3m SE Edenbridge off B2026)
☎ *Edenbridge (0732) 865224*

The gardens of the 13th-century castle were
created early this century. Within the 30 acres
a wide variety of plants and landscapes can
be seen, but the gardens are probably best-
known for the topiary and maze and the 4-
acre Italian garden with a large collection →

of classical statuary. The roses, rhododendrons, azaleas, spring bulbs, and trees
are also worth seeing. Guided tours by prior
arrangement. Some plants labelled.

*Open Apr–1 Nov Gardens 11–6 (last entry
5). Castle open from noon.*

* *Gardens £1.75 (ch 90p); Castle & gardens
£3 (ch £2.50) Party.*
P ⬚ *(licensed)* ✝ & *(gardens & ground
floor; wc) wc Garden centre*

Aster novi-belgii

Highdown
West Sussex   **Map 4 TQ00**
HIGHDOWN
*(N off A259 halfway between Worthing and
Littlehampton)* ☏ *Worthing (0903) 501054*

Attractive gardens situated in a chalk pit on
Highdown Hill, with good views of the
surrounding countryside. There are flowering shrubs, a rock garden and many
daffodils.

*Open all year Mon–Fri 10–4.30; wknds &
BHs Apr–Sep 10–8.*

Free.
P ⬚ ⛩ 🚐 &

Hoar Cross
Staffordshire   **Map 7 SK12**
HOAR CROSS HALL
*(off A515 & B5234 near Newborough &
Abbots Bromley)* ☏ *(028375) 224*

The 20 acres of mid-Victorian gardens at
Hoar Cross were allowed to decay in the mid
20th century, but are now being restored.
There are woodland walks including rhododendron glades, yew hedges, borders, lime
alleys and enclosed gardens. These include a

water garden, a rock garden and a sunken
garden. Some plants labelled. Guided tours
of house and gardens by arrangement. House
also open.

*Open Spring BH–early Sep. Sun, also some
weekdays (please phone for details) and for
educational parties by arrangement.*

* *£1.40 (ch 60p).*
P ⬚ & *wc*

Hockley Heath
Warwickshire   **Map 7 SP17**
PACKWOOD HOUSE
(2m E off A34)

Timber-framed 16th- to 17th-century house
with remarkable topiary yew garden
representing the Sermon on the Mount, and
a flower garden.

*Open Apr–Sep Wed–Sun & BH Mon 2–6;
Oct Sat & Sun 12.30–4 (closed Good Fri).*

£1.60.
⬚ ✝ *(NT)*

Hodnet
Shropshire   **Map 7 SJ62**
HODNET HALL GARDENS
*(6m SW Market Drayton, 12m NE
Shrewsbury)* ☏ *(063084) 202*

Sixty acres of landscaped gardens surround
the hall, which is not open to the public. The
gardens include a chain of pools fed by
underwater springs extending along a cultivated valley. Some plants labelled. Collection of big game trophies also on show.

*Open daily Apr–29 Sep, weekdays 2–6.30,
Sun, BH Mon and Tue following 12–6.*

£1.40 (ch 70p). Party 25+.
P ⬚ & *(wc) wc Plants for sale*

Hoghton
Lancashire   **Map 7 SD62**
HOGHTON TOWER
(5m SE Preston on A675) ☏ *(025485) 2986*

The 16th-century hilltop mansion with fine
views is surrounded by three walled gardens.

One garden, known as 'The Ramparts' is mainly laid to grass and has brightly coloured herbaceous beds. Another garden has old English roses. The third garden was once a formal garden but is now a more informal wilderness. There is also mature woodland with spring daffodils and rhododendrons. House also open.

Open Etr Sat, then every Sun to Oct 2-5; also Sat in Jul & Aug and BH 2-5. Parties other times by appointment.

£1.50 (ch 50p).
P ⌂ ⌖

Holdenby

Northamptonshire   **Map 4 SP66**

HOLDENBY HOUSE GARDENS
☎ *Northampton (0604) 770786*

Under the grass of the outer gardens, the outlines of various features such as terraces, arches and ponds can be seen. These are the only remaining traces of Sir Christopher Hatton's great Elizabethan Palace of Holdenby. The inner garden of the present house has restored borders and shrubberies including an Elizabethan herb garden and silver borders. Some plants labelled. Guided tours of the house are available by prior arrangement.

Open Etr-Sep, Sun & BH Mon (2-6) and also Thu in Jul and Aug (2-6).

* *£1.20 (ch 60p, pen £1).*
P ⌂ *wc Plants for sale*

Holker

Cumbria   **Map 7 SD37**

HOLKER HALL AND PARK
☎ *Flookburgh (044853) 328*

Within the 122 acres of deer park are 22 acres of formal and woodland gardens which aim to provide colour, scent and interest all the year round. The gardens contain many unusual and attractive herbaceous plants, shrubs and trees, some of which are very rare. Seeds and cuttings of many of these are available during the period of flowering (such plants being indicated by signs). There are collections of rare cut leaf beeches, oaks and many shrubs and trees of Eastern origin, and also a fine collection of rhododendrons.

Guided tours by prior arrangement. Plants labelled. Various special events in grounds during the year. Hall also open.

Open Etr Sun-last Sun in Oct, Sun-Fri 10.30-6 (last admission 4.30).

£1.65 (ch £1.00, ch 6 free) for grounds, gardens and exhibitions. Party 20+.
P ⌂ *(licensed)* ⌖ & *(gardens & ground floor) wc Plants for sale*

Holkham

Norfolk   **Map 9 TF84**

HOLKHAM GARDENS
(1½m W of Wells-next-the-Sea off A149, entrance by Almhouses Gate in Holkham village) ☎ *Fakenham (0328) 710227*

The gardens at Holkham are essentially as Samuel Wyatt designed them in 1780 and are particularly valuable because of the insight they give to life and gardening in the late 18th and 19th century. They comprise over 6 acres of walled kitchen garden divided into six squares, as well as glasshouses and vineries. The gardens are used to grow a wide range of plants for sale and also unusual ornamental varieties. Most plants labelled. Large park, Palladian mansion and bygones collection also open to public.

Open Sun, Mon & Thu 28 May-Sep & also Wed in Jul & Aug (1.30-5), and Spring and Summer BH Mon (11.30-5).

Gardens free; Hall £1.30 (ch 5-15 50p, pen £1).
P ⌂ & *(gardens & ground floor; wc) wc Garden centre*

Holt

Wiltshire   **Map 3 ST86**

THE COURTS
☎ *North Trowbridge (0225) 782340*

These 7-acre gardens include herbaceous borders, a large lily pond, a conservatory, a wild flower area, and an arboretum, and are of interest to plantsman and amateur alike. Guided tours for parties by prior arrangement with the Head Gardener.

Open Apr-Oct, Mon-Fri 2-6.

£1.
P *(NT)*

Holy Island (Lindisfarne)

Northumberland **Map 12 NU14**

LINDISFARNE CASTLE

☎ Berwick (0289) 89244

In the grounds of this 16th-century castle, which was restored by Lutyens in 1903, is a delightful walled garden. The original layout was designed by Gertrude Jekyll and the garden was restored by the National Trust.

Open Apr–Oct 11–5; 1–16 Apr Wed, Sat & Sun; 17 Apr–Sep daily (ex Fri, but open Good Fri); Oct Sat & Sun only. Last entry 4.30. Island not accessible two hours before and four hours after high tide.

£2.20 Jun–Aug, other times £1.70. Party.
P *(nearby)* 🐕 *(NT)*

Horringer

Suffolk **Map 5 TL75**

ICKWORTH

(2½m SW of Bury St Edmunds)
☎ (0263) 734077

The 100 acres or so of formal garden and parkland surrounding the elliptical rotunda at Ickworth are noted for their fine trees and shrubs including holm oaks, copper beeches, yews, cedars, cypressus and magnolias. The formal garden, planted in the 19th century 'Italian'-type style, has a long terrace with a box hedge and fine views over the park (probably planted by 'Capability' Brown). Guided tours are available by arrangement. Plants labelled.

Park open daily. Gardens and house open Apr and Oct wknds only. May–Sep Tue, Wed, Fri, Sat, Sun and BH Mon 1.30–5.30 (though gardens usually open from 12).

Garden & house £1.50 (ch 75p) plus 50p access.
P ☕ 🐕 ♿ *(wc) wc (only when house open) (NT)*

Horsham

West Sussex **Map 4 TQ13**

HORSHAM MUSEUM

9 The Causeway ☎ (0403) 54959

This small walled garden approached via the museum, and covering about 30ft by 60ft, is mainly planted with old cottage garden plants, old roses, cyclamen species and some rare herbs. There are also hop and grape vines, and jasmines, and local paving stone is used in the herb garden. A 'Garden Week' is usually held each summer. Plants labelled.

Open Apr–Sep Tue–Sat 10–5, Oct–Mar Tue–Fri 1–5 & Sat 10–5 Coach parties by prior arrangement only.

Free.
P *(at rear)* 🐕 ♿ *Plants for sale*

Howick

Northumberland **Map 12 NU21**

HOWICK HALL GARDENS AND GROUNDS

☎ Longhoughton (066577) 285

Lovely garden with a variety of flowers and shrubs. It is particularly noted for its beautiful show of rhododendrons.

Open Apr–Sep daily 2–7.

50p (ch & pen 30p).
P

Hull

Humberside **Map 8 TA02**

WILBERFORCE HOUSE

23–25 High Street ☎ (0482) 222737

This small and secluded walled garden in the Old Town area of the city has mulberry trees, herbs and old roses. The garden was constructed after the war to form a setting for the 17th-century house which is also open to the public. Some plants are labelled.

Open daily Mon–Sat 10–5, Sun 1.30–4.30 (ex 1 Jan, Good Fri, 25 & 26 Dec).

Free.
P ⛺ 🐕 *wc*

Ilfracombe

Devon **Map 2 SS54**

CHAMBERCOMBE MANOR

(1m E off A399) ☎ (0271) 62624

One of England's oldest houses, dating from the 11th century, with 4 acres of gardens set in a peaceful wooded valley. The main garden has lawns, a shrubbery, herbaceous borders and rose and herb gardens. Stone steps lead down to the water garden where various water fowl can be seen. House also open.

Open Good Fri–Sep Mon–Fri 10.30–12.30 & 2–4.30, Sun 2–4.30 (closed Sat).

£1.50 (ch 75p, pen £1.25).
P ⌂ ♿ ✕ ♿ *(ground floor & gardens)*

Ilminster
Somerset   Map 3 ST31

BARRINGTON COURT GARDENS
(3m N off B3168)
☎ *South Petherton (0460) 41480*

Gertrude Jekyll influenced the design of this series of garden 'rooms'. The orchard is carpeted with daffodils in the spring whilst the separate iris, rose and lily gardens provide colour and interest throughout the summer. Plants labelled.

Open 19 Apr–Sep, Sun–Wed 2–5.30.

£1.50 Party 15+.
P ⌂ ♿ ✕ ♿ *wc Plants for sale (NT)*

Instow
Devon   Map 2 SS43

TAPELEY PARK
☎ *(0271) 860528*

Home of the Christie family of Glyndebourne, the grounds cover an area of about 10 acres, two of which are taken up by lawns. The formal Italian gardens are laid out in three terraces and include some rare plants from various countries around the world. The 18th-century kitchen garden, sheltered by a wall, has old varieties of fruit trees, plums, apples etc and soft fruit. An ice

house and shell house are some of the unusual features of this garden.

* Open Etr–Oct Tue–Sun & BH Mon, 10–6. During winter, gardens only in daylight hours. Conducted tours of the house when numbers permit.

* Garden £1 (ch 50p). Tour of house & gardens £2 (ch £1).
P ⌂ *(licensed)* ♿ ♿ *(ground floor & gardens) wc Plants for sale*

Inveresk
Lothian *Midlothian*   Map 11 NT37

INVERESK LODGE GARDEN

Two acres of gardens with attractive displays of plants familiar to most gardeners. Some plants labelled.

Open daily Mon–Sat 10–4.30, Sun 2–5.

50p (ch accompanied by adults 25p).
wc (NTS)

Inverness
Highland *Inverness-shire* Map 14 NH64

DOCHFOUR GARDENS
(6m SW on A82) ☎ *(046 386) 218*

These terraced gardens, dating from Victorian times, have mature trees, rhododendrons, naturalised daffodils, a water garden and yew topiary.

* Open daily Apr–Oct (not always open on Mon), 2–5.

* £1 (for garden walk) (collection box) (ch 16 free).
P *Plants for sale*

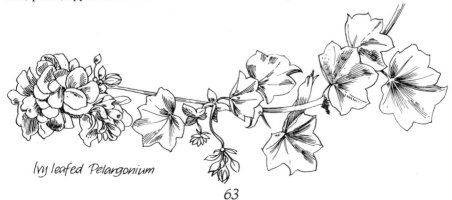

Ivy leafed Pelargonium

Ipswich

Suffolk   Map 5 TM14

CHRISTCHURCH MANSION
Soane St (south side of Christchurch Park)
☎ (0473) 53246

Mansion set in beautiful parkland with fine trees, formal gardens and ponds. House also open.

Open all year (ex Xmas, Good Fri & some BH) Mon–Sat 10–5, Sun 2.30–4.30 (dusk in winter).

Free.

P ✗ ⟁ (ground floor & gardens)

Irvine

Strathclyde Ayrshire   Map 10 NS34

EGLINGTON CASTLE & GARDENS
Irvine Rd, Kilwinning
☎ (0294) 74166 ext 373

The late 18th-century castle ruins are set in a loop of the River Lugton which meanders through the 13-acre park. There are formal gardens, rock gardens, large rhododendrons, azaleas, heathers and 2 small wooded areas. Archery competitions early May and mid Sep. Castle also open.

Open all year during daylight hours.

Free.

P ⟁ (gardens only) wc

Isleworth

Gt London   Map 4 TQ17

SYON PARK GARDENS
(follow A315 off A310 to Busch Corner, and enter via Park Rd, Isleworth entrance).
☎ 01-560 0881

Extensive gardens, originally landscaped by 'Capability' Brown, with specimen trees and lakeside plantings. The Great Conservatory, built c1826 by Dr Fowler, was the first large glass and metal construction of its kind in the world; it now contains many interesting plants and cacti. There is a beautiful 6-acre rose garden and a large garden centre. Advisory service.

* Open all year daily 10–6 (dusk in winter) closed xmas, Conservatory closed in winter.

* Garden £1 (ch & per 80p); combined ticket for house & park £1.50 (ch & pen £1). Rose garden 10p.
P ⟐ ✗ ⟁ (ex Rose garden; wc) wc

Jarrow

Tyne and Wear   Map 12 NZ36

THE BEDE MONASTERY MUSEUM
Jarrow Hall ☎ Tyneside (091) 4892106

A small garden with spring bulbs, shrubs, lawns and fine trees. The main feature here is the well-established herb garden which has separate beds of aromatic, culinary and medicinal herbs, and some known to have existed in the Anglo-Saxon period. Most herbs labelled. Advisory service. Museum also open.

* Open Apr–Oct, Tue–Sat 10–5.30, Sun 2.30–5.30; Nov–Mar Tue–Sat 11–4.30, Sun 2.30–5.30 (closed Mon ex BH).

* 45p (ch, pen & reg unemp 20p; students 30p).
P (400yds) ⟐⟁ (ground floor & garden) wc
Herbs for sale   ·

Jodrell Bank

Cheshire   Map 7 SJ77

JODRELL BANK VISITOR CENTRE
(3m NE of Holmes Chapel off A535)
☎ Lower Withington (0477) 71339

In sight of the 250ft radio telescope is a 35-acre arboretum containing several thousand species of trees and shrubs. Native ground flora has been planted on the banks of one of the several naturalised ponds. Plants labelled. Garden centre. Planetarium also open.

Open Etr–Oct daily 10.30–5.30; winter wknds 2–5.30.

£2 (ch & pen £1).
P ⟐ (licensed) ⟑ ✗ ⟁ (wc) wc

Keighley

West Yorkshire   Map 7 SE04

EAST RIDDLESDEN HALL
Bradford Rd ☎ (0535) 607075

Lovely peaceful gardens which extend to around 12 acres and include a 13th-century tithe barn and a large fish pond with ducks. There is a formal garden of one acre, part of which is walled, and plants here are in keeping with the period of the Hall. Old varieties of apple and pear trees form well-kept avenues and there are spacious lawns for picnics and relaxing. House also open. Special events first Sun in each month.

Open wknds in Apr & Nov; Etr (ex Good Fri); May, Jun, Sep & Oct Wed–Sun & BH Mon 2–6; Jul & Aug 12–6.

£1.30 (ch 60p) Party.
P ☕ 🐕 *(NT)*

Kellie

Fife **Map 12 NO50**

KELLIE CASTLE AND GARDENS
(2m N of St Monans off B9171)
☎ Arncroach (03338) 271

The garden at Kellie Castle, which dates from the late 16th & 17th century, is a walled late Victorian garden of about 2½ acres designed by Mrs Lorimer and her architect sons. It consists of gardens within a garden divided by a series of pleasant, plant-laden pathways edged with box. Old roses and herbaceous plants are particular specialities. Guided tours for parties by prior arrangement. Plants labelled. Castle also open.

Gardens and grounds open daily 10–sunset; Castle Etr, Apr & Oct Sat & Sun 2–6; May–Sep daily 2–6.

Gardens 80p (accompanied ch 40p); Castle & gardens £1.80 (ch 90p) Party 20+.
P ⛺ *wc (NTS)*

Kelmarsh

Northamptonshire **Map 4 SP77**

KELMARSH HALL
(on A508) ☎ Maidwell (060128) 276

The grounds surrounding this palladian mansion, built between 1726 and 1732 by James Gibbs, extend to about 20 acres with extensive herbaceous borders, old-fashioned roses and a wooded wilderness garden. The beautiful Spring Garden has an impressive display of bulbs etc in the early months of the year. A large lake with swans completes this interesting area.

* *Open Etr–Sep; Sun & BH, 2.15–5.30.*

Gardens 50p; House and gardens £1.
P ☕ *wc*

Kelso

Borders *Roxburghshire* **Map 12 NT73**

FLOORS CASTLE
☎ (0573) 23333

The grounds of this castle, the home of the Duke and Duchess of Roxburgh, contain a magnificent walled garden with herbaceous borders, vines and peach house. Pipe bands 3 & 24 May; 7 June; 12 Jul. Massed pipe bands 30 Aug. Scottish Driving Trials 4 & 5 Jul.

Gardens open all year daily 9.30–5; castle open Etr Sun & Mon & 3 May–Sep Sun–Thu (also Fri in Jul & Aug) 10.30–5 (last admission 4.45).

Gardens £1.20 (ch free) Castle & gardens £2 (ch £1.30) Party 25+.
P *(200 yds)* ☕ *(licensed)* ⛺ ♿ *(ground floor & gardens; wc) wc Plants for sale*

Kemerton

Hereford & Worcester **Map 3 SO93**

THE PRIORY
☎ (038689) 258

This attractive 4-acre garden offers something of interest for everyone. Long, herbaceous borders planted in colour groups, a large collection of unusual trees, and many shrubs and plants. The sunken garden has raised beds for alpine plants and a stream. Plants labelled. The house is not open.

Open May–Sep each Thu, also the following Suns: 24 May, 21 June, 12 July, 2 & 23 Aug & 6 Sep 2–7pm.

£1 (accompanied ch free) Party 20+.
P ☕ *(Sun openings only)* ♿ *wc Plants for sale*

Keswick

Cumbria **Map 11 NY22**

LINGHOLM
(turn off A66 for Portinscale & continue 1m on road to Grange) ☎ (07687) 72003

Situated on the west side of Derwentwater, Lingholm consists of a largely terraced formal garden spreading out into an extensive woodland garden. In the woodlands there are many rhododendrons and azaleas, together with other interesting shrubs, primulas and specimen trees. Daffodils, begonias, →

gentians and fine autumn colours are other features for which the gardens are noted. Guided tours for 'garden groups' on application. Plants labelled.

Open daily Apr–Oct 10–5.

£1.25 (accompanied ch free).
P ☕ ⛺ ♿ *wc Plants for sale*

MIREHOUSE
(4m NW on A591) ☎ (07687) 72287

A manor house dating from the 17th century with a beautiful woodland shrub garden. Rhododendrons, azaleas, buddleias and hydrangeas provide a constant display of colour from early spring to late autumn. The parkland borders Bassenthwaite Lake. House also open.

Open Apr–Oct, Grounds daily 10.30–5.30; House Sun, Wed & BH Mon 2–5.

** Grounds 50p (ch & students 35p) House & grounds £1.30 (ch & students 65p).*
P *(¼m)* ☕ *(daily 10.30–5.30)* ⛺ 🐕 *(house & tea room)* ♿ *(ground floor & gardens)*

Kettering

Northamptonshire **Map 4 SP87**

BOUGHTON HOUSE
☎ (0536) 82248

The delightul gardens and grounds of this 15th-century monastic building include a walled garden, a fish pond, Victorian rose beds and herbaceous borders. There is also a woodland play area and a nature trail.

** Gardens open 2–31 Aug 12.30–5.*

** £1 (pen & students 50p).*
⛺ ♿

Kew

Gt London **Map 4 TQ17**

KEW GARDENS
(Royal Botanic Gardens)
☎ 01-940 1171 ext 4622

Essentially a scientific research centre, the gardens, which cover a 300-acre site encompassing lakes, greenhouses, walks, garden pavilions, museums etc., have something for all visitors. More than 50,000 plant species are grown and include notable collections of arum lillies, ferns, orchids, aquatic plants, cacti, mountain plants, palms and water lilies. At all times of year there is something to see, from the spring bulbs through to winter heath plants. Guided tours for parties up to 20 by prior arrangement. Plants labelled. 15 & 16 May Library, herbarium and laboratories open day. Autumn 1987 (date to be announced) official opening of new 'Tropical Conservatory'.

Open daily (ex 25 Dec & 1 Jan) 10–between 4 & 8 (depending on season). Museums and glasshouses may have more limited opening as do Kew Palace and Queens Cottage.

25p (ch 10 free).
P ☕ 🐕 *(ex guide dogs)* ♿ *(wc) wc*

Kilchrenan

Strathclyde *Argyll* **Map 10 NN02**

ARDANAISEIG
(3m NE at end of unclass rd) ☎ (08663) 333

A mainly woodland and shrub garden with rhododendrons, azaleas and eucalyptus. In the spring, daffodils and bluebells carpet the grounds immediately surrounding the house, which is now a hotel. Some plants labelled.

Open 30 Mar–Oct daily 8.30–dusk.

75p (ch free).
P ☕ 🐕 🚌 *Plants for sale*

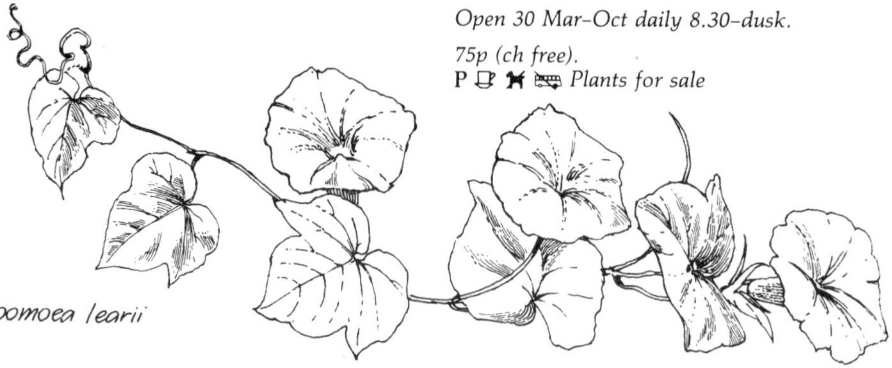

Ipomoea learii

Kildrummy

Grampian *Aberdeenshire* **Map 15 NJ41**

KILDRUMMY CASTLE GARDEN TRUST
(Alford-Strathdon rd, A97, off A944)
☎ *(03365) 264, 277 & 203*

The gardens, dating from 1904, are dominated by the medieval castle ruins. The alpine and shrub gardens, situated in the ancient quarry, are sheltered by fine, mature trees. There is an attractive shrub bank, and a water garden with a copy of the 14th-century 'Auld brig o'Balgownie. Plants labelled.

Open Apr–Oct daily 10–5.

* *£1 (ch free).*
P ⚓ ♿ *(wc) wc Plants for sale*

Killerton

Devon **Map 3 SS90**

KILLERTON HOUSE AND GARDEN
(5m NE of Exeter on B3185 off B3181)
☎ *Exeter (0392) 881345*

An interesting and well-tended hillside garden with large open lawns backed by trees and shrubs. The gardens, particularly beautiful in the spring, always provide a colourful display of flowers and foliage. There are many herbaceous plants, magnolias, azaleas, oaks and conifers. Good views of the Clyst and Culm Valleys. House also open. Plants labelled.

Open House & Garden Apr–Oct daily 11–6 (last admission 5.30), garden only Nov–Mar during daylight hours.

House & Garden £2.40 (ch £1.20); garden only £1.50 (ch 75p) Party.
P ⛩ *(licensed)* ♿ *wc Plants for sale (NT) (NGS)*

Kilmun

Strathclyde *Argyll* **Map 10 NS18**

KILMUN ARBORETUM & FOREST PLOTS
☎ *(036984) 666*

Established by the Forestry Commission in 1930, and extended to cover 100 acres on a hillside overlooking the Holy Loch. A large collection of conifer and broad leaf tree species, planted in plots and specimen groups.

Woodland walks. Some plants labelled.

Open all year during daylight hours.

Free.
P 🚐

Kingsdon

Somerset **Map 3 ST52**

LYTES CARY MANOR
☎ *Somerton (0458) 223297*

A formal garden set out in Elizabethan style with yew hedges and topiary. The long border of shrubs, roses and clematis is at its best from early summer onwards. There is an orchard of ornamental trees underplanted with bulbs.

Open Apr–Oct Wed & Sat 2–6, last admission 5.30.

£1.50.
P *(NT)*

Kingswear

Devon **Map 3 SX85**

COLETON FISHACRE GARDEN
(1¾m E on unclass roads) ☎ *(080425) 466*

An 18-acre garden set in a stream-fed valley and created by Lady Dorothy D'Oyly Carte between 1925 and 1940. Planted with a wide variety of uncommon trees and rare and exotic shrubs.

Open Apr–Oct, Wed, Fri & Sun 11–6.

£1.20 (ch 60p) Party.
P *Garden centre (NT)*

Kington

Hereford and Worcester **Map 3 SO25**

HERGEST CROFT GARDENS
(¼m W off A44) ☎ *(0544) 230160*

Large gardens with a fine collection of trees and shrubs including many rhododendrons almost 30ft tall. The old-fashioned kitchen garden has flowers and herbaceous borders. Good autumn colour. Plants labelled.

Open 19 Apr–20 Sep daily; 21 Sep–25 Oct Sun only 1.30–6.30.

£1.20 (ch 60p).
P ♿ *wc Plants for sale*

Kirkbean

Dumfries and Galloway Map 11 NX95
Dumfriesshire
ARBIGLAND GARDENS
(1m SE, adjacent to Paul Jones' Cottage)
☎ *(038788) 213*

Fifteen acres of woodland, water and shrub gardens containing many rare trees and some tropical plants. Some plants labelled.

Gardens open May–Sep, Tue, Thu & Sun 2–6; House open 23–31 May, 22–30 Aug.

Gardens £1 (ch 50p), House £1 (ch 50p). Parties by prior arrangement.
P & *wc*

Kirkoswald

Strathclyde *Ayrshire* **Map 10 NS20**
CULZEAN CASTLE GARDENS
(4m N) ☎ *(06556) 269*

The gardens surrounding the 18th-century castle form part of the 563-acre Country Park. Mixed woodland and colourful gardens with ponds and streams are set against a background of the Firth of Clyde and the Isle of Arran. The Fountain Court Garden lies adjacent to the castle and nearby are the Camellia House and a 4-acre Walled Garden. There are many daffodils, rhododendrons and azaleas. Special events throughout the year. Plants labelled. Castle also open.

Open Gardens all year daily; Castle 17 Apr–Sep daily 10–6; Oct daily 12–5 (last admission ½hr before closing).

Gardens: pedestrians free. Parking charges to be decided. Castle: £1.80 (ch 90p) Party (ex Jul & Aug).
P ☕ & *wc Plants for sale (NTS)*

Knebworth

Hertfordshire **Map 4 TL22**
KNEBWORTH HOUSE GARDENS
(direct access from A1(M) at Stevenage (South) roundabout)
☎ *Stevenage (0438) 812661*

The gardens in their present form are mainly the work of Edwin Lutyens. They include a sunken lawn with pleached lime avenues, a rose garden, formal yew hedges, two mounds and various herbaceous borders.

Gertrude Jekyll designed the herb garden and two long herbaceous borders are in her style. There is a 'blue garden', a 'gold garden' and a wilderness area. House also open.

Open Apr–May, Sat, Sun, BH & school holidays then daily (ex Mon) 23 May–13 Sep & 19, 20, 26, 27 Sep. House & gardens 12–5, Park 11–5.30.

* House, Park & Gardens £2.50 (ch & pen £2). Park only £1.50. Party 20+.
P ☕ *(licensed)* 🍴 ✖ & *(ground floor & gardens) wc*

Knutsford

Cheshire **Map 7 SJ77**
PEOVER HALL AND GARDENS
(4m S off A50)
☎ *Lower Peover (056581) 2135*

Beautiful gardens and landscaped parkland with many interesting features including a wild garden, an Azalea Dell and Rhododendron Walks. The formal walled gardens have roses, a lily pond, herbs and white and pink gardens. Some plants labelled. Country Fair 16 Aug. House also open.

Open Gardens May–Oct Mon & Thu 2–5, House May–Sep Mon 2–5.

Gardens £1 (ch & pen 50p); House & Gardens £2.
P ☕ *(Mon only)* 🍴 & *wc*

TATTON PARK
(3½m from M6, junc 19; or M56, junc 7; entrance by Rostherne Lodge on Ashley Rd; 1½m NE of junc of A5034 with A50)
☎ *(0565) 54822*

Stately home set in beautiful ornamental gardens which have been enlarged and improved over the years with extensive parkland landscaped by Humphrey Repton. There are wonderful displays of colour throughout the year from many bulbs, azaleas, rhododendrons, roses and the autumn foliage. Perhaps the most famous feature here is the authentic Japanese Garden, a tranquil area complete with a Shinto Temple. The formal Italian gardens, many water features, a maze, arboretum and the Orangery are also of interest. Plants labelled. Advisory service. Special events throughout the year.

Open Gardens 17 May–6 Sep Mon–Sat 11–5.30, Sun 10.30–6; Apr–16 May & 7 Sep–Oct

Peony — protection against witches?

GARDEN LORE AND LEGEND

By Jennifer Westwood

Although the ordinary garden probably has more varieties in it today than at any time in the past, individual plants hold less significance. Once plants were seen more as people — talking to them is no new thing and the well-known custom of 'telling the bees' was extended to favourite plants. They had to be informed of a death in the family and put in mourning by having bits of black crepe tied to them or draped round their flowerpots. If not, they would die. They had their own preferences as to owners. One old man when asked about a fine bush of rosemary caustically replied: 'They do say that it only grows where the missis is master — and it do grow here like wildfire.' Myrtle likewise throve best if planted by a woman. A lady in the 1840s was advised during planting to spread her skirt over it and 'look proud'.

From time immemorial stories have been told accounting for the origins of flowers. The violet received its Greek name, Ion, when the philandering Jove turned the nymph Io into a white cow to save her from Hera, his wife, The Poet's Narcissus was once a beautiful youth who fell in love with his own reflection in a pool. Thinking it was a nymph he saw, but unable to reach her, he pined to death on the spot and was transformed into a flower. Another beautiful youth was Hyacinthus, Apollo's favourite, whom he accidentally slew. In memory of him, the sun-god caused a purple flower to spring from his blood which bore on its petals the letters Ai, Ai, his cry of grief. Whether this flower was our modern hyacynth is debated: many say the cry 'Ai! Ai!' is actually borne by the martagon lily, or else the gladiolus or larkspur. Later, the poet Herrick tells the romantic tale of a maiden shut up in a castle on the Tweed because she loved the heir of a rival family. She and her lover planned her escape by climbing down the wall on an improvised rope.

Up she got upon a wall,
Attempted down to slide withal,
But the silken twist untied,
So she fell and, bruised, she died.

Love changed her to a wallflower — which is why it grows best on walls.

Some flowers have changed their colour. The flowers of rosemary used to be white until, during the Flight into Egypt, Mary spread the Christ Child's clothes to dry on a rosemary bush and they turned blue. An ancient tradition says the first roses were likewise white but turned red when stained with blood. For Muslims, this was the blood of Mohammed; for Christians, the blood of Christ, whose crown of thorns — made of briars — caused blood to drip from his forehead to the ground where it sprang up again at the foot of the Cross as red roses.

In the British Isles several different plants were said to have sprung from the blood of the Danes. The purple Pasque Flower is in eastern England called Dane's Flower and supposed to bloom on sites of ancient battles between Danes and Saxons. In Sussex, in St. Leonard's Forest, lilies of the valley annually marked the spots sprinkled with the blood of the hermit-saint Leonard in a dragon-fight.

Because it was a symbol of love, the rose, particularly the old common moss, was once much used in love-charms. An unfaithful lover could be brought to heel by gathering three roses on Midsummer Eve and very early next morning burying one under a yew, another in a fresh-dug grave, and putting the third under your pillow. If you left it there for three nights and then burnt it, you would haunt your sweetheart's dreams and he would get no rest until he returned to you. Along the Welsh Border, a girl who wanted to know the name of the man she would marry would make a cowslip ball and toss it in the air, saying 'Tisty, tosty, tell me true, who shall I be married to?' She then recited the names of likely young men in the parish and the ball fell to the ground when the right one was mentioned.

The Narcissus—whose legend is well-known.

Traditionally linked with Easter, the Pasque flower has more sinister connections.

Above: the lovely Peony 'Plena', below: Primroses — another of the flowers said to give protection against witchcraft.

Other flowers were less prophetic than downright magical. Golden rod according to tradition is a divining rod which points to hidden treasure. One still sees on old cottage roofs houseleeks, originally lightning charms. More sinister are the herbs and flowers connected with the supernatural and witchcraft. The souls of the dead were once believed to inhabit thyme, and its scent was associated with the ghosts of the murdered. If a smell of thyme clung to a spot where no thyme grew, it was a sign that someone has been murdered there. At Dronfield in Derbyshire a young man killed his sweetheart while she was carrying a bunch of thyme and ever after the scent of it lingered about the place. The poisonous monkshood with its brilliant blue spires was an ingredient in witches' 'flying ointment', a hellish brew including babies' fat, with which they anointed their foreheads and wrists in order to fly. Protection *against* witches was given by marigolds and other yellow flowers. In the Isle of Man, little bunches of primroses used to be laid on the doorstep of houses and cowsheds on May Eve, a night when witches were specially active.

Peony Suffraticosa.

Even the humble cabbage stalk was once the favourite steed of fairies and there is much food for thought in a handful of parsley. Notoriously slow to germinate, it is reputed to go nine times to the Devil before coming up — and they say it grows best for the wicked!

The delightful Narcissus — but a sad story.

'Vervain and dill hinder witches of their will' and peony seeds and roots could be worn against them. But you had to be careful gathering peony — for, like the mandrake, its cry as it was uprooted was fatal to all who heard it.

Jennifer Westwood is a well-known authority in the field of folklore and legend. Among her recent publications are *Albion: A Guide to Legendary Britain* and articles for the AA's *Secret Britain*.

Mon–Sat 11.30–5, Sun 10.30–5.30; Nov & Mar Sun only 1–4. Times vary for House, Old Hall and Farm.

Garden 85p, House £1.20, Old Hall 95p, Farm 85p. Park £1 per car. An additional charge may be made for special events.
P ⬚ ✱ *(in house)* & wc *Plants for sale (NT)*

Lamarsh
Suffolk   **Map 5 TL83**
PARADISE CENTRE
(on Ballingdon road from Sudbury to Bures)
☎ *Twinstead (078 729) 449*

These gardens, which specialise in unusual tuberous and bulbous plants, cover 5 acres. The site is on a slope in the Stour Valley and many mature trees have been retained. Crocus, fritillaries and autumn-flowering colchicums are grown, and ponds (with plants and fish) and small livestock are other attractions. Most plants labelled. Advisory service available.

* *Open Etr–1 Nov Sat, Sun & BH 10–5 (weather permitting). Other days by appointment.*

* *80p (ch 50p, pen 60p). Party.*
P ⬚ ☂ ✱ wc *Plants for sale (incl mail order)*

Lamberhurst
Kent   **Map 5 TQ63**
OWL HOUSE GARDENS
(1m NE off A21) ☎ *01-235 1432*

Thirteen acres of romantic walks, spring flowers, azaleas, roses, rhododendrons, rare flowering shrubs and ornamental fruit trees surround the 16th-century smugglers' haunt, the Owl House (not open to public). Wide expansive lawns lead to woodlands of oak, birch, and informal sunken water gardens. Guided tours by prior arrangement. Some plants labelled.

Open daily including BH weekends 11–6.

£1.50 (ch 75p).
P ✱ & wc *Plants for sale*

SCOTNEY CASTLE GARDEN
(1m SE) ☎ *(0892) 890651*

The romantic-style castle, dating from the

14th century, but altered in the 19th century, is set in a picturesque landscaped garden. The gardens were started in the 1840s and are an example of early (pre-Jekyll) natural landscaping. They include an old quarry, which provided the stone for the house, and a lily-filled moat. Castle ruins also open.

Open Gardens Apr–15 Nov, Wed–Fri 11–6, Sat & Sun 2–6 (closed Good Fri). Old Castle May–25 Aug same times.

£1.90 (ch £1).
P & *(NT)*

Lamport
Northamptonshire   **Map 4 SP77**
LAMPORT HALL
(8m N of Northampton on A508)
☎ *Maidwell (060128) 272*

This garden includes a remarkable 20ft high alpine rock garden built in the late 19th century by Sir Charles Isham. There is also a small Italian garden, a pool, a rose garden and fine woodland walks. Much of the 5 acres of gardens consists of herbaceous borders and expansive lawns with some old cedars and sycamores, and an avenue of Irish yews. Parkland surrounds the formal gardens. House also open to public.

Open Etr–Sep Sun & BH Mon 2.15–5.15; Jul & Aug Thu 2.15–5.15.

£1.50 (ch 16 75p, pen £1.20) admission includes Hall and museum. Party 30+ (by appointment).
P ⬚ ☂ ✱ wc *Plants for sale*

Langbank
Strathclyde *Renfrewshire* **Map 10 NS37**
FINLAYSTONE COUNTRY ESTATE
(1m W) ☎ *(047554) 285*

The 4-acre garden consists of a large landscaped area with herbaceous plants and shrubs, expecially rhododendrons and azaleas, and mature ornamental trees. There are also lawns with spectacular spring daffodil displays, and bog and water gardens. Celtic paving is featured in part of the garden, and the old kitchen garden is now a nursery. House also open summer Sun afternoons. →

Guided tours by arrangement. Some plants labelled. Advisory service available.

Open daily. Coach parties by prior arrangement only.

Woodland and Gardens 80p (ch 50p); House 80p (ch 40p).

P ⚑ *(Apr–Sep, Sat & Sun 2–5)* ⚘ *wc Plants for sale*

Lanhydrock

Cornwall   Map 2 SX06

LANHYDROCK GARDENS

☎ *Bodmin (0208) 3320*

The formal gardens at Lanhydrock were originally laid out in 1857 and feature spring and summer bedding. There is also an extensive informal garden with large tree magnolias, hardy hybrid rhododendrons, azaleas, and about 300 different camellia cultivars. The herbaceous garden is best Jun–Oct. Guided tours available in Apr & May. Most plants labelled.

Open daily until dusk (house open Apr–Oct 11–6).

Gardens £1.60. House & Gardens £3.

P ⚑ *(part of year) wc Plants for sale (NT)*

Iris xiphioides

Largs

Strathclyde *Ayrshire*   Map 10 NS25

KELBURN COUNTRY CENTRE

(2m off A78) ☎ *Fairlie (047556) 685 or 554*

On the Firth of Clyde, these beautiful gardens contain rare trees and exotic and unusual shrubs from all over the world. Among the trees are weeping larches and yew trees over 1,000 years old. Part of the grounds include Kelburn Glen, part cultivated, part left wild with waterfalls, pools and glen walks. Spectacular views over this historic estate of the Earls of Glasgow. Guided tours (by prior arrangement).

Open Etr–mid Oct daily, 10–6 Sun only in winter 11–5.

£1.50 (ch & pen £1) party.

P ⚑ *(licensed)* ⚘ *Garden centre*

Lavenham

Suffolk   Map 5 TL94

THE PRIORY

Water Street ☎ *(0787) 247417*

The gardens of this medieval timber-framed house include a herb garden of unique design with over 100 varieties of herbs grown. Within the 3 acres there is also a garden walk with a viewing point, and a wild flower meadow. Guided tour, by appointment, includes garden and priory.

Open daily Etr–Oct (ex Sun), 10.30–12.30 & 2–5.30.

£1.25 (ch 11–16 50p, ch 11 free).

P *(in surrounding streets)* ⚑ ✖ *wc Plants for sale*

Lea

Derbyshire   Map 8 SK35

LEA GARDENS

☎ *Dethick (062984) 380*

These 4 acres of gardens were started in 1935 in an old quarry. An extensive collection of hybrid and specie rhododendrons are grown in mixed woodland. The excellent rock garden contains a huge variety of alpine plants with acers, dwarf conifers, heathers and spring bulbs. The beds of massed azaleas are colourful in May & June. Guided tours by request. Some plants labelled.

Open 20 Mar–Jul, daily, 10–7.

Season ticket £1.00 (ch 50p, disabled free).

P ⚑ ⚘ ♿ *(wc) wc Garden centre (NGS)*

Leeds

West Yorkshire   Map 8 SE33

CANAL GARDENS Roundhay Park
☎ (0532) 661850

At 700 acres, Roundhay Park is one of Leeds finest and largest parks. It offers a variety of attractions including 2 large rose gardens (with over 10,000 plants), a large conservatory (Coronation House) full of flowering plants, herbaceous borders, tropical gardens and special gardens for the blind and disabled. There are also large areas of parkland, lakes (with boating), fountains and aviaries. Plants labelled. 7–9 Aug The Leeds Show.

Open daily 7.30–dusk, conservatories 10–dusk.

Free.
P ⌷ ☶ ᕃ *(wc)* wc

TEMPLE NEWSAM PARK
(on SE outskirts of city) ☎ (0532) 645535

The 917 acres of grounds surrounding the Tudor and Jacobean house of Temple Newsam were landscaped by 'Capability' Brown. The park includes seven varied gardens, namely: a herb garden, a spring garden (with 15 species of bulbs), an Italianate garden, a rhododendron walk (with azaleas), an arboretum, a bog garden and a rose garden (in former walled kitchen garden). Spring Bulb Festival (late Apr), Summer Festival (end May). House also open.

Open daily (ex 25 & 26 Dec), Tue–Sun & BH Mon 10.30–6.15 or dusk, Wed May–Sep 10.30–8.30.

Free (park & gardens). House 60p (ch & pen 25p).
P ⌷ ☶ ᕃ *(wc) Plants for sale*

Leicester

Leicestershire   Map 4 SK50

BELGRAVE HALL
(off Thurcaston Rd) ☎ (0533) 666590

A fine early 18th-century house with attractive rock and water gardens and botanic gardens. House also open.

Open all year Mon–Thu & Sat 10–5.30; Sun 2–5.30 (closed Fri, Good Fri & Xmas).

Free.
P *(in street)* ✘ *(ex guide dogs)* ᕃ *(ground floor and gardens)*

UNIVERSITY OF LEICESTER BOTANIC GARDENS
Beaumont Hall, Stoughton Drive South, Oadby (3½m SE A6) ☎ (0533) 717725

The gardens were originally four separate gardens belonging to large houses (now student residences). The 16 acres have been landscaped to form one site, but still retain some of the characters of the individual properties. The grounds include formal gardens and pool, rock gardens, heather and herb gardens, and glasshouses. Guided tours by appointment (charge made). Plants labelled.

Open throughout year Mon–Fri 10–4.30 (Children must be accompanied).

Free.
P *(nearby roads)* ✘ ᕃ *wc Plants for sale*

Leuchars

Fife   Map 12 NO42

EARLSHALL CASTLE
☎ (033483) 205

This garden, designed by Sir Robert Lorimer in the late 19th century is famous for its topiary in the form of four Scottish saltire crosses (though often said to be in the form of chessmen). Other attractions within the 3½-acre grounds of the castle (also open to the public) include woodland walks, espaliered fruit trees, kitchen garden, rose terrace, orchard, pleached lime avenue, herb garden and secret garden. Some plants are labelled.

Open Etr Sat–Mon and then until last Sun of Sep Thu–Sun 2–6. At other times by prior arrangement for booked parties.

Castle and gardens £2 (ch 5–16 £1, pen £1.50) Party.
P ⌷ ☶ ✘ ᕃ *(gardens only) wc*

Levens

Cumbria   Map 7 SD48

LEVENS HALL
☎ Sedgwick (05395) 60321

Levens Hall is famous for its topiary, the masterpiece of Monsieur Beaumont, who laid out the garden in 1692. There are magnificent tall trees clipped into fantastic shapes, vast beech hedges, colourful formal →

bedding and herbaceous borders, and the first ha-ha introduced into England. Plants labelled. House and working steam engine collection also open to public.

Open Etr Sun–11 Oct, Sun–Thu 11–5, Steam Collection 2–5. '

Garden £1.30 (ch 70p); House & Garden £2.20 (ch £1.10) Party.
P ⬚ *(licensed)* ⅋ ✗ ⅋ *(gardens only; wc)*
wc Garden centre

Leyburn
North Yorkshire   Map 7 SE19
CONSTABLE BURTON HALL
(3½m E on A684, 6m W of A1)
☎ *Bedale (0677) 50428*

Large, informal garden with something of interest all through the spring and summer. Splendid display of daffodils, rockery with some rare alpine plants and many shrubs and roses. There is also a small lake with wildfowl. House not open.

Open Apr–1 Aug daily 9–6.

50p (ch 10 & pen free) Party.
P ⅋

Lichfield
Staffordshire   Map 7 SK10
HANCH HALL
(3m NW on B5014, Handsacre)
☎ *Armitage (0543) 490308*

The gardens extend to some 6 acres, with lawns and flower beds typifying the first half of this century, whilst other features are of an earlier date. These include a fine 18th-century ha-ha and an ancient stewpond which has been restored. Other pools form an important part of the gardens, the largest containing a colourful display of yellow water-lilies. There are two more pools and a 12-acre lake. A perennial walk is being developed in part of the old kitchen garden. House also open.

Open 5 Apr–27 Sep Sun BH Mon & following Tue 2–6; Jun, Jul, Aug & Sep also open Tue, Wed, Thu, Sat & Sun 2–6.

£2 (ch £1) Party 20+.
P ⬚ ✗ ⅋ *(gardens and ground floor only)*
wc

Lincoln
Lincolnshire   Map 8 SK97
LINCOLN CASTLE
Castle Hill ☎ *(0522) 25951*

About 5 acres of grounds are contained within the walls of the great limestone castle, with lawns, flower beds and a newly-formed Butterfly garden.

Open Apr–Oct, Mon–Sat 10–6 (5 in Oct); Nov–Mar Mon–Sat 10–4 (5 in Mar); Suns Apr–Oct 11–6 (5 in Oct).

Grounds & Castle 50p (ch 14 & pen 30p) Party 20+.
P ✗ *wc*

Liphook
Hampshire   Map 4 SU83
BOHUNT MANOR
☎ *(0428) 722208*

This 20-acre woodland garden has lakeside walks and the lake has a large collection of ornamental waterfowl. Bulbs, rhodo-dendrons, a water garden, roses and herba-ceous borders provide plenty of colour. It also has one of the tallest tulip trees in the south of England and a handkerchief tree which flowers in June. Some of the plants are labelled.

Open daily Mon–Fri 12–5, Sat & Sun by appointment only.

£1 (ch 10p) Party.
P ✗ ⅋ *(wc) wc*

HOLLYCOMBE HOUSE STEAM COLLECTION, RAILWAYS AND WOODLAND GARDENS
(1½m SE on unclass Midhurst rd)
☎ *(0428) 724900*

As well as the steam collection, there is much to see in the gardens at Hollycombe. The 10-acre woodland garden was laid out at the turn of the century and includes many fine and rare trees and shrubs with some of the tallest cathedral beeches in the country. In late spring the azaleas offer a spectacular show of colour. Plants labelled.

Open Etr wknd, Sun & BH from 12 Apr–11 Oct, also daily 16–31 Aug, 1–6.

£2 (ch & pen £1.50) Party 20+.
P ⬚ ⅋ ✗ ⅋ *wc*

Littledean

Gloucestershire   Map 3 SO61

LITTLEDEAN HALL
☎ Dean (0594) 24213

New landscaping, and the restoration of shrubberies and borders, has created an attractive and interesting garden here in the heart of the Forest of Dean. There are terraced lawns and specimen trees, including a group of very old sweet chestnuts. The water garden is being developed and will eventually be a showpiece for cold-water ornamental fish. House and Roman Temple also open.

* Open Apr–Oct daily 2–6. BH weekends and peak holiday periods 11–6.

* £1 (ch over 8 50p, pen 90p).
P & (gardens only)

Little Ness

Shropshire   Map 7 SJ41

ADCOTE SCHOOL
(7m NW Shrewsbury off A5)
☎ Baschurch (0939) 260202

Around 12 acres of attractive landscaped gardens surround the Grade I listed building. There are many fine trees including tulip trees, oaks, beeches, cedars, Wellingtonia etc. There are also rhododendrons and azaleas and there is a small lake. House also open.

Open 22 Apr–9 Jul & 6–30 Sep 2–5. (Closed 23–25 May) Other times by appointment.

Free (ex on NGS open days) but Governers of the Trust reserve the right to make an admission charge.
P ✻ & (gardens only) wc

Llanfair P.G.

Gwynedd   Map 6 SH57

PLAS NEWYDD
(1m SW on A4080 to Brynsiencyn)
☎ Llanfairpwll (0248) 714795

The present layout of the gardens mostly dates from the late 18th- and early 19th-century, partly influenced by Humphrey Repton. During the 20th-century many tender and exotic flowering shrubs have been planted as well as azaleas, Japanese maples and magnolias. Camellias are also grown, and more recent plantings in the gardens include great 'hedges' of Viburnum tomentosum, Chilean fire bushes and hydrangeas. Other attractions include an Italianate garden created in the 1920's, rose beds, mixed borders and summer-flowering shrub beds. House also open.

Open 17 Apr–Sep, Sun–Fri 12–5; 2–25 Oct, Fri & Sun 12–5.

Garden £1 (ch 50p); House & Garden £1.80 (ch 65p, family ticket £4.50) Party 20+.
P ⌂ ✻ (ex guide dogs) & wc (NT)

Llanrug

Gwynedd   Map 6 SH56

BRYN BRAS CASTLE
(½m SE of A4086)
☎ Llanberis (0286) 870210

The delightful castle grounds cover an area of 32 acres, the lower gardens gradually blending into the higher woodlands, which in turn merge into the foothills of the Snowdonia mountains. Graceful sweeping lawns, flowering trees and shrubs, pools, streams and statuary combine to create a relaxing environment and there are superb views. There are marked walks and a knot garden. Castle also open.

Open Spring BH–Sep, Mon–Fri & Sun 1–5; mid Jul–Aug 10.30–5.

£1.20 (ch 15 60p) inclusive.
P ⌂ ✻ wc

Lochaline

Highland Argyll   Map 13 NM64

ARDTORNISH HOUSE GARDENS
☎ Morvern (096784) 288

The gardens extend to around 28 acres and have been sculpted out of a rocky hillside with fine views along Loch Aline to the Isle of Mull. There are areas of mature woodland, lawns, primulas and a rockery. Of particular interest is the fine collection of rhododendrons. Some plants labelled.

Please telephone for opening times and admission charges.
P

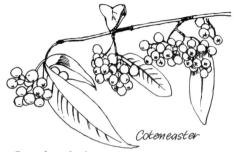

Cotoneaster

Lochgilphead

Strathclyde *Argyll*   **Map 10 NR88**

KILMORY CASTLE GARDENS
☎ (0546) 2127

The 30 acres of grounds which surround the castle were begun in the 18th-century, but later suffered years of neglect before being acquired by the present owners. Miraculously, a number of rare trees and shrubs survived and the gardens are now being restored to their former glory. There are woodland walks and nature trails.

Open all year 9–dusk.

Free.
P ☗ ☖ ☗

Lode

Cambridgeshire   **Map 5 TL56**

ANGLESEY ABBEY
(6m NE Cambridge on B1102)
☎ *Cambridge (0223) 811200*

Impressive gardens which extend to around 100 acres. The Hyacinth Garden has 4000 bulbs and there is a superb Herbaceous Garden. Sweeping lawns, unusual trees, avenues and viewpoints are augmented by fine statuary and there is something of interest throughout the year. Visitor Centre explains how these gardens were developed. Watermill demonstrated on first Sun in each month. Plants labelled.

Open Apr–Oct: Gardens 1 Apr–28 Jun (ex 4 Apr) Wed–Sun; 29 Jun–18 Oct daily 1.30–5.30. Abbey 11/12 Apr & 18 Apr–18 Oct Wed–Sun & BH's 1.30–5.30.

Garden £1 (ch 50p); Abbey & Garden £2.50 (ch £1.50) Party 15+.
☗ (from 12.30 pm) ☗ (ex guide dogs) wc (NT)

London

Greater London   **Map 4 TQ37**

CHELSEA PHYSIC GARDEN
66 Royal Hospital Road SW3 ☎ *01-352 5646*

The second oldest botanic garden in the UK, this 3½-acre garden was set up in 1673 to grow plants for recognition and study for medicinal and general scientific use. The present garden includes ponds, a herb garden, a rock garden, a perfumery border, family order beds and a collection of over 5000 trees, shrubs and herbaceous plants, many rare or unusual. Plants labelled. Guided tours by arrangement (charge). Advisory services and courses available. Special planting to commemorate founding of Curtis' *Botanical Magazine* on 12 Apr.

Open Wed & Sun 12 Apr–18 Oct 2–5. Additional opening during Chelsea Flower Show week (19–22 May, 12–5); parties at other times by appointment.

£1.50 (ch and students £1).
P ☗ *(Sun)* ☗ ☗ ☖ wc Plants for sale

CHISWICK HOUSE
Burlington Lane W4 ☎ *01-995 0508*

Built 1725–30 with interior decoration by William Kent. This mansion is considered to be the finest example of Palladian architecture in Great Britain. Formal garden created in the 17th-century in the Italian style, with a lake, yew hedges and conservatory with a collection of camellias.

* *Open mid Mar–mid Oct, daily 9.30–6.30, mid Oct–mid Mar, Sun & Wed–Sat 9.30–4.*

* *75p.*
P ☗ ☖ *(gardens & ground floor) (AM)*

FENTON HOUSE
Hampstead Grove NW3 ☎ *01-435 3471*

A small walled garden consisting of a terrace, a formal garden and a rustic garden situated on three different levels. There are formal lawns, herbaceous borders, climbers and a rose garden with many areas enclosed by box hedging. William and Mary house also open.

Open Mar, Sat & Sun 2–6; Apr–Oct Sat–Wed (inc BH Mon) 11–6. (last admission 5).

Gardens free; House £1.80 (£1.30 Mon & Tue ex BH's).
(NT)

HORNIMAN GARDENS
Forest Hill SE23 (on S Circular Road)
☏ 01-699 8924

Run by the Inner London Education Authority (ILEA), this 11-acre hillside garden has good views over central London. There is a colourful sunken garden with annual bedding displays, rose and water gardens, a greenhouse and a fine collection of trees, some of which are labelled. Other attractions include animal and bird enclosures, nature trails etc. Horticultural demonstrations are held on the first Wed in each month, Mar–Sep.

Open all year from 7.30 (or 8 on Sun). Greenhouse open Sun Jun–Aug.

Free.
P *(nearby roads)* 🍴 *(in Horniman Museum)* 🎠 🕭 wc

KENSINGTON ROOF GARDENS
99 Kensington High St, W8 ☏ *01-937 7994*

The 1½-acre roof garden is divided into 3 gardens; Woodland, Spanish and Tudor. There are many exotic plants as well as flamingos, ducks, pheasants and bantam hens. The gardens were established in 1938. Some plants labelled.

Open daily Mon–Fri 10–6.

Free.
P 🍴 *(licensed restaurant) no pushchairs* 🍴 🕭 *(lift available) no pushchairs*

KENWOOD HOUSE AND GARDENS
Hampstead Lane, Hampstead NW3
☏ 01-348 1286

The grounds of Kenwood House are bordered by woodland giving access to Hampstead Heath. Sheltered gardens, with pleached walks, an extensive shrubbery and sloping lawns leading to an ornamental lake form a tranquil surround to the 18th-century mansion.

Open Apr–Sep daily 10–7; Feb, Mar, Oct 10–5; Nov–Jan 10–4; closed Good Fri, Xmas Eve, Xmas Day.

Free.
🍴 🍴 🕭 *(ground floor & gardens only) (AM)*

LEIGHTON HOUSE
12 Holland Park Road W14 ☏ *01-602 3316*

An enclosed London garden, mostly laid down to grass. It is gradually being restored to re-create the original plantings and borders of the 1890's. The grounds are also used to display sculpture.

Open all year daily 11–5 (6pm during temporary exhibitions) garden open Apr–Sep 11–5 (closed Sun & BH).

Free.
P 🍴 wc

TRADESCANT TRUST MUSEUM OF GARDEN HISTORY
St Mary-at-Lambeth, Lambeth Palace Rd, SE1 ☏ *01-261 1891*

This small garden in the grounds of the church of St Mary-at-Lambeth was established in 1981. It is a replica of a 17th-century knot garden and only includes plants introduced into this country by the Tradescants, or known to have been grown by them in their garden. It was designed by Lady Salisbury. Plants labelled. The church itself houses the Museum of Garden History with lectures and exhibitions. Spring Gardens Fair 26 Apr.

Open early Mar–mid Dec Mon–Fri 11–3, Sun 10.30–5 Children must be supervised.

Free (donations appreciated).
P *(50–100yds)* 🍴 🍴 🕭 *Plants for sale*

Long Ashton
Avon   Map 3 ST57
ASHTON COURT ESTATE
☏ *Bristol (0272) 633438*

This large estate of 864 acres has signposted pathways and trails through the woods and deer park. There are rose gardens and a sunken garden with an ornamental pond, and one of the oak trees on the estate is said to be over 900 years old. Some plants labelled. Various events held in the grounds during the year.

Open all year daily.

Free.
P 🍴 🎠 🕭 *(wc) wc*

Longleat
Wiltshire   Map 3 ST84
LONGLEAT HOUSE
(Entrance on Warminster–Frome road A362)
☏ *Maiden Bradley (09853) 551*

More famous, perhaps, for its Safari Park and other attractions, Longleat does have →

79

fine gardens which were designed by Russell Page. The 2-mile long Azalea Drive is spectacular in May/June and there is a maze and a superb orangery designed by Wyatville. The gardens give way to many acres of 'Capability' Brown parkland and there are outstanding views from Heaven's Gate and Sheerwater Lake. Garden centre specialising in fuchsias and pelargoniums. House and other attractions also open.

Open all year (ex 25 Dec): Etr–Sep daily 10–6; Oct–Etr daily 10–4. Safari Park, Boat Ride and Pets Corner 14 Mar–1 Nov 10–6, other attractions 4 Apr–1 Nov. Closing times may vary in Mar, Oct & Nov.

House £2.50 (ch £1, pen £2) Discount ticket for all attractions £7 (ch £4, pen £5) Safari Park £3 (ch £2, pen £2.50).
P ⏚ (licensed) ⏀ ⅋ Garden centre

Lotherton Hall
West Yorkshire   **Map 8 SE43**
LOTHERTON HALL
(10m E of Leeds, off B1217 near Aberford)
☎ *Leeds (0532) 813259*

This Edwardian house is now a country house museum, with gardens laid out in the same period as the house, a bird garden and deer park. Museum also open.

Open May–Sep, Tue–Sun 10.30–6.15 or dusk. Thu 8.30. Also open BH Mon.

60p (ch & pen 25p) students with union card free.
P ⏚ (licensed) ⏀ ✗ (park only)

Lower Beeding
West Sussex   **Map 4 TQ22**
LEONARDSLEE GARDENS
(at S junc of A279 & A281) ☎ *(040376) 212*

A Grade I listed garden of about 80 acres set in a beautiful valley. Renowned for its spring display of rhododendrons and azaleas. In the autumn, maples of all colours and other shrubs are well worth seeing. A series of lakes and waterfalls give rise to delightful views and reflections. Plants labelled. Plants for sale.

Open 18 Apr–28 Jun 10–6; 28 Jun–28 Sep wknds only 2–6 & Oct, wknds only 10–5.

£2.50 (ch £1) May, other times £1.50 (ch £1) Party.
P ⏚ ✗ wc

Luton
Bedfordshire   **Map 4 TL02**
LUTON HOO
Entrance at Park St gates ☎ *(0582) 22955*

18th-century house with many art treasures, set in landscaped gardens by 'Capability' Brown. There are 2 terraces, one planted with roses, yew hedges and topiary. House also open.

Open 16 Apr–11 Oct daily 2–5.45, last admission 5 (closed Mon ex BH Mon).

£2 (ch £1) Party 30+.
P ⏚ ⏀ ✗ ⅋ (NGS)

Lydney
Gloucestershire ·   **Map 3 SO60**
LYDNEY PARK GARDENS
(entrance off A48 Gloucester to Chepstow between Lydney and Aylburton)
☎ *Dean (0594) 42844*

Extensive rhododendron, azalea and flowering shrub gardens in a lakeland valley. The gardens around the house contain magnolias and daffodils and have fine views across the Severn. Deer park. Roman temple. Museum. Plants labelled.

Open Etr Sun & Mon, 25 May–31 May 11–6, Sun, BH & Wed 26 Apr–14 Jun.

£1 (ch free) Party.
P ⏚ 🚌 (except by appointment) wc Plants for sale

Hibiscus syriacus

Macclesfield

Cheshire **Map 7 SJ79**

HARE HILL
(4m NW off B5087)

Walled garden with pergola, rhododendrons and azaleas. Also parkland.

* *Open Apr–Oct, Wed, Thu, Sun & BH Mon 2–5.30. Parties by written appointment with Head Gardener.*

* *80p.*
♿ *(wc) wc (NT)*

Madron

Cornwall **Map 2 SW43**

TRENGWAINTON GARDEN
(2m W of Penzance on B3312)
☎ *Penzance (0736) 63148*

A woodland garden, mainly spring flowering, daffodils, primroses, magnolias, rhododendrons and azaleas. A series of walled gardens contain a wide selection of trees, shrubs and perennials. There is a colourful stream garden along the main drive with spring-flowering shrubs. Extensive lawns with colourful borders surround the house. House not open. Guided tours (by prior arrangement).

Open 4 Mar–Oct, Wed–Sat, also BH Mon 11–6.

£1.30.
wc (NT)

Maidstone

Kent **Map 5 TQ75**

LEEDS CASTLE
(5m E on B2163 off A20) ☎ *(0622) 65400*

Leeds Castle has 500 acres of parkland and gardens. The Culpeper Garden, a traditional English walled garden, is filled with a mixture of cottage plants providing scent and colour throughout the summer. There are good collections of old-fashioned shrub roses, herbaceous perennials, flowering shrubs, and herbs. Lakes, streams, waterfalls and a woodland garden lie within the parkland. Plants labelled. Special events throughout the year. Castle also open.

Open Apr–Oct, daily 11–5; Nov–Mar Sat & Sun 12–4.

Grounds £2.85 (ch 5–15 £1.85, pen & students £2.35) Castle & Grounds £3.85 (ch 5–15 £2.85, pen & students £3.35).
P ☕ *(licensed)* ⛺ 🐕 ♿ *(ground floor & gardens; wc) wc Plants for sale*

Malton

North Yorkshire **Map 8 SE77**

CASTLE HOWARD
(6m SW of Malton)
☎ *Coneysthorpe (065384) 333*

Gardens and extensive landscaped grounds, with lakes and an ornamental fountain surround this famous house designed by Sir John Vanbrugh. A grassy terrace above the lakes leads to the Temple of the Four Winds, from where there are magnificent views over the park and to the Mausoleum designed by Hawksmoor. There are peacocks in the grounds, a walled rose garden and a plant centre. The house is also open.

Open House & Garden 25 Mar–Oct daily, house 11–5, garden 10–5 (last admission 4.30).

Admission charges not known for 1987.
P ☕ *(licensed)* 🐕 ♿ *Plants for sale*

Manchester

Gt Manchester **Map 7 SJ89**

FLETCHER MOSS BOTANICAL GARDENS
Didsbury ☎ *061-434 1877*

The location and southerly aspect of this garden has made it possible to create a haven of botanical beauty for the professional and amateur gardener. Protection from cold winds allow many specimen trees and shrubs to be grown. The garden contains many uncommon alpines, bulbs, screes, with aquatic and marginal plants around the natural pond and water features. A peat bed contains miniature conifers and rhododendrons. A wild garden with colchichums and rose species. Orchid House. Many of the plants and shrubs are labelled. An information board displays the names of the plants of the week, for visitors to look out for. Museum shortly to be re-opened.

Open all year, daily 8–dusk.

Free.
P *(limited)* 🐕 ♿ *wc*

Mawnan Smith

Cornwall   Map 2 SW72

GLENDURGAN

A Valley garden, leading down to the Helford River, planted with camellias, rhododendrons, magnolias, fine specimen trees and an unusual laurel maze. Some plants labelled.

Open 2 Mar–Oct Mon, Wed & Fri 10.30–6 (closed Good Fri).

£1.40.

wc (NT)

Melbourne

Derbyshire   Map 8 SK32

MELBOURNE HALL

☎ *(03316) 3347 & 2502*

These famous, early 18th-century formal gardens, covering 16 acres, were designed by Henry Wise in the style of French landscape gardener, Le Nôtre. Terraces and avenues lined with yew and lime hedges provide a beautiful setting for fountains, ponds, statues and garden ornaments. A wrought iron pergola, a Victorian grotto and a 200yd-long yew tunnel are some of the many interesting features here. Lakeside walks. Hall also open.

Open Gardens Apr–Sep Wed, Sat, Sun, BH Mon 2–6; House Jun–Oct Wed 2–6. Other times by appointment.

Gardens £1; House £1.50 (ch 16 75p). Family ticket for House.

P *(limited)* ⬩ ✖ ⬩ *(ground floor & gardens)*

Melrose

Borders *Roxburghshire*   Map 12 NT53

ABBOTSFORD GARDENS

(2m W off A6091) ☎ *Galashiels (0896) 2043*

The grounds of Sir Walter Scott's home slope down to the River Tweed and contain many fine trees, some of which are believed to have been planted by Scott himself. Near to the house are 2 acres of formal gardens with yew hedges, sculptures and fountains, and rhododendrons, azaleas, viburnums and old shrub roses are also grown. There is a 19th-century fern house with begonias, pelargo-

niums and ferns. Guided tours for parties by prior arrangement. House also open.

Open 3rd Mon in Mar–Oct, Mon–Sat 10–5, Sun 2–5.

House and gardens £1.50 (ch 75p) Party.

P ⬩ ✖ ⬩ *(wc) wc*

PRIORWOOD GARDEN

☎ *Melrose (089682) 2965*

This small garden specialises in flowers suitable for drying. The gardens are formal in design and have herbaceous and everlasting annual borders. In the orchard there is a walk illustrating 'Apples through the ages'.

Open Apr & Nov–24 Dec, Mon–Sat 10–1 & 2–5.30; May–Jun & Oct, Mon–Sat 10–5.30, Sun 1.30–5.30, Jul–Sep, Mon–Sat 10–6, Sun 1.30–5.30.

Admission by donation.

(NTS)

Mersham

Kent   Map 5 TR03

SWANTON MILL

☎ *Aldington (023372) 223*

Three acres of gardens surround this beautifully restored mill. Rose, herb, iris and water gardens, and a trout lake, are among the attractions. The mill can be seen working.

Open Mill & Gardens Apr–Oct, Sat & Sun 3–6, parties by appt.

£1 (ch 12 50p).

P ⬩ ✖ ⬩ *(gardens & ground floor only) wc*

Plants for sale

Mickleton

Gloucestershire   Map 4 SP14

HIDCOTE MANOR GARDEN

(½ SE) ☎ *(038677) 333*

Ten acres of beautiful English gardens divided by superb hedges into many formal and informal garden 'rooms'. Many rare trees, and a wide variety of plants and shrubs including old-fashioned roses. Plants labelled.

Open Apr–Oct Sat–Mon, Wed & Thu 11–8 (last admission 7pm, or 1 hr before sunset).

£2.50 (ch £1.25) Parties by prior written arrangement.

⬩ ✖ *wc Plants for sale (NT)*

KIFTSGATE COURT
(½m S off A46, adjacent Hidcote Garden)

Unusual shrubs and plants are the features of this fine garden created between 1920 and 1950 by Mrs. J. B. Muir. The collection of old-fashioned and specie roses includes R. Filipes Kiftsgate, believed to be the largest rose in England.

Open Garden only Apr–Sep, Wed, Thur, Sun & BH Mon 2–6. Parties by appt.

£1.50 (ch 50p).

P ✖ *Plants for sale on open days*

Middle Woodford
Wiltshire   Map 4 SU13
HEALE HOUSE GARDENS
☎ *(072273) 207 & 504*

Attractive gardens bordering the River Avon with an interesting and varied collection of shrub roses and perennials. The Water Garden, at its best in the spring and autumn, has an authentic Japanese tea house and bridge sited among the acers, magnolias and flowering cherries. Some plants labelled. Nursery. Advisory service.

Open Good Fri–autumn, Mon–Sat & 1st Sun in the month & BH 10–5. Nursery Feb–Dec, Mon–Sat & 1st Sun in month & BH, 11–5 (closed 1–2 in winter).

£1 (accompanied ch 14 free). Party.
P ⚹ *wc*

Milton
Oxfordshire   Map 4 SU49
MILTON MANOR HOUSE
☎ *Abingdon (0235) 831287 & 831871*

A simple Georgian garden with sweeping lawns, fine trees and a one acre walled garden.

Open Etr Sat–25 Oct, Sat, Sun & BH 2–5.30.

Gardens 50p; House and gardens £1.30 (ch 60p).
P ⬚ ⚹ *(ground floor & gardens) wc*

Minard
Strathclyde *Argyll*   Map 10 NR99
CRARAE GLEN GARDENS
☎ *(0546) 86633 or 86274 (evenings and wknds)*

This wild, highland glen on the shores of Loch Fyne is planted with many flowering shrubs and rare trees. There are beautiful views of the tumbling burn and steep banks planted with massed azaleas, rhododendrons, eucalyptus and magnolias. Plants labelled. Advisory service.

Open daily 9–6.

Admission fee payable.
P *wc Plants for sale*

Minstead
Hampshire   Map 4 SU21
FURZEY GARDENS
☎ *Southampton (0703) 812464*

Delightful, informal gardens of 8 acres which are full of interest throughout the year. Spring is a mass of crocus, snowdrops, daffodils and bluebells followed by a spectacular show of azaleas. The collection of heathers ranges from ground cover to giant tree varieties. There are also many trees →

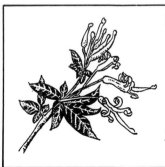

and shrubs, a water garden, lake and fernery. Plants labelled. Forest Cottage and Art Gallery in gardens also open.

Open daily 10.30-5 (dusk in winter) (closed Xmas).

Gardens, cottage and gallery £1.50 (ch 5-14 75p) Nov-Feb reduced admission charge. Party 25+.

P ✖ wc

Minterne Magna

Dorset   Map 3 ST60

MINTERNE HOUSE
(on A352) ☎ *Cerne Abbas (03003) 370*

A wild, woodland garden laid out in the 18th century with small lakes, streams and cascades. Many rare trees, rhododendrons, azaleas and magnolias. Excellent autumn colour. Some plants labelled.

Open Apr-Oct daily 10-7.

£1 (accompanied ch 16 free).
P wc Plants for sale

Moniaive

Dumfries & Galloway   Map 11 NX79
Dumfriesshire

MAXWELTON HOUSE
☎ *(08482) 385*

Herbaceous borders, vegetable plots, ponds and greenhouses are amongst the attractions of these gardens. There are also interesting old summer huts. Beyond the more formal gardens the grounds are wooded, and include a colourful variety of rhododendrons. House, chapel and museum also open.

Open Garden Apr-Sep, Mon-Thu 2-5; Chapel, Apr-Sep daily 10-6; House & Museum Jul & Aug Mon-Thu 2-5 (house also open by arrangement all year).

Garden 50p (ch 10-16 & pen 25p) House £1.50 (ch 10-16 & pen £1).
P ⚲ *(parties only)* ⚶ ✖ ⚹ *(gardens & ground floor) wc*

Monksilver

Somerset   Map 3 ST03

COMBE SYDENHAM HALL
☎ *Stogumber (0984) 56284*

An Elizabethian house (undergoing restoration) with herbaceous borders and individual herb, rose, knot and secret gardens divided by tall yew hedges. Woodland walks through the large estate. Some plants labelled. Hall also open.

Open Etr Mon-Oct, Mon-Fri 11-4.30.

* *£1.80 (ch 80p, pen £1.60) Party.*
P ⚲ ✖ *(in house)* ⚹ *(gardens & ground floor) wc Plants for sale*

Montacute

Somerset   Map 3 ST41

MONTACUTE HOUSE
☎ *Martock (0935) 823289*

Elizabethan house with 12 acres of formal Victorian gardens set in attractive parkland. There are sweeping lawns, large yew hedges, mixed borders, old-fashioned roses, an orangery and a lily pond. Fine garden stonework includes 2 handsome pavillions. Some plants labelled.

Gardens open all year daily. House Apr-Oct Wed-Mon 12.30-6, (last admission to house 5.30). Parties by written appointment with the Administrator.

Gardens Jun-Sep 80p (ch 40p), Oct-May 60p (ch 30p) House & gardens £2.50 (ch 17 £1.20, under 5 free). Party.
⚲ ⚹ wc (NT)

Moreton-in-Marsh

Gloucestershire   Map 4 SP23

BATSFORD ARBORETUM
(2m NW) ☎ *(0608) 50722 & Blockley (0386) 700409 (wknds)*

Delightful walks among 50 acres of many rare and exotic trees and shrubs, including large collections of acers and magnolias. In spring there are daffodils and early flowering trees. Autumn brings a further blaze of colour from Japanese maples, beeches and chestnuts. Plants labelled.

Open Apr-Oct, daily 10-5.

£1.50 (ch & pen 75p) Party.
P ⚹ *(ex Mon)* ⚶ wc Plants for sale

CHASTLETON HOUSE
(5m SE off A44)
☎ *Barton-on-the-Heath (060874) 355*

A 17th-century garden with cut box and yew topiary. House also open.

Open Good Fri–27 Sep, Fri, Sat, Sun & BH Mon 2–5 (last admission 4.30).

* £2 (ch £1) Party 20+.
P wc

SEZINCOTE
(3m SW)
The house, built in 1805, with its copper dome, pinnacles and temples, was the inspiration for the Brighton Pavilion. The 10-acre water gardens, by Humphrey Repton and Thomas Daniell, continue the Indian theme with canals representing the rivers of life and a Hindu temple set beside a pool.

Open Garden all year (ex Dec) Thu, Fri & BH Mon 2–6 (or dusk); House May–Jul & Sep, Thu & Fri 2.30–5.30.

Gardens £1.50 (ch 50p) House and garden £2.50.
P (100 yds) ✘ wc

Morpeth
Northumberland   **Map 12 NZ18**
MELDON PARK
(6m W on B6343) ☏ Hartburn (067072) 661

The house, built in 1832, is in an attractive woodland setting with colourful displays of rhododendrons. The gardens have herbaceous borders, roses and a Camellia House, Part of house also open.

Open 23 May–21 Jun daily, also 22–24 Aug, 2–5.

£1.50 (ch & students 50p).
P ✘ & (wc) wc

Moseley
Staffordshire   **Map 7 SJ90**
MOSELEY OLD HALL
☏ Wolverhampton (0902) 782808

The small garden of this Elizabethian house has been reconstructed since 1962 in 17th-century style with formal, box parterre. Only plants known in the 17th-century are grown here. Other features include an arbour, a small herb garden and an orchard. Guided tours of house and garden by prior arrangement.

Open 14 Mar–Jun & 12 Sep–15 Nov, Sat & Sun 2–6; Jul–6 Sep Wed–Sun 2–6; 15 Nov–20 Dec, Sun 2–4.30; also BH Mon & following Tue 2–6. Parties at other times by prior arrangement.

£1.80 (ch 90p) family and party rates.
P ☐ (licensed) ✘ & (wc) (NT)

Mottisfont
Hampshire   **Map 4 SU32**
MOTTISFONT ABBEY
☏ Lockerley (0794) 40757

The garden at Mottisfont Abbey, near the River Test, is particularly famous for the collection of old-fashioned roses, especially shrub roses and climbers, in the walled garden. These are usually at their best during June and July. Herbaceous plants are also grown, and the surrounding parkland has extensive lawns and fine, mature trees. Part of house also open.

Grounds including rose garden, open daily (ex Fri & Sat), Apr–Sep 2–6. Rose garden also open 7–9pm Wed & Sun during rose season. House Apr–Sep Wed & Sun 2–6. Coach parties by appointment only.

Grounds £1.50 (rose season), £1 at other times. House 30p extra.
P ✘ & (wc) wc (NT)

Lamium maculatum
'Dead nettle'

Mull, Isle of
Strathclyde *Argyll*   Map 10 NM73
TOROSAY CASTLE & GARDENS
Craignure ☎ *(06802) 421*

The terraced gardens, covering 11 acres, testify to the benefits of the Gulf Stream, and include many unexpected plants, for example, Australian gum trees and a Japanese garden. The famous statue walk is embellished with 18th-century Italian statues. House also open.

Open House & Garden mid Apr–early Oct, daily 10.30–5.30 (last admission 5).

* House & Garden £1.50 (pen & students £1.20, ch over 5 90p); garden only (pen, students & ch over 5 50p).
P ⌷ ⅋ *(wc)*

Muncaster
Cumbria   Map 6 SD19
MUNCASTER CASTLE
☎ *Ravenglass (06577) 614 or 203*

Famous rhododendron garden with azaleas, magnolias and a good collection of rare trees. The land has been owned by the Pennington family since the 13th century. The grounds also contain a bird garden and there are extensive views over the Esk valley from the ½-mile-long grass terrace. Garden centre. House also open.

Open Good Fri–Sep, Tue–Sun & BH; Garden 12–5; House 1.30–4.30. Parties in morning also, if booked in advance.

Gardens £1.10 (ch 14 70p); House & Gardens £2.20 (ch 14 £1.10). Party.
P ⌷ ⅋ *(ground floor & gardens) wc*

Muthill
Tayside *Perthshire*   Map 11 NN81
DRUMMOND CASTLE GARDENS
(1m N) ☎ *(076481) 257*

The beautiful formal gardens of Drummond Castle were originally laid out around the year 1630. In 1830 the parterre was remodelled in the Italian style and embellished with fine figures and statues including a large sundial. The design of the gardens takes the form of a St. Andrew's Cross. Garden Centre.

* Open Apr & Sep Wed & Sun, May–Aug daily 2–6.

* £1 (ch & pen 50p).
P ⅋

Ness
Cheshire   Map 7 SJ37
LIVERPOOL UNIVERSITY BOTANIC GARDENS
(off A540) ☎ *051-336 2135*

Fine trees and shrubs, herbaceous borders, a rock terrace, water gardens and an extensive collection of roses, are among the delights of this beautiful garden. The Visitor Centre has educational indoor exhibitions and a slide sequence.

Open daily 9–sunset (closed Xmas Day).

£1.60 (ch 8–16 & pen £1).
P ⌷ *(Etr–Oct)* ⅋ *(wc) Plants for sale*

Newby Bridge
Cumbria   Map 7 SD38
GRAYTHWAITE HALL GARDENS
(4m N on W side of Lake Windermere)
☎ *(0448) 31248*

Seven acres of landscaped gardens which were among the first to be designed and laid out by Thomas Mawson. Rhododendrons and azaleas are the main feature of the garden and some of the species are quite rare. There are also mixed herbaceous plants, a Dutch garden and examples of topiary. Another attraction is the delightful terraced rose garden which affords fine views of the surrounding grounds.

Open Apr–Jun, daily 10–6.

75p (ch 14 free).
P *wc*

Newcastle Upon Tyne

Tyne and Wear **Map 12 NZ26**

JESMOND DENE

☎ *(091) 2328520 ex 6217*

A Victorian/Edwardian park set in a river valley about 2 miles long. Exotic trees, shrubs and rhododendrons help to provide colour all year round. There are also magnolias, evergreens, walnut trees and redwoods. A woodland stream runs through the park which borders the Ouseburn Valley, currently being developed into a leisure area. Pets corner.

Open all year daily.

Free.
♿ *wc*

Newick

East Sussex **Map 5 TQ42**

NEWICK PARK

☎ *(082572) 2915*

The home of Lord Brentford and his family, this 18th-century mansion is set in 200 acres of beautiful gardens, parkland and farmland. Mainly a spring garden with azaleas and rhododendrons, it also has herbaceous plants, lakeside walks and an ice house. In the grounds is Siselle Nursery which specialises in wild flowers, herbs and old-fashioned plants, some of which are endangered species. Some plants labelled. Plants for sale.

Open Mar–Oct, daily 2–5.30, coaches by appointment only.

£1 (ch 50p) Party 4+.
P *wc*

Newport

Gwent **Map 3 ST38**

TREDEGAR HOUSE & COUNTRY PARK

(Coedkernew, SW of Newport, signed from A48 & M4 junct 28) ☎ *(0633) 62275*

The extensive grounds of this magnificent Restoration house comprise flower gardens, a fishing and boating lake, a visitor centre and some craft workshops. Newport Show is held here 4–6 Sep. House also open.

Open House Etr–last Sun in Sep, Wed–Sun & BHs; (guided tours every 30 mins from 12.30–4.30); grounds all year daily dawn–dusk.

* *Grounds free; house & grounds £1.50 (ch 75p, students, reg unemp & pen 90p) Party.*
P ☕ *(licensed)* ♿

Newstead

Nottinghamshire **Map 8 SK55**

NEWSTEAD ABBEY

☎ *Mansfield (0623) 792822*

Former 12th-century priory, rebuilt as a house which is famous for its associations with Lord Byron. The beautiful grounds contain a number of feature gardens including Iris, Fern, Rose, and Japanese Gardens. There are two large lakes, fed by the River Leen, streams, ponds, waterfalls and cascades. Some plants labelled.

Open Gardens all year daily 9.30–dusk; Abbey Etr–Sep daily 1.45–5.

* *Gardens 75p (ch 25p); Abbey & Gardens £1.75 (ch 45p).*
P *(300 yds)* ☕ *wc*

Northampton

Northamptonshire **Map 4 SP76**

DELAPRE ABBEY

☎ *(0604) 762129*

Built on the site of a Cluniac nunnery, a 16th–19th century house with 8 acres of attractive grounds and gardens. In one part of the grounds is a walled garden with herbaceous borders, backed by wall shrubs. Topiary hedges divide the annuals and summer flower borders. A collection of herbs; glasshouses with grapes and peaches. The →

outer garden has pools and a stream, arboretum and shrubs. A ha-ha boundary has views of Delapre Woods. House also open.

Walled garden open May–Sep (during daylight hours) Abbey grounds open all year until dusk. Certain parts of the interior shown Thu only, May–Sep 2.30–5, Oct–Apr 2.30–4.30.

Free.

P ✖ 🚌 ᕼ *(grounds only; wc) wc*

Northenden
G Manchester   **Map 7 SJ89**
WYTHENSHAWE HORTICULTURAL CENTRE
Wythenshawe Park ☎ 061-945 1768

Large horitcultural centre set in beautiful parkland with rare trees, shrubs and woodland walks. Many glasshouses including a Tropical House, Cactus House and Alpine House. There is also a model fruit and vegetable garden and a large area of bedding plant trials. Plants labelled. Advisory service.

Open all year daily 10–4.

Free.

P ✖ ᕼ *(wc) wc*

Northiam
East Sussex   **Map 5 TQ82**
GREATER DIXTER
☎ *(07974) 3160*

The beautiful gardens of this timber-framed manor house were originally laid out in 1910, largely by Edwin Lutyens, but the choice of plants seen today are the work of the well-known gardening expert Christopher Lloyd, who has introduced a wide variety of interesting and unusual plants. House also open.

Open House & Gardens Apr–11 Oct & 17/18, 24/25 Oct, daily ex Mon (but open BH Mon) 2–5; Gardens open from 11am 24/25 May, Suns in Jul & Aug, & 31 Aug. Parties at other times by arrangement.

House & Garden £2 (ch 50p; reduced rate Fri for pen & NT members £1.50); garden only £1.20 (ch 30p).

P 🌳 ✖ *Plants for sale*

Northwich
Cheshire   **Map 7 SJ67**
ARLEY HALL AND GARDENS
(5m N of Norwich, 5m from M6 junc 19 & 20; M56 junc 9 & 10) ☎ *(056585) 284 or 353*

Gardens of great variety overlooking extensive parkland. Notable features include double herbaceous borders, a unique avenue of holm oaks trimed into cylinder shapes, a collection of shrub and specie roses and walled gardens. Other features are areas of rhododendrons and azaleas, a scented garden and a herb garden. A newly created woodland leads to a woodland walk. Plants for sale. House also open.

Open Good Fri–early Oct, Tue–Sun & BH Mons 2–6. Jun, Jul & Aug, gardens open at 12 noon.

House & garden £2.20 (ch 8 free, ch 17 £1.10), gardens only £1.40 (ch 8–17 70p). Party 20+.

P 🍴 *(licensed)* 🌳 ᕼ *(gardens & ground floor; wc) wc*

Nottingham
Nottinghamshire   **Map 8 SK53**
WOLLATON HALL
(2½m W of city centre) ☎ *(0602) 282146*

Around 10 acres of formal gardens, within the 500-acre deer park, with a variety of ornamental displays. As well as lawns and herbaceous beds, there are wall shrubs, rhododendrons and erica borders. A number of unusual trees can be seen and there is also a camellia house. Trees and shrubs labelled. Flower shows as part of the City Festival (late May) and City Show (late Aug/Sep). Natural history museum also open.

Open daily throughout the year, dawn–dusk.

Free.

P 🍴 *(summer wknds only)* 🌳 ᕼ *(wc) wc*

Nuneaton
Warwickshire   **Map 4 SP39**
ARBURY HALL
(2m SW) ☎ *(0203) 382804*

Tree-lined drives lead through the large park surrounding this fascinating house, the home of Lord and Lady Daventry. The grounds are notable for their copper beeches, lime trees and pines. The gardens include fine herbaceous borders, roses and a bog garden.

Open House, Park & Gardens Etr–Sep Sun; Jul–Aug BHs, Tue & Wed; gardens 1–6, house 2–5.

House & grounds £2 (ch £1); grounds only £1 (ch 50p) Party 25+.
P ⌂ ⅋ (ground floor & garden only)

Nuneham Courtenay
Oxfordshire   Map 4 SU59
JOHN MATTOCK ROSE NURSERIES
☎ (086738) 265

Over 200,000 roses are grown annually in the rose fields at Nuneham Courtenay. In the 3-acre display gardens mature specimens of many varieties can be seen and all types of roses are grown. Rose pruning demonstrations Sats in March. Guided tours by arrangement for horticultural societies etc. Advisory service available. Plants labelled.

Open Jun–Sep, daily Mon–Sat 9–6, Sun 10.30–6.

Free.
P ⅋ wc garden centre

NUNEHAM COURTENAY ARBORETUM
☎ (0865) 242737

An outstation of the University of Oxford Botanic Garden housing a collection of conifers, broadleaf trees, rhododendrons and other plants for teaching and research purposes. Plants labelled.

Open May–Oct Mon–Sat 8.30–5 & Sun 2–6.

Free.
P ⅋ ⅋

Oakwell Hall
West Yorkshire   Map 8 SE22
OAKWELL HALL & COUNTRY PARK
(Nova Lane nr Birstall Smithies, 6m SE Bradford) ☎ Batley (0924) 474926

The 67-acre country park includes interesting period gardens representative of the history of the moated manor house which dates back to Elizabethan times and also has associ-

ations with the Civil War and, later, the Brontës. House also open.

Open House & Grounds Mon–Sat 10–5, Sun 1–5.

Free.
P ⌂ ⅋ ⅋ (ground floor & grounds only; wc)

Old Dailly
Strathclyde *Ayrshire*   Map 10 NX29
BARGANY GARDENS
(4m NE on B734 from Girvan)
☎ (046587) 227 or 274

Woodland walks with snowdrops, bluebells and daffodils. Fine display of azaleas and rhododendrons round the lily pond in May and June. Many ornamental trees. Autumn colours.

Gardens open Mar–Oct daily until 7pm (or dusk).

Contribution box.
P ⅋ ⅋ Plants for sale

Fuchsia

Old Warden

Bedfordshire Map 4 TL14

SWISS GARDEN

(2m W from roundabout on A1 Biggleswade bypass) ☎ *Bedford (0234) 228330*

An unusual "Romantic" garden dating from the early 19th-century, inspired by the writings of J. B. Papworth. The garden contains a great variety of plants and trees, some quite rare, such as early examples of English rambling roses, fine specimens of Cedar, Arolla Pine and Wellingtonia. A series of picturesquely contrived vistas are created by shrubberies, ponds, groves and winding paths. A summerhouse, grotto and fernery complete the effect of this attractive garden. Guided tours (evenings only) by arrangement.

Open Apr–Oct Wed, Thu, Sat, Sun (ex last Sun of each month); Good Fri & BH Mons 2–6 (last admission 5.15).

* 50p (ch14 & pen 25p) family ticket £1.25. Party (by prior arrangement).
P 🕀 ঝ *(wc)*

Ormesby

Cleveland Map 8 NZ51

ORMESBY HALL

☎ *Middlesbrough (0642) 324188*

18th-century mansion set in a small attractive garden with many plants and shrubs. There is a spring garden and a holly walk. House also open.

Open Apr–Oct Wed, Thu, Sat & Sun 2–6.

£1 (ch 50p) Party.
P *(NT)*

Ottery St Mary

Devon Map 3 SY19

FERNWOOD

☎ *(040481) 2820*

A woodland garden of 2 acres with a wide selection of flowering shrubs, particularly rhododendrons and azaleas. Many spring bulbs. Plants labelled.

Open Apr–Sep daily.

50p (ch free).
P   wc

Oxborough

Norfolk Map 5 TF70

OXBURGH HALL

☎ *Gooderstone (036621) 258*

The main feature of these gardens is the large parterre laid out in 1845 by the Bedingfeld family who copied the design seen in a Paris garden. Beyond this lies a traditional herbaceous border backed by climbing roses. There are many spring flowers in the 'Wilderness' area. Hall also open.

Open 11 Apr–18 Oct; Apr & Oct wknds only, May–Sep Sat–Wed 1.30–5.30; also BH Mon 11–5.30.

£2 (ch £1) party 15 +.
✱ *(NT)*

Oxford

Oxfordshire Map 4 SP50

Many of the colleges have nice gardens to which the public may sometimes have access.

UNIVERSITY BOTANIC GARDEN

Rose Lane ☎ *(0865) 242737*

The oldest botanic garden in Britain, founded in 1621, in a beautiful setting by the River Cherwell. The wide range of plants, used for teaching and research, includes roses, alpines, ferns, orchids, succulents and tropical water lilies. Plants labelled.

Open all year, weekdays 8.30–5 (9–4.30 Oct–Mar), Sun 10–12 & 2–6 (2–4.30 Oct–Mar). Greenhouses open daily 2–4 (closed Good Fri & Xmas day).

Free.
P *(St Clements Car Park)* ✱ ঝ

Jasminium rex
'Jasmine'

Paignton

Devon　　　　　　　Map 3 SX86

OLDWAY MANSION GARDENS

☎ (0803) 550711

Mansion built in reproduction style of the Palace of Versailles. The gardens are similarly styled with knot garden, grotto and ponds, sweeping lawns dotted with trees and a rock garden featuring some maturing dwarf conifers. House also open.

Open Gardens all year daily; house May–Sep, Mon–Sat 10–1 & 2.15–5.15, Sun 2.30–5.30; winter Mon–Fri 10–1 & 2.15–5.15 (Closed Sat & Sun).

Free.
P ⊟ *(Summer only)* ✹ *(ground floor & gardens)* & wc

Parceval Hall

North Yorkshire　　　Map 7 SE06

PARCEVAL (PERCIVAL) HALL GARDENS

(8m SW of Pateley Bridge)

☎ Burnsall (075672) 214

Twenty acres of gardens, sheltered by mixed woodland, include terrace gardens with fish pools, overlooking lovely Wharfdale countryside. Because of its sheltered position, the garden includes many plants and shrubs, such as rhododendrons, crinodendrons and camellias, which are unusual this far north. There is a spring display of daffodils and heathers in the autumn as well as herbaceous plants, herbs, climbers and a rock garden. An old orchard, where visitors can picnic, has interesting varieties of apples.

Open Etr–Oct daily 10–6.

* *50p (ch 25p).*
P ⟤

Peebles

Borders *Peebleshire*　　Map 11 NT23

KAILZIE

(2½m SE on B7062) ☎ (0721) 22054

Beautifully recreated within the last nineteen years this varied garden contains a double herbaceous border, many shrub borders and an interesting collection of old-fashioned shrub roses. Also of interest is a formal rose garden, laburnum alley and 15 acres of wild garden, with woodland, burnside and laburnum walks set amongst many fine old trees. Plants labelled.

Open 4 Apr–11 Oct daily 11–5.30.

£1 (ch 35p).
P ⊟ ⟤ & wc *Plants for sale*

Penshurst

Kent　　　　　　　Map 5 TQ54

PENSHURST PLACE

(on B2176) ☎ (0892) 870307

This magnificent medieval manor house is set in a 10-acre walled and terraced garden with hedged enclosures and is largely the inspiration of the Tudor owners and their immediate successors. Each enclosure is laid out and planted to form a garden of its own, containing many varieties of roses and with herbaceous borders. Large open parkland with delightful walks. House also open.

Open Apr–4 Oct daily (Closed Mon ex BH Mons) Grounds 12.30–6. House 1–5.30.

Grounds £2 (ch £1, pen £1.60); House & Grounds £2.50 (ch £1.50, pen £2.25) Party
P⊟ ⟤ ✹ & *(gardens only)* wc

Perth

Tayside *Perthshire*　　Map 11 NO12

BRANKLYN GARDEN

(on Dundee Rd, A85) ☎ (0738) 25535

A fine 2-acre garden noted for its outstanding collection of plants, especially rhododendrons, herbaceous and alpines from all over the world. All are arranged in the setting of a small personal garden which can be enjoyed by both specialist gardeners and the ordinary visitor. Plants labelled.

Open Mar–Oct, daily 9.30–sunset.

£1 (ch 50p).
wc *Plants for sale (NTS)*

Petworth

West Sussex　　　　Map 4 SU92

PETWORTH HOUSE

☎ (0798) 42207

One of the finest surviving 'Capability' Brown landscape parks, providing a superb →

setting for the great house. The Pleasure Grounds, a rectangular plantation dissected by straight paths comprise many trees and shrubs including American and Japanese maples, trumpet flowers, rhododendrons, roses, sweet chestnuts, limes and sycamores. The ideal growing conditions have enabled several trees to attain record heights. House also open.

Open Apr–Oct, Tue (ex Tue following BH Mons), Wed, Thu, Sat, Sun & BH Mons 2–6. Deer park open daily 9–sunset.

£2.40 (ch £1.20).
❏ (NT)

Picton

Dyfed   **Map 2 SN01**

PICTON CASTLE GARDENS AND GROUNDS
☎ Rhos (043786) 201

The castle, home of the Philipps family since the 12th century, has extensive grounds with delightful walks through shrub gardens and woodlands. Castle and art gallery also open.

Open Gardens, woodland walks and Gallery Etr–Sep daily (ex Mon but open BH Mon) 10.30–6. (Gallery 10.30–5) Castle open mid July–mid Sep Sun & Thu, also Etr Sun & Mon and Aug BH's.

* Garden £1 (ch & pen 50p), gallery 50p (ch & pen 30p). Castle, admission fee payable.
P ❏ ⇞ ⅋ (ground floor & gardens)

Pitmedden

Grampian *Aberdeenshire* **Map 15 NJ82**

PITMEDDEN GARDEN
☎ Udny (06513) 2352

A reconstruction of the original 17th-century garden with the addition of elaborate floral designs, sundials, pavilions and fountains. There is also a Museum of Farming Life and rare breeds of livestock.

Open Gardens and grounds all year daily 9.30–sunset; Museum May–Sep daily 11–6 (last admission 5.15).

Gardens 80p (ch 40p); Museum & garden £1.50 (ch 75p).
⅋ (NTS)

Plympton

Devon   **Map 2 SX55**

SALTRAM HOUSE
(S of bypass) ☎ *Plymouth (0752) 336546*

An 8-acre garden leading away from the west front of the house, comprising fine tree specimens, a spring garden and rhododendrons. There is also an avenue of limes and plantings of young trees and shrubs. Of particular interest is the 18th-century orangery and an octagonal garden house which house orange and lemon trees and other tender plants. Plants labelled. Advisory service. House also open.

Open Garden daily 11–6 (Nov–Mar during daylight hours). House Apr–Oct Sun–Thu, Good Fri & BH Sats 12.30–6.

Garden £1 House & Gardens £2.60 (ch £1.30) Party.
❏ ⅋ wc (NT) (NGS)

Pocklington

Humberside   **Map 8 SE84**

BURNBY HALL GARDENS & STEWART COLLECTION
☎ (07592) 2068

Gardens with outstanding collection of water lilies in two lakes developed over the last forty years. Today, 5,000 blooms of many species and varieties fill the Burnby Hall water with summer glory, July being the most colourful month. The lakeside and walk by the stream are planted with hundreds of different marginals and bog plants, while rock gardens by the wayside display alpines and rock plants. Museum also open.

Open Etr–Sep 10–7.

60p (ch 10–16 20p, ch 10 free, pen 40p). Party
P ❏ (daily Jun–Sep, Sat & Sun & BH only Etr–May) ⇞ ⅋ (wc) wc Plant sales

Poolewe

Highland   **Map 14 NG88**
Ross and Cromarty

INVEREWE GARDEN
☎ (044586) 200

In 1864 Osgood Mackenzie planted a windbreak of fir trees around the perimeter of Inverewe and thus began to transform this bleak and barren Highland peninsula into magnificent gardens full of shrubs, trees and many rare and sub-tropical plants. There are rhododendrons, large herbaceous borders and bulbs. Magnificent mountain views.

Garden open all year daily 9.30–sunset.

£1.80 (ch 90p) Party.
P *(10p)* & *(NTS)*

Portishead
Avon   Map 3 ST47

BRACKENWOOD NURSERIES
131 Nore Rd ☎ *(0272) 843484*

Over 6 acres of mature woodland with grassy pathways which meander through areas inter-planted with camellias, rhododendrons, azaleas, maples and other rare and spectacular plants and trees. The Garden Centre has one of the widest retail selection of trees, shrubs and lesser known plants in the South West. Pool and pond plant section. Plants labelled. Advisory service.

Open Apr–mid Oct daily 11–4.30.

60p (ch 30p).
P ⊡ ⚶ ✗ &*(Garden Centre only) wc*
Plants for sale

Port Logan
Dumfries & Galloway   Map 10 NX04
Wigtownshire

LOGAN BOTANIC GARDEN
☎ *Stranraer (0776) 86231*

An annexe of the Royal Botanic Garden, Edinburgh containing a wide range of rare and exotic plants from mild, temperate regions. The walled garden has various tree ferns, and palms and rhododendrons grow

alongside unusual shrubs and climbers. The woodland garden has a good collection of trees and shrubs from New Zealand, Australia and Chile. Plants labelled.

Open Apr–Sep daily 10–5.

50p (admits car & all passengers).
P ⊡ ✗ & *(wc) wc*

Powderham
Devon   Map 3 SX98

POWDERHAM CASTLE
(entrance off A379 Exeter/Dawlish road)
☎ *Starcross (0626) 890243*

Home of the Earl of Devon, with its one-acre garden containing a particularly attractive terraced rose garden with small lawns overlooking a deer park. Fine views across the Exe estuary. Plants labelled. House also open.

Open 24 May–10 Sep Sun–Thu 2–5.30.

Sun & Mon ground floor & gardens £1.75 (pen £1.50, ch 8–16 £1, ch 8 free); Tue, Wed & Thu whole house & gardens £2 (pen £1.75, ch 8–16 £1.25, ch 8 free).
P ⊡ ⚶ ✗ &*(gardens & ground floor) wc*
no pushchairs

Probus
Cornwall   Map 2 SW94

COUNTY DEMONSTRATION GARDENS & RURAL STUDIES CENTRE
☎ *Truro (0872) 74282 ext 3400*

Established to illustrate, in the form of permanent demonstrations and planting displays, a comprehensive range of garden →

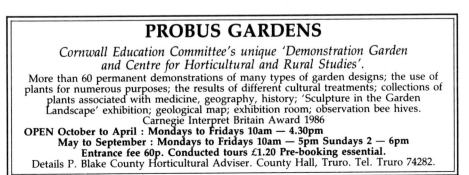

PROBUS GARDENS
Cornwall Education Committee's unique 'Demonstration Garden and Centre for Horticultural and Rural Studies'.
More than 60 permanent demonstrations of many types of garden designs; the use of plants for numerous purposes; the results of different cultural treatments; collections of plants associated with medicine, geography, history; 'Sculpture in the Garden Landscape' exhibition; geological map; exhibition room; observation bee hives.
Carnegie Interpret Britain Award 1986
OPEN October to April : Mondays to Fridays 10am — 4.30pm
May to September : Mondays to Fridays 10am — 5pm Sundays 2 — 6pm
Entrance fee 60p. Conducted tours £1.20 Pre-booking essential.
Details P. Blake County Horticultural Adviser. County Hall, Truro. Tel. Truro 74282.

practices, plant utilisation and the results of modern gardening techniques and research. Exhibits of fruit, herbs and vegetables. Historical plant collection. Plants labelled. Advisory service. Thu 2–5.

Open May–Sep Mon–Fri 10–5, Sun 2–6; Oct–Apr Mon–Fri 10–4.30.

60p (ch free)
P ⊼ ✻ ⅋ wc

TREWITHEN HOUSE & GARDENS
☞ *St Austell (0726) 882585*

These gardens, covering 20 acres, are internationally renowned for their magnificent collection of camellias, rhododendrons, magnolias and many rare trees and shrubs seldom found elsewhere in Britain. Enchanting walled garden and original water gardens. Plants labelled. House also open.

Open Gardens Mar–Sep Mon–Sat & BH 2–4.30, House Apr–Jul Mon & Tue 2–4.30.

* Gardens Mar–Jun £1.20 (pen £1), Jul–Sep £1 (pen 90p); House £2.
P ⅋ (wc) wc Plants for sale

Pulborough
West Sussex   Map 4 TQ01
PARHAM HOUSE AND GARDENS
(3m SE off A283)
☞ *Storrington (09066) 2021*

Tudor gabled and mullioned house with a 4-acre walled garden containing box, coloured gravels and yew sentinels, with mixed herbaceous borders of silver, purple and grey. Also features orchards and a herb garden. 7 acres of grounds with a lake and a temple garden. Plants labelled. House also open.

Open Etr Sun–first Sun in Oct, Wed, Thu, Sun & BH's garden 1–6, house 2–6.

* Gardens £1 (ch 75p) House & Gardens £2.50 (ch £1.50, pen £2). Party.
P ⌷ ⊼ ⅋ (ground floor & gardens) wc Plants for sale

Pusey
Oxfordshire   Map 4 SU39
PUSEY HOUSE GARDENS
☞ *Buckland (036787) 222*

Landscaped in the mid-18th-century and with new garden terraces added in 1935,

Pusey has three main features. Close to the house, fine herbaceous borders are richly stocked with roses, clematis and other plants. Across the lake are a series of luxuriant water gardens and passing through glades there are pleasure gardens and shrubberies. Many, fine trees include cedar, beach, new and vigorous magnolias, sorbus and maples. Plants labelled.

Open 18 Apr–25 Oct Tue–Thu, Sat, Sun & BH Mons 2–6.

£1.30 (ch 11 free) Party.
P ⌷ ⅋ (wc) wc Plants for sale

Quatt
Shropshire   Map 7 SO78
DUDMASTON
☞ *(0746) 780866*

A late 17th-century house, in extensive gardens, with a rock garden and a bog garden at either end of a large lake. There is a long border with American plants. House also open.

Open Apr–Sep Wed & Sun 2.30–6 (last admission 5.30) Parties by appointment only.

Garden 80p; House and garden £2 Party.
⌷ ✻ (in house) ⅋ (NT)

Queensferry (South)
Lothian *West Lothian*   Map 11 NT17
HOPETOUN HOUSE
(2m W on unclass road) ☞ *031–331 2451*

The extensive (100-acre) grounds of the great Adam mansion of Hopetoun House are landscaped and contain fine trees and shrubs. They also offer walks with views over the deer park and the River Forth. The 4 acres of walled ornamental gardens are divided into a number of smaller gardens, and illustrate the use of the wide variety of plants available from the Garden Centre. Plants labelled in walled gardens. Guided tours for parties by prior arrangement. Advisory service available. House also open.

Walled gardens and garden centre open daily. Grounds open May–Sep 11–5.30.

* Walled garden/garden centre free. Grounds 60p (ch 40p). House and grounds £2 (ch £1).
P ⌷ (licensed) ⊼ ⅋ Garden centre

Saintpaulia ionantha

Radcliffe-on-Trent

Nottinghamshire **Map 8 SK63**

HOLME PIERREPONT HALL

(¾m W on unclass road) ☏ (06073) 2371

There are two distinct gardens at the old manor house of Holme Pierrepont Hall. The formal garden was laid out in 1875 and contains an elaborate box parterre, rose beds, and a long old-fashioned berbaceous border. The outer garden of about 1½ acres has lawns, yew hedges and shrub and rose borders. Guided tours by prior arrangement. Open for Gardeners Sunday 19 May. House also open.

Open Etr Sun–Tue, Spring and Summer BH Sun–Tue, Jun–Aug, Sun, Tue, Thu & Fri, 2–6. Pre-booked parties at other times.

Garden 40p; house and gardens £1.50 (ch 75p).
P ☕ 🐕 ♿ *(gardens & ground floor; wc) wc*

Reading

Berkshire **Map 4 SU77**

CAVERSHAM COURT GARDENS

☏ (0734) 477917

These 3½-acre gardens extend to the bank of the River Thames, with lawns and a number of island perennial beds and also a herbaceous border. Interesting trees, allotments, a herb bed and rose garden can also be seen. Plants labelled.

Open daily Apr–Sep 7.30am–8pm, Sep–Mar 7.30am–dusk. Coach parties by prior arrangement only.

Free.
P ♿ *wc*

Rhuddlan

Clwyd **Map 6 SJ07**

BODRHYDDAN HALL

(1½m E on A5151) ☏ (0745) 590414

These 3-acre gardens include a formal parterre on the South Front of the 17th-century manor house, surrounded by lawns, clipped yews, and old oak trees. Two ponds, which will form the focus of a garden walk, are under construction. House also open.

Open Jun–Sep Tue & Thu 2–5.30. Coach parties by appointment only.

£1 (ch 50p).
P ☕ 🐕 ♿ *(gardens only)*

Rhynie

Grampian *Aberdeenshire* **Map 15 NJ42**

LEITH HALL & GARDEN

(3½m NE on B9002)
☏ Kennethmont (04643) 216

The hall is set within extensive grounds with a loch and countryside walks. The two main features of the gardens are the long herbaceous border and a fine rock garden. There are also many roses, shrubs and trees. Hall also open.

Gardens & grounds open all year 9.30–sunset; house May–Sep daily 2–6 (last admission 5.15).

Admission to grounds by donation; house and gardens £1.80 (ch 90p).
(NTS)

Richmond

North Yorkshire **Map 7 NZ10**

ST NICHOLAS

☏ (0748) 2328

The gardens at St Nicholas were laid out in 1910 and contain many rare Tibetan rhododendrons. Although these are now huge plants, they were nearly all grown from seed collected on Himalayan expeditions. Shrub roses and topiary can also be seen in the 6-acre gardens.

Open Mar–Oct daily, all day. Coach parties by prior arrangement only.

** 30p (ch 15p).*
P

Rievaulx

North Yorkshire   Map 8 SE58

RIEVAULX TERRACE

The half-mile long landscaped terrace at Rievaulx provides sweeping views of the 13th-century Rievaulx Abbey, and Ryedale and the Hambleton Hills beyond. The grass terrace, which dates from 1758, has a garden temple at either end. Exhibition of English landscape design in Ionic Temple.

Open daily (ex Good Fri) Apr–Oct 10.30–6. Last admission 5.30.

£1.20 (ch 60p).
P & wc (NT)

Ripley

North Yorkshire ·   Map 8 SE26

RIPLEY CASTLE
☎ *Harrogate (0423) 770152*

The 14 acres of grounds include a walled garden of 6 acres. There is also a large greenhouse, and herbaceous borders. Specimen trees from around the world can be seen. Heathers are a speciality. Guided tours available by prior arrangement. Plants labelled. Castle also open.

Open Apr–Oct daily 11–5.30.

Gardens 85p (ch, pen & reg unemp 60p); Castle & Gardens £2.
P ☐ (licensed) ₮ & wc Plants for sale

Ripon

North Yorkshire   Map 8 SE37

FOUNTAINS ABBEY & STUDLEY ROYAL COUNTRY PARK
(2m SW off B6265) ☎ *Sawley (076586) 333*

The large monastic ruins are set in a landscaped garden laid out by John Aislabie in 1720–40 with lake, formal water gardens and temples. There is also an extensive deer park. Guided tours available (in summer) by prior arrangement.

Deer park open throughout year during daylight hours. Abbey and gardens open daily (ex 24 & 25 Dec). Jan–Mar & Nov & Dec 10–5 or dusk, Apr–Jun & Sep 10–7, Jul & Aug 10–8, Oct 10–6 or dusk.

£1.70 (ch 80p) Party 40+.
P (50 yds) ☐ & (wc) (NT)

NEWBY HALL & GARDENS
☎ *Boroughbridge (09012) 2583*

Late 17th-century house set in 25 acres of gardens with a wide variety of trees and shrubs, and many 'theme' gardens. The grassed walk leading down from the house to the River Ure is backed by double herbaceous borders believed to be the longest in England. Paths, lined with rhododendrons lead to the Circular, Tropical, Orchard and White Gardens. House also open.

Open Apr–25 Oct (house closes 4 Oct) Tue–Sun (closed Mon ex BH Mon.). Gardens 11–5.30; Hall 12–5.

* Gardens £1.50 (ch & disabled £1.10, pen £1.40); House & Gardens £2.30 (ch & disabled £1.20, pen £2.10) Party.
P ☐ (licensed) ₮ ✗ & (ground floor & gardens) wc Plants for sale

NORTON CONYERS
☎ *Melmerby (076584) 333*

The large (2 acre) 18th-century walled garden of this Jacobean manor, with Bronte connections, has an orangery at its centre. There are wide borders, backed by high yew hedges, a gold/silver border, and an '18th-century patch'. A variety of plants for drying and also paeonies are grown. 'Meet the Gardener' visits for small groups by prior arrangement. House also open.

Garden and garden centre open Mon–Fri all year, and Sat & Sun Etr–Oct (2–5). House Etr, May & Spring BH Sun & Mon; 31 May–6 Sep every Sun; 25 Jul–3 Aug daily 2–5.30.

Garden free, House £1.20 (ch 60p, pen 80p).
P & Garden centre and Pick-your-own soft fruit

Rockingham

Northamptonshire   Map 4 SP89

ROCKINGHAM CASTLE
☎ *(0536) 770240*

The formal gardens comprise 3 terraces leading to a rose garden enclosed by a yew hedge on the site of the old keep. As well as extensive rose beds there are herbaceous borders and an Elizabethan garden mound, and the snowdrops, daffodils and autumn colour are particularly fine. The lawns beyond extend to 6 acres and are enclosed with trees, and there is also a ravine garden planted with over 200 species of trees and shrubs dating from the early 19th-century. Plants labelled. Castle also open.

Open Etr Sun–Sep, Sun, Thu, BH Mon and following Tue, 2–6. Also Tue in Aug 2–6. Other times for prebooked groups.

Castle & gardens £2 (ch £1, pen £1.60); Gardens £1 Party.
P 🖫 ⅃ *wc*

Coleus blumei

Rougham Green
Suffolk　　　　　　　　　**Map 5 TL96**

NETHERFIELD HERBS
📞 *Beyton (0359) 70452*

The 60 × 40 ft herb garden is designed to illustrate the atmosphere of tranquility that an enclosed herb garden can create. Over 200 herbs and wildflowers are grown, with the emphasis on aromatic plants. Many unusual herbs are grown, and visitors may find it useful to be able to compare a number of varieties of the more common herbs. Plants labelled. Guided tours/lecture by prior arrangement (charge made).

Open daily (ex Christmas) 10.30–5.30 or dusk. Children must be accompanied and under control. Coach parties by prior arrangement only.

Free.
P 🗶 ⅃ *Plants for sale*

Rothbury
Northumberland　　　　**Map 12 NU00**

CRAGSIDE
(entrance for cars 2m N on B6341)
📞 *(0669) 20333*

The castle at Cragside is, as its name suggests set high up above its rocky gardens. These cover over 900 acres in total and grow numerous rhododendrons and azaleas. Many large North American conifers are also grown, and other features of the gardens include banks of heather, and lakes, streams and waterfalls. House also open.

Country Park open daily Apr–Sep 10.30–6, Oct 10.30–5 and Nov–Mar Sat & Sun 10.30–4. House 1–16 Apr & Oct Wed, Sat & Sun 1–5, 17 Apr–Sep Tue–Sun & BH Mon 1–5. Coach parties by arrangement only.

Country Park only £1, house & country park £2.40 Party 20+.
P 🖫 ⅋ 🗶 *(in house)* ⅃ *(wc) wc (NT)*

Rousham
Oxfordshire　　　　　　**Map 4 SP42**

ROUSHAM HOUSE PARK AND GARDEN
(off A423) 📞 *Steeple Aston (0869) 47110*

This 18th-century garden, landscaped by William Kent, adjoins the River Cherwell, and within its 25 acres has a number of buildings, statues and ponds. Other features include a 1635 walled garden, herbaceous borders, roses, a small parterre, a pigeon house, and a kitchen garden. Herd of long-horn cattle in park. House also open.

Gardens open daily 10–4.30 (house Wed, Sun & BH afternoons in summer only). Coach parties by prior arrangement only. Ch 15 not admitted.

* *House £1.50, Gardens £1. Party.*
P 🗶 *wc*

Rowland's Castle
Hampshire　　　　　　　**Map 4 SU71**

STANSTED PARK
📞 *(0705) 412265*

The arboretum at Stansted Park contains over 120 trees (some labelled), the oldest of which, a cedar of Lebanon, dates back to c1575. There are also extensive lawns, and a 2 mile-long beech avenue, cutting through part of the ancient Forest of Bere. The 2 acres of cultivated gardens include two walled gardens used to cultivate organic vegetables and other plants, an early 19th-century rose garden and greenhouses growing vines, peaches, etc. House also open.

Open 24 May–29 Sep Sun–Tue 2–6. Coach parties by appointment only.

Gardens £1 (ch 12 50p, pen 80p). House & Gardens £1.80 (ch 80p, pen £1.20).
P 🖫 🗶 ⅃ *(gardens & part of ground floor; wc) wc Plants for sale*

Rufford

Lancashire   Map 7 SD41

RUFFORD OLD HALL

☎ (0704) 821254

Outstanding 15th-century building set in period garden which includes some fine species of trees many rare and individual. Also of interest is a waterside walk. Plants labelled. Hall also open.

Open Apr–1 Nov, Sat–Thu Garden 12–5, Hall 1–5.

£1.40 (ch 70p) Party.

⌇ & wc (NT)

Runcorn

Cheshire   Map 7 SJ58

NORTON PRIORY MUSEUM GARDENS

Warrington Road ☎ (09285) 65029

The 7 acres of woodland garden adjoining the medieval monastic remains were laid out in Georgian and Victorian times. Features include a stream glade, a Victorian rock garden and two summerhouses. The replanted late 18th-century walled garden, with herbaceous plants, fruit trees and vegetables has the plants labelled, and should be open to the public after May 1987. Guided tours by prior arrangement.

Open Mar–Oct Mon–Fri (12–5), Sat, Sun & BH Mon (12–6); Nov–Feb daily (ex 24–26 Dec) 12–4.

Woodland garden and museum £1 (ch, pen, students 50p, ch 5 free).

P ⌇ ₮ & (wc) wc

Rydal

Cumbria   Map 11 NY30

RYDAL MOUNT

☎ Ambleside (0966) 33002

The grounds of the house, home of William Wordsworth between 1813 and 1850, were landscaped by the poet. The 4½-acre semi-natural garden has lawns surrounded by trees and shrubs, including some fairly rare trees. There are also terraces, rock pools, a wildlife area, and fine views of Windermere and Rydal Water. Guided tours by prior arrangement only. Some plants labelled. House also open.

Open daily (ex Tue) Mar–Oct 10–5, Nov–Feb 10–4.

£1.50 (ch 16 50p, ch 5 free, pen and students £1).

P ✹ wc

Rye

East Sussex   Map 5 TQ92

LAMB HOUSE AND GARDEN

West Street

A small attractive walled garden forming the grounds to the 18th-century house which was the home of Henry James between 1898 and 1916.

Open Apr–Oct Wed & Sat 2–6. Last admission 5.30

£1 (three rooms of house & garden).

✹ (NT)

Ryton-on-Dunsmore

Warwickshire   Map 4 SP37

RYTON GARDENS

(The National Centre for Organic Gardening) (on B4029 N from A45 towards Wolston) ☎ Coventry (0203) 303517

These recently opened gardens aim to illustrate gardening according to organic principles. As well as demonstrating methods of composting and weed and pest control, the gardens also aim to show disease resistant varieties of roses, soft fruit, etc. Vegetables, including a number of unusual varieties, fruit, shrubs and trees are grown, and experimental 'no dig' plots and raised beds can also be seen.

Open daily (ex 25 & 26 Dec) Apr–Sep 10–6, Oct–Mar 10–4, Coach parties by prior arrangement.

£1.20 (ch 18, pen, students, reg unemp, and reg disabled 75p), Family and party rates.

P ⌇ ₮ ✹ & (wc) wc Plants for sale

Saffron Walden

Essex   Map 5 TL53

BRIDGE END GARDENS

☎ Great Dunmow (0371) 5411

Important 18th-century gardens containing recently restored pavilions, lawns, Dutch

Garden and old-fashioned rose garden. Maze under restoration.

Open all year daily.

Free.

&

St Albans

Hertfordshire   Map 4 TL10

THE GARDENS OF THE ROSE
(2m S off Watford Rd in Chiswell Green Lane) ☎ *(0727) 50461*

The showground and collection of historic roses of The Royal National Rose Society. There are some 30,000 plants in over 1,650 different varieties. Modern roses of all kinds, and a fine planting of old garden roses, all displayed at their best in the attractive land-scaped gardens. New varieties from all over the world are on trial in the Trial Grounds. Plants labelled. Advisory Service. The British Rose Festival 11 & 12 Jul.

Open mid Jun–mid Oct, Mon–Sat 9–5, Sun & BH 10–6.

£1.30 (accompanied ch free, reg disabled 60p) Party 20+.
P ⬚ *(licensed)* & *(wc) wc Plants for sale*

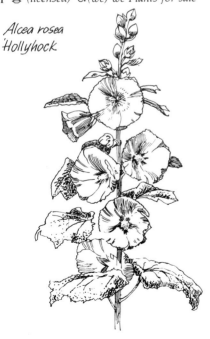

Alcea rosea
Hollyhock

St Andrews

Fife   Map 12 NO51

UNIVERSITY OF ST ANDREWS BOTANIC GARDEN
☎ *(0334) 76161 ext. 8448*

Eighteen acres of impressively landscaped gardens which have won international recog-nition both for design and for the wide range of plants. At the western end there are large plantings of trees and shrubs; to the east are extensive rock and peat gardens and a lake. Plants labelled. Advisory service.

Open all year Apr–Oct daily; Apr & Oct 10–4; May–Sep 10–7; Nov–Mar, Mon–Fri 10–4.

50p (ch 16 25p).
P *(wknds)* ✗ & *wc*

St Boswells

Borders *Roxburghshire*   Map 12 NT53

MERTOUN GARDENS
☎ *(0835) 23236*

Twenty acres of gardens with sweeping lawns, herbaceous borders, shrub roses and azaleas. The arboretum, established over the past 25 years, has many varieties of conifers and hardwoods. Paths and grass walks lead through all parts of the garden and the surrounding woodland. The well-maintained Walled Garden is situated on a south-facing slope and contains a great variety of fruit trees, vegetables and flowers. Plants labelled.

Open Apr–Sep Sat, Sun & BH Mon 2–6 (last admission 5.30).

80p (ch 14 & pen 30p).
P ✗ *wc*

St Margarets at Cliffe

Kent   Map 5 TR34

THE PINES GARDEN
St Margarets Bay (off Beach Rd)
☎ *Dover (0304) 853229*

Beautiful 6½ acre garden comprising of a rockery, waterfall and lake, together with a bog garden and a variety of trees, shrubs, aquatic plants and spring flowers.

Open all year daily summer 10–7, winter 10–5.

* *50p (ch & pen 30p) Party.*
P ⬚ ⛩ & *Plants for sale*

St Nicholas

South Glamorgan   Map 3 ST07

DYFFRYN GARDENS
☎ *Cardiff (0222) 593328*

Approximately 55 acres of formal and informal gardens designed by Thomas Mawson. There are extensive collections of trees, shrubs and herbaceous plants, many of which are uncommon. Part of the garden is divided into a series of 'rooms' each enclosed by clipped yew hedges and individually planted. Some plants labelled. Special events throughout the year. Courses available.

* *Open end Mar–end May & Sep daily 1–6, late May–Aug daily 10–7, Oct wknds only 1–6 (last admission 1hr before closing).*

* *£1 (ch 16 accompanied free, unaccompanied & pen 50p). Party.*
P ⌂ ⊼ ᚹ wc Plants for sale

St Tudy

Cornwall   Map 2 SX07

TREMEER GARDENS
(off A39) ☎ *Bodmin (0208) 850313*

This colourful garden was built by Major-General E G W Harrison between 1947 and 1978 and comprises mainly trees and shrubs. It is a camellia and rhododendron enthusiasts garden and from it have come many of the finest new hybrids in recent years. The walls of the house are clothed with shrubs and climbers with low-growing plants at their feet. There are two small lakes supplied by natural spring water. Plants labelled.

Open Mar–Sep daily 9–6.

Free (Donation for charity).
P

Salcombe

Devon   Map 3 SX73

OVERBECKS MUSEUM & GARDEN
Sharpitor (½m SW on unclass rd)
☎ *(054884) 2893*

A terraced, hillside garden 200ft above the Salcombe estuary with many rare and tender plants which thrive in the mild climate. Plants labelled. Edwardian house with museum also open.

Gardens always open. Museum Apr–Oct daily 11–1 (last admission 12.45) & 2–6 (last admission 5.30).

Gardens £1; Museum & gardens £1.50. Parking charge refundable on purchase of entrance ticket.
P ⊼ wc (NT) (NGS)

Salisbury

Wiltshire   Map 4 SU12

MOMPESSON HOUSE
☎ *(0722) 335659*

Fine 18th-century house in Cathedral Close with peaceful garden with herbaceous borders surrounding a lawn. Enclosed to the north by the imposing wall of the Close.

Open Apr–Oct, Mon–Wed Sat & Sun 12.30–6 or sunset if earlier.

£1.20.
P ✗ ᚹ (NT)

QUEEN ELIZABETH GARDENS
☎ *(0722) 334956*

Mature gardens, famous as the foreground of Constable's view of Salisbury Cathederal.

Open all year daily, dawn to dusk.

Free.
ᚹ

Sandringham

Norfolk   Map 9 TF62

SANDRINGHAM HOUSE & GARDENS
☎ *Kings Lynn (0553) 772675*

Beautiful royal gardens full of interest with enormous lawns, magnificent trees, woodland glades with shrubberies and formal gardens. Colour is provided by camellias, daffodils, rhododendrons, azaleas, lavender and many more. Formal gardens have box hedges which create enclosures some containing small lawns, others hardy plants and roses. Rock garden, lakes and moisture-loving plants. Plants labelled.

Open 19 Apr–24 Sep, Sun–Thu, grounds 10.30 (11.30 Sun)–5, house 11(12 Sun)–4.45. (House closed 20 Jul–8 Aug, grounds 24 July–5 Aug).

Grounds only £1.30 (ch 70p, pen £1); house and grounds £1.80 (ch £1, pen £1.40).
P ⌂ ⊼ ✗ ᚹ (wc)

Saxthorpe
Norfolk   Map 9 TG13
MANNINGTON HALL GARDENS
☎ (026387) 284

The gardens surrounding the moated Hall include the Heritage Rose Gardens where a special collection of hundreds of roses are planted in small gardens reflecting their periods. Also of interest are the walled garden, the chapel garden, woodland walks, the lake and various follies. Mannington Rose Festival 3-5 Jul. Plants labelled. Advisory service.

Open Jun–Aug Wed–Fri 11–6, also Sun 2–5 May–Sep.

£1 (students & pen 75p accompanied ch 16 free).
P ⊡ ⊼ ✗ ⅋ (wc) wc Plants for sale

Scarborough
North Yorkshire   Map 8 TA08
EBBERSTON HALL
☎ ((0723) 85516

Palladian villa with water gardens formed by three small lakes joined by cascades at the rear of the house. House also open.

Open Good Fri–Oct daily 10–6.

House & grounds £1 (ch free).
P ⅋ wc

Scholar Green
Cheshire   Map 7 SJ85
LITTLE MORETON HALL
(on E side of A34)
☎ Congleton (0260) 272018

A small moated garden adjacent to a fine Elizabethan Hall. The area of garden to the north of the house is an Elizabethan-style Knot garden with a yew tunnel alongside. It is in the form of an open knot with the borders containing many varieties of herbs and flowers. Elsewhere most of the garden is planted as a small orchard with herbaceous borders. Plants labelled. Hall also open.

Open Mar–Oct: Mar & Oct, Sat & Sun 1.30–5.30; Apr–Sep daily (ex Tue) 1.30–5.30; BH Mons 11.30–5.30 (closed Good Fri).

£2 wknds & BH, £1.60 weekdays.
P (150 yds) ⊡ ⅋ (gardens & ground floor) wc Herbs for sale (NT)

Scilly, Isles of
Cornwall   No Map
TRESCO ABBEY GARDENS
Tresco ☎ Scillonia (0720) 22849

These famous sub-tropical gardens were started by Augustus Smith in the mid 19th-century and have been maintained by his descendants since then. Monterey Cypress and pine trees are used to provide shelter for the 14-acre gardens where many unusual Mediterranean and southern Hemisphere plants, including palms, acacias, pelargoniums and cinerarias are grown.

Open daily 10–4.

* £2 (ch £1).
⅋ wc

Scolton
Dyfed   Map 2 SM92
SCOLTON MANOR MUSEUM & COUNTRY PARK
(on B4329) ☎ Clarbeston (043782) 328

Georgian country mansion set in 40 acres of grounds, specially rich in fine trees and ornamental shrubs. The landscaped grounds demonstrate a wide range of types with laurel, fir and spruce plantations and mature deciduous woodland. Spring colour is provided by various rhododendrons and azaleas. Plants labelled. Museum also open.

Open Country Park all year, Etr–Oct 10.30–7, winter 10.30–4.30; Museum Jun–Sep Tue–Sun 10.30–6.

50p (ch & pen 25p) Party.
P ⊡ ⊼ ✗ ⅋ wc

Scone
Tayside *Perthshire*   Map 11 NO02
SCONE PALACE
☎ (0738) 52300

Scone Palace is set on grand lawns surrounded by parkland leading down to the River Tay. In spring there is a succession of snowdrops, primroses and bluebells in the woodlands, with daffodils in the Lime Avenue. Colourful displays of azaleas and rhododendrons. David Douglas was born at Scone and his introduction of the first Douglas fir in 1824 led to the planting of the →

magnificent pinetum. Some plants labelled. House also open. Special events during the year.

Open 17 Apr–12 Oct, Mon–Sat 9.30–5, Sun 1.30–5 (Jul & Aug 10–5).

Grounds £1.10 (ch 90p); House & grounds £2.20 (ch £1.80) Family £8 Party 20+. P ☕ (licensed) 🍴 ♿ wc

Scunthorpe

Humberside   **Map 8 SE81**

NORMANBY HALL

Normanby Country Park (5m N on B1430)

Regency mansion set in 350 acres of gardens and parkland, the main attraction being the rhododendron walks. Close to the hall are formal lawns and a sunken garden. The vast parkland is graced by fine examples of mature trees including oak, Scots pine and Lebanon cedar. Advisory service.

Open Country Park all year during daylight hours; Hall Apr–Oct Mon–Fri 10–12.30 & 2–5.30 (5pm Nov–Mar) Sun 2–5.30 (5pm Nov–Mar). Closed Good Fri, Xmas & New Years Day.

Helleborus argutifolius

* Country Park free: Hall 55p (ch & pen 25p).
P ☕ (Apr–Oct) 🍴 ✖ (ex guide dogs house only) ♿ (gardens & ground floor; wc) wc

Selborne

Hampshire   **Map 4 SU73**

GILBERT WHITE MUSEUM GARDENS

The Wakes ☎ (042050) 275

Historic 18th-century garden comprising lawns and ha-ha, old-fashioned rose garden, 19th-century topiary and a wild garden in an old orchard with naturalised flowers and plants including snowdrops, daffodils and wild tulips. In recent years emphasis has been on re-introducing plants and features of the garden that were known to Gilbert White. Plants labelled. Advisory service.

Open Museum & Garden Mar–Oct Tue–Sun 12–5.30.

£1 (ch 50p, pen 70p).
P (200 yds) ✖ ♿ wc Plants for sale

Selsley

Gloucestershire   **Map 3 SO80**

SELSLEY HERB & GOAT FARM

☎ Stroud (04536) 6682

Formal herb gardens and demonstration borders with nursery. Barn shop selling gift products allied to herbs. Plants labelled. Advisory service.

Open Apr–Sep Tue–Sun 2–5.30.

Free.
P ♿ wc Plants for sale

Shallowford

Staffordshire   **Map 7 SJ82**

IZAAK WALTON COTTAGE

☎ Stafford (0785) 760278

Small, period garden with main speciality being in 17th-century herbs. Plants labelled. Cottage also open.

Open all year mid Mar–late Oct, Fri–Tue 12.30–5.30, winter wknds only 12.30–4.30.

20p (ch 10p).
P 🍴 ♿ wc Plants for sale

Sheffield Park

East Sussex Map 5 TQ42

SHEFFIELD PARK GARDENS
(5m E of Haywards Heath off A275)
☎ *Danehill (0825) 790655*

Magnificent gardens and lake-watered park of nearly 150 acres laid out by 'Capability' Brown in the 18th century, and modified early in the 20th century. The gardens and grounds contains many rare trees, shrubs and fine waterlilies including rhododendrons, azaleas, maples and many species of conifers. Plants labelled.

Open Apr–8 Nov Tue–Sat 11–6, Sun & BH 2–6 or sunset (Sun, Oct & Nov 1pm–sunset) Last admission 1hr before closing (Closed Good Fri & Tue after BH).

£2 (ch £1) Apr & Jun–Sep £2.60 (ch £1.30) May, Oct & Nov.
P ♿ ✖ wc (NT)

Shepreth

Cambridgeshire Map 5 TL34

THE CROSSING HOUSE
78 Meldreth Road ☎ Royston (0763) 61071

Small cottage garden with many old-fashioned and some rare plants grown in mixed beds including shrubs, bulbs and alpines. The design is full of original touches, incorporating a tiny lawn, pools with a cascade, banks for alpines and two hexagonal greenhouses. Plants labelled.

Open all year daily during daylight hours.

Free (Donation box).
P ♿

Shepton Mallet

Somerset Map 3 ST64

OAKHILL MANOR
(Entrance by 'Mendip Inn' on A37)
☎ *(0749) 840210*

The grounds of this country estate extend to 45 acres situated high in the Mendip Hills. Fine country house set in 8 acres of delightful gardens.

* *Open late Mar–early Nov daily 11–5.*

Admission fee payable.
P ♿ ⛱ ♿

Sherborne

Dorset Map 3 ST61

SHERBORNE CASTLE ESTATE
☎ *(0935) 813182*

Sixteenth-century house, with 20 acres of landscaped lakeside grounds planned by 'Capability' Brown. The gardens, with lawns, wooded valleys and open views contain many native trees. House also open.

* *Open House & grounds Etr Sat–last Sun in Sep; grounds Thu 1.30–6, Sat, Sun & BH Mons 12–6; house Thu, Sat, Sun & BH Mon 2–6.*

* *Grounds only 80p (ch 40p) House & grounds £2.20 (ch £1.20, pen £1.70).*
P ♿ ✖ (ex guide dogs) wc

Sheringham

Norfolk Map 9 TG14

SHERINGHAM HALL
(¼m W of town off A149) ☎ (0263) 823074

Extensive park landscaped in 1812 by Humphrey Repton. It has a mile-long drive through spectacular rhododendron woods, planted in the 19th century.

* *Open Park & rhododendron woods open May–Jun Mon–Sat 10–6; Sun 2–6 (mid May–mid June).*

* *£1 (ch 50p).*
P 🚌 ♿

Phlox paniculata

Shipton

Shropshire Map 7 SO59

SHIPTON HALL
(6½ SW of Much Wenlock on B4378)
☎ *Brockton (074636) 225*

Elizabethan manor in picturesque setting with attractive stone-walled garden and medieval dovecote.
Open May–Sep, Thu 2.30–5.30; Sun 2.30–5.30 Jul & Aug, also BH wknds 19 & 20 Apr; 3 & 4, 24 & 25 May; 30 & 31 Aug.
£1.20 (ch 14 60p) Party.
P ⏚

Rhododendron

Shrewsbury

Shropshire Map 7 SJ41

QUARRY PARK
☎ *(0743) 61411*

The Quarry Park (26 acres) is located in a beautiful setting in Shrewsbury town centre, adjoining the River Severn. The centrepiece of the park is the Dingle Garden, which has a wide range of trees, shrubs and rock-garden plants, together with an outstanding example of Victorian-type annual bedding. Guided tours available by prior arrangement. 14–15 Aug Shrewsbury Flower Show.
Open daily throughout year during daylight hours.
Free.
P ⏛ ⅋ *(wc) wc*

Shugborough

Staffordshire Map 7 SJ92

SHUGBOROUGH HALL & COUNTY MUSEUM
(5m E of Stafford off A513)
☎ *Little Haywood (0889) 881388*

Notable landscape includes Chinese garden house, classic temple, riverside gardens, beautiful trees and shrubs. Near the house are terraced lawns, a rose garden and beside the river a wild garden. House, museum & farm also open.
Open 14 Mar–25 Oct, Tue–Fri & BH Mon 10.30–5.30, Sat & Sun 2–5.30. Winter Grounds, Museum & Farm Tue–Fri 10.30–4.30 & Sun 2–4.30 (House open to pre-booked parties only).
Grounds £1 per car (summer only), House £1 (ch 50p), Museum £1 (ch 50p), Farm £1 (ch 50p).
P ⏚ ⅋ *(NT)*

Silsoe

Bedfordshire Map 4 TL03
☎ *Silsoe (0525) 60152*

WREST PARK GARDENS

Fine gardens much of which were laid out early in the 18th-century in the French style with a long canal pond sited between groups of trees. An Italian style garden was made in the 19th-century with formal terraces, parterres, statues and clipped evergreens. Gardens, still being historically restored; orangery. Part of house also open.

Open Good Fri–Sep, Sat, Sun & BH's Gardens 9.30–6.30; House 10–6.

75p.
P ⏚ *wc (AM)*

Sissinghurst

Kent Map 5 TQ73

SISSINGHURST CASTLE GARDEN
(1½m NE of town)
☎ *Cranbrook (0580) 712850*

Beautiful gardens, created by the late Vita Sackville-West. Series of garden rooms each one furnished differently with rich collections of plants and linked by vistas, walks and hedged paths. Themes throughout the seasons, a red border, white garden, spring walk and an old orchard massed with bulbs. Famous for roses in Jun & Jul. Plants labelled.

Open Apr–14 Oct Tue–Fri 1–6.30; Sat, Sun & Good Fri 10–6.30.

£2.60 (ch £1.30) Tue–Sat; £3.20 (ch £1.60) Sun.
P ⏚ ✻ *wc Plants for sale (NT)*

Sizergh

Cumbria   Map 7 SD48
SIZERGH CASTLE
☎ Sedgwick (0448) 60070

Fifteenth-century building with a series of gardens with a collection of trees, shrubs, herbaceous and alpine plants including magnolias and shrub roses. Fine ¼ acre limestone rock garden comprising Japanese maples, dwarf conifers, hardy ferns and many perennials. Also water garden with bog and aquatic plants, rose garden and a Dutch garden. Plants labelled.

Open Apr–29th Oct Sun, Mon, Wed & Thu, Garden 12.30–5.45; House 2–5.45.
Garden 75p (ch 40p), House & Garden £1.50 (ch 75p) Party 15+.
wc Plants for sale (NT)

Skelton

Cumbria   Map 12 NY43
HUTTON-IN-THE-FOREST
☎ (08534) 500

The spacious grounds covering 10 acres include a walled garden, a topiary terrace, a woodland garden, ponds, and park and forest walks. Many fine specimen trees. Guided walks by prior arrangement. House also open.

Grounds open daily (ex 25 Dec) dawn to dusk. House Etr Sun & Mon, 3 & 4 May, 21 May–13 Sep Thu, Fri & Sun, 1–4, and for parties at other times.
Grounds £1 (ch 50p), in 'Honesty Box', house £2 (accompanied ch free, pen £1.50).
P ⏚ wc

Sledmere

Humberside   Map 8 SE96
SLEDMERE HOUSE GARDENS
☎ Driffield (0377) 86208

The formal garden is set within a 'Capability' Brown landscaped parkland. It includes a walled 18th-century rose garden, a 'rambling garden', herbaceous borders, and the 'Vicars Walk' (a secret walk between the vicarage and church through the gardens). House also open.

Open 17–20 Apr & Suns to 3 May, then daily (ex Mon & Fri) to Sep, and Suns in Oct, 1.30–5.30. Also BH Mons.

* Gardens only 70p (ch 40p). House and gardens £1.50 (ch 80p, pen £1.30) Party 20+.
P ⏚ (licensed) & wc Plants for sale

Small Hythe

Kent   Map 5 TQ82
TENTERDEN VINEYARDS & HERB GARDEN
☎ Tenterden (05806) 3033

A formal herb garden, containing over 400 different herb and cottage garden plants. All the plants in the ⅓-acre garden are labelled, and there are seats and a summerhouse where visitors may sit and enjoy the gardens. Guided tours of herb garden, vineyard and winery for parties 15+ by appointment May–Oct (charge made).

Open daily 2 May–1 Nov 10–6 (10–5 in Oct); shop open Etr–Christmas.
Vineyards, Winery and herb garden £1 (ch 16 free, pen 75).
P ⏚ 🍴 & wc Plants for sale

Somerleyton

Suffolk   Map 5 TM49
SOMERLEYTON HALL
(off B1074) ☎ Lowestoft (0502) 730224

Twelve acres of gardens surrounding splendid Hall, comprising sweeping lawns, yew and box hedges, azaleas, rhododendrons and some fine trees including eucalyptus, cedars, pines and an avenue of 25-year-old lime trees. A notable feature is the maze planted in 1846 and an interesting statuary. Plants labelled.

Open Etr Sun–27 Sep; gardens only daily (ex Sat) 2–5.30; Hall & gardens Thu, Sun & BH's also Tue & Wed in Jul & Aug 2–5.30.
* Garden only (when hall is not open) £1.20, (ch 70p) hall & gardens £1.90 (ch £1, pen £1.40) Party.
P ⏚ 🍴 ✗ & wc

Southampton

Hampshire   Map 4 SU41
TUDOR HOUSE MUSEUM
Bugle St, St Michael's Sq ☎ (0703) 332513

Half-timbered, 16th-century house, now a museum, with gardens formally laid out →

in Elizabethan style, featuring Tudor knot garden.

Open Tue–Fri 10–5, Sat 10–4, Sun 2–5 (Closed 25–27 & 31 Dec & BH Mon).

Free.
P (150yds) ✸

South Harting
West Sussex   Map 4 SU71
UPPARK
(1m S on B2146) ☎ *(073085) 317 or 458*

Five acres of gardens designed by Humphrey Repton in 1810 consist mainly of lawns, with flowering shrubs and many mature trees. House also open.

Open Apr–Sep, Wed, Thu, Sun & BH Mons 2–6.

House & gardens, Sun & BH Mons £2.20 (ch £1.10), Wed & Thu £1.80 (ch 90p) Party.
P (150 yards) ⚑ ✸ & (NT)

South Molton
Devon   Map 3 SS72
CASTLE HILL
(3½m W on A361) ☎ *Filleigh (05986) 227*

Palladian mansion with fine ornamental garden, shrub, woodland garden and arboretum.

Open Apr–Oct by appointment for conducted tours by owners for parties of 20 or more.

Garden only 50p (seen at any time by telephoning ☎ *(05986) 336). House & garden £2.*
P ✸

South Walsham
Norfolk   Map 9 TG31
FAIRHAVEN GARDEN TRUST
☎ *(060 549) 449*

These large gardens (170 acres including Bird Sanctuary and Inner Broad) include a number of rare shrubs and plants as well as many azaleas and rhododendrons. There is a beech walk which features spring bulbs and primroses and another attraction is the mass displays of candelabra primulas. Within the gardens is the King Oak reputed to be over 900 years old. The parts of the garden are linked by a series of bridges over dykes populated with beds of water-loving plants.

Open 12 Apr–10 May & 13–27 Sep Sun & BH, 13 May–6 Sep Wed–Sun & BH 2–6. Also 'Autumn Colour Day' in late Oct/early Nov (please phone to check date).

80p (accompanied ch & pen 50p) Season tickets available.
P ⚑ & wc

Spalding
Lincolnshire   Map 8 TF22
SPRINGFIELDS GARDENS
(on eastern outskirts of town (A151)
☎ *(0775) 4843*

These 25-acre gardens are famous for their springtime bulb displays, when over a million blooms of tulips, daffodils, hyacinths, pansies, etc. can be seen. In summer there are magnificent displays of around 250,000 bedding plants and 10,000 roses. As well as these massive displays, the gardens also have lawns, slabbed paths, trees, a lake, woodland walks, greenhouses and a maze. Plants labelled. 7 & 8 Feb Springfields Forced Flower Show, 9 May Spalding Flower Parade, 9 & 10 May Springfields Country Fair, 12 July & 16 Aug Gardeners' Day Out.

Open daily 10–6, 27 Mar–Sep.

£1.50 (ch free), special events £2.
P ⚑ ✸ & (wc) wc Garden centre

Speke
Merseyside   Map 7 SJ48
SPEKE HALL
☎ *051-427 7231*

Tudor house with grounds laid out in mid-19th century. Herbaceous borders in moat garden. Rose garden, surrounding shrubberies and woodland with raised walk overlooking the Mersey. House also open.

Open Apr–Oct daily (ex Mon but open BH Mons) Tue–Sat 1–5.30, Sun & BH Mon 12–6. Nov–20 Dec Sat & Sun 1–5. Closed Good Fri.

£1.50 (ch 75p).
P ⚑ (Etr & summer afternoons) ✸ (NT)

Spetchley
Hereford & Worcester **Map 3 SO85**

SPETCHLEY PARK GARDENS
☎ (090565) 213 & 224

A 30-acre garden with a large collection of rare and unusual trees, shrubs and plants. It is basically a Victorian garden of formal design coupled with informal planting. Spring bulbs are a feature as are the large herbaceous borders around the kitchen garden. There is also a fine landscape park and lake with a deer herd. Plants labelled.

Open Apr–Sep, Mon–Fri 11-5, Sun 2-5; BH Mons 11-5.

* £1.20 (ch 60p).
P ⚑ (Sun & BH Mons only) ✖ ♿ wc
Plants for sale

Staindrop
Co Durham **Map 12 NZ12**

RABY CASTLE
☎ (0833) 60202

As well as parkland, Raby has a large walled garden first planned in the mid-18th-century, and recently replanted. Ancient yew hedges, and established herbaceous and shrub borders blend with the informal garden, containing ericas and shrubs. There is also a formal rose garden, and raised beds beside the pergola. The White Ishia Fig, brought to Raby in 1781, still grows and fruits in the fig house. Guided tours by advance arrangement with the Curator. Plants labelled. Castle also open.

Open Etr, May, Spring & August BH weeks Sat–Wed, Wed & Sun in May & Jun, daily (ex Sat) Jul–Sep. Park & gardens 11-5.30, castle 1-5 (last admission 4.30).

Gardens, park & carriage collection only 75p (ch & pen 50p), with castle £1.80 (ch & pen £1).
P ⚑ ⅌ ✖ (ex park) ♿ (wc) wc

Stapeley
Cheshire **Map 7 SJ65**

STAPELEY WATER GARDENS
☎ Nantwich (0270) 623868

This is Europe's largest water garden centre and extends to over 45 acres. Many of the plants, pools and other equipment on sale can be seen in landscaped garden settings. Over 60 varieties of water lillies are grown, together with hundreds of other water and poolside plants. Also at Stapeley are the 2-acre Palm Gardens, housed within fully enclosed glass pavilions where visitors can experience an exciting world of palms, hardy and subtropical aquatic plants, streams and fountains. Guided tours by prior arrangement. Plants labelled. Advisory service available

Open daily (ex 25 Dec): Water Gardens open Etr–Aug Mon–Fri 9-6, Sat & Sun 10-7; Sep–Etr Mon–Fri 9-5, Sat & Sun 10-5. BH hours as Sat & Sun. Palm Gardens Etr–Aug Mon–Fri 10-6, Sat & Sun 10-7; Sep–Etr 10-5.

Water gardens free. Charge made for Palm Gardens.
P ⚑ ✖ ♿ (wc) wc Garden Centre

Staplehurst
Kent **Map 5 TQ74**

IDEN CROFT HERBS
Frittenden Road ☎ (0580) 891432

Herb farm specialising in fragrant, culinary, decorative and medicinal herbs. Traditional and modern gardens illustrating a fresh approach to planting for colour and design. Aromatic garden for visually handicapped. Plants for sale. Advisory service. Special events.

Open all year Mon–Sat 9-5, Sun 11-4.

Free (donations).
♿ wc Plants for sale

Alstroemeria aurantiaca

Stevenage

Hertfordshire   Map 4 TL22

BENINGTON LORDSHIP GARDENS
☎ *Benington (043885) 668*

An Edwardian terraced garden of 7 acres overlooking lakes and parkland. Spectacular double herbaceous borders, sweeping lawns, spring rock-and-water garden, rose garden and greenhouse display. The site includes a ruined Norman castle and a Victorian folly. Some plants labelled. Slide show of 'The garden at other seasons' available for prebooked parties. Snowdrop Sundays last weekend of Feb and first of Mar (please confirm).

Open for Snowdrop Sundays, Etr Mon & Summer BH, Sun May–2 Aug, 2–5; Wed May–end of summer time 11–5. Parties by prior appointment at other times.

£1 Wed, Sun & BH, £1.20 at other times.
P ⊡ *(Sun & BH & for parties)* ✗ *wc Plants for sale*

Stobo

Borders *Peeblesshire*   Map 11 NT13

DAWYCK BOTANIC GARDEN
(on B712, 8m SW of Peebles) ☎ *(07216) 254*

Impressive arboretum, noted for its collection of trees, shrubs and bulbs. A larch is believed to have been planted in 1725 and of particular interest are the Dawyck beeches. Specie and hybrid rhododendrons flourish in the sheltered 'glen'. An annexe of the Royal Botanic Garden, Edinburgh.

Open Apr–Sep daily 9–5.

50p per car.
P ✗

Stockbridge

Hampshire   Map 4 SU33

HOUGHTON LODGE
☎ *Andover (0264) 810502*

Eighteenth-century 'cottage orné' with lawns leading down to the River Test, and fine views over the valley. Unusual walls surround the kitchen garden. Extensive glasshouses with fine displays of flowers.

* *Open Mar–Aug, Wed & Thu 2–5; also Etr Sun & Mon.*

£1 (ch 50p).
✗ & *Plants for sale*

Stoke-on-Trent

Staffordshire   Map 7 SJ84

TRENTHAM GARDENS
(2m SW on A34) ☎ *(0782) 657341*

Beautiful gardens with extensive wooded parkland, with a large lake, landscaped by 'Capability' Brown. There are rose and rock gardens, an elaborate Italian garden, statues and fountains. Special events throughout the season.

* *Gardens open daily Etr–mid Sep 9–dusk.*
Admission fee payable.
P ⊡ *(licensed)* &

Stone

Hereford & Worcester   Map 7 SO87

STONE HOUSE COTTAGE GARDENS
☎ *Kidderminster (0562) 69902*

This sheltered ¾-acre walled garden is full of rare wall shrubs, climbers and interesting herbaceous plants, with over 2000 different plants being grown. A network of formal hedges and paths lead to hidden and secret gardens. Three towers, built into the walls, give superb views over the gardens and surrounding countryside. Guided tours for gardening societies etc. by prior arrangement. Plants labelled. 18 July 16th-century music event.

Open Mar–Nov Wed–Sat 10–6, also Sun in May & Jun plus 12 Jul & 30 Aug. Coaches by prior appointment only.
Admission by donation (50p–£1) in charity collection box.
P ✗ & *Plants for sale (NGS)*

Stonor

Oxfordshire   Map 4 SU78

STONOR HOUSE & PARK
(4m NW of Henley-on-Thames on B480)
☎ *Turville Heath (049163) 587*

House dating from 12th century, with beautiful gardens commanding wide views over the park. Terraced rose garden, scenic walk, spring bulbs. House also open.

Open Apr, Sun 2–5.30; May–Sep, Wed, Thu & Sun (Sat in Aug) 2–5.30, also BH Mons 11–5.30.
* *£1.80 (ch 14 free, 14–18 & pen £1.50).*
Party.
P ⊡ ⍥

Campanula medium
'Canterbury Bell'

Stourton
Wiltshire **Map 3 ST73**

STOURHEAD HOUSE & PLEASURE GARDENS
(off B3092)
☎ Bourton (Dorset) (0747) 840348

Celebrated landscape garden laid out 1741–85 with lakes and temples in a woodland setting. Many trees and shrubs including rhododendrons, magnolias, acers and pines.

Open garden open daily all year 8–7 or dusk. House Apr & Oct Sat–Wed; May–Sep Sat–Thu 2–6.

Garden £1.50 (ch 80p) 15 May–Jun £2, (ch £1); House £2 (ch £1).
P ⊞ ✶ ⅀ *(wc) wc (NT)*

STOURTON HOUSE GARDEN
(just before NT garden at Stourhead — look out for blue signs on approach to Stourhead)
☎ Bourton (Dorset) (0747) 840417

This 4-acre plant-lovers' garden sometimes gets overlooked by visitors to its famous neighbour, but is well worth visiting in its own right. It is colourful all the year round, and grass paths lead past trees, shrubs, herbaceous borders and a semi-wild garden. Of particular interest are the unusual daffodils, over 60 varieties of hydrangeas, and dried flower plants. The owners or gardeners are usually present and willing to answer any questions and show visitors plants. 4 May

Daffodil Day, 28 Jun Delphinium Day & Singers Sunday.

Open Apr–Nov Wed, Thu, Sun & BH Mon, 11–6 or dusk. Also Sat 9 May & 6 Jun (NGS). Parties at other times by prior appointment.

£1 (ch 25p). Reduced prices very early and late in season.
P *(same car park as Stourhead)* ✶ ⅀ wc
Plants for sale

Stowe
Buckinghamshire **Map 4 SP63**

STOWE HOUSE LANDSCAPE GARDEN
☎ Buckingham (0280) 813650

The grounds of the 18th-century mansion (now a school) were landscaped by 'Capability' Brown. There are many fine trees and lakes within the 750 acres, as well as 32 garden temples and follies. Guided tours available by prior arrangement.

Open daily 1–21 Apr and 20 July–6 Sept, 11–5. Other times by prior appointment.

House and grounds 75p (ch & pen 60p) Party.
P ⊞ wc

Stratford-upon-Avon
Warwickshire **Map 4 SP15**

NEW PLACE & NASH'S HOUSE
Chapel St ☎ (0789) 204016

The Knot Garden, which occupies part of the site of New Place, is a replica of an enclosed Elizabethan garden, and is modelled on designs shown in contemporary gardening books. A gateway leads from the Knot Garden to a terrace overlooking the Great Garden with its box and yew hedges. An ancient mulberry tree, descended from the one planted by Shakespeare, can be seen on the lawn.

Open Apr–Oct weekdays 9–6 (5 in Oct) & Sun 10–6 (5 in Oct); Nov–Mar weekdays 9–4.30 (last admission 20 mins before closing). Closed 24–26 Dec, 1 Jan am & Good Friday am

* 80p (ch 30p), but entry to Great Garden free. Combined ticket to all 5 Shakespearian properties £3.80 (ch £1.50). Party.
P *(in street)* ✶ ⅀ wc

Lavatera trimestris

Sudbury

Derbyshire **Map 7 SK13**

SUDBURY HALL GARDENS

☏ (028378) 305

The landscaped gardens consist of three terraces running down to the lake edge. There are two small borders of roses and shrubs, and also clipped yews. A particularly unusual feature of 'classic' design is the Quincunx — a plantation of lime trees creating an arbour. House and museum also open.

Open Apr–Oct Wed–Sun & BH Mon, hall and museum 1–5.30, grounds open till 7.

Grounds free, Hall £2 (ch £1), Museum 60p (ch 30p).
P ☕ 🧺 ♿ *(museum & grounds; wc in museum by request) wc (NT)*

Sutton-at-Hone

Kent **Map 5 TQ57**

ST JOHN'S JERUSALEM GARDEN

A 6½-acre garden encircled by the River Darenth, with borders bright in spring and summer with bulbs, herbaceous plants, dahlias and buddleias.

Open Garden & former chapel Apr–Oct. Wed 2–6.

40p.
🐕 ♿ *wc (NT)*

Sutton-on-the-Forest

North Yorkshire **Map 8 SE56**

SUTTON PARK

(on B1363) ☏ Easingwold (0347) 810249

To the south of this early Georgian house are about 4 acres of terraced gardens descending to a water lily canal. A variety of interesting and rare plants are grown, including roses, clematis, scented plants and willow-leaf pear trees. Beyond the terraces is landscaped parkland. Other attractions are a semi-wild glade and the Temple Walk which is especially good in spring. Most plants labelled. Guided tours by prior arrangement. Flower Festival 28–31 Aug. House also open.

Gardens open daily from Etr to Oct (11–5) House open Etr & BH Mons, Sun & Tue 3 May–4 Oct (1.30–5.30). Parties at other times by prior arrangement.

Gardens only 80p (ch 35p, pen 75p). House and gardens £1.80 (ch 70p, pen £1.50), Party 20+.
P ☕ 🐕 ♿ *(gardens only) wc*

Swainshill

Hereford & Worcester **Map 3 SO44**

THE WEIR

The garden, with fine views over the River Wye, is laid out on a steep bank with winding paths between trees and shrubs. Also of interest are the rock and water gardens and a riverside walk that is at its best in spring.

Open Mar–Oct, Wed–Sun & BH Mons 2–6 (closed Good Fri).

** 50p.*
🐕 *(NT)*

Swallowfield

Berkshire **Map 4 SU76**

SWALLOWFIELD PARK

☏ 01-836 1624 (Country Houses Association)

17th-century house with walled garden of about 4 acres containing a variety of flowering shrubs, roses and many interesting trees. House also open.

Open May–Sep Wed & Thu 2–5.

£1 (ch 50p).
P 🐕 ♿ *(gardens & ground floor)*

Swinford

Leicestershire   Map 4 SP57

STANFORD HALL

☎ *Rugby (0788) 860250*

The Hall is surrounded by lawns and trees, all set in a Park. There is a walled Rose Garden containing about 1,000 roses. House also open.

Open Etr-Sep, Thu, Sat & Sun, 2.30-6; BH Mon & following Tue grounds 12-6.

Grounds 95p (ch 45p). House & Grounds £1.80 (ch 85p). Party.
P ♿ & *wc*

Symonds Yat (West)

Hereford & Worcester   Map 3 SO51

JUBILEE MAZE & MUSEUM OF MAZES

☎ *(0600) 890360*

This award-winning garden is the creation of brothers Lindsay and Edward Heyes, who designed and built the maze themselves. The maze is in the style of the 'Labyrinths of Love' which were popular between 1560 and 1650 and the best romantic effect is obtained on August evenings when the maze is illuminated. Lindsay Heyes is the author of our special colour feature on page 14. The entrance garden was designed by Julian Dowle. Maze museum.

Open Good Fri-end Oct daily 11-5.30, Maze illuminated Jul-Aug each evening (ex Sun) 8-10.30.

* 80p, Jul-Aug evenings £1.20 (ch 80p).
P ♿ ✗ & *wc*

Tal-y-Cafn

Gwynedd   Map 6 SH77

BODNANT GARDEN

(8m S of Llandudno & Colwyn Bay on A470. Entrance ½m along Eglwysbach Road)
☎ *Tyngroes (049267) 460*

Situated above the River Conwy, this beautiful 80-acre garden falls into three main sections; the Italianate terraces in front of the house, the shrub borders above the River Hiraethlyn and the Dell full of great conifers, rhododendrons and primulas. The summer display is concentrated on the terraces, roses, water-lilies and clematis. Plants labelled.

Open 14 Mar-Oct daily 10-5.

£1.70 (ch 85p).
P ♿ ✗ *(ex guide dogs)* & *wc Plants for sale (NT)*

Taunton

Somerset   Map 3 ST22

HESTERCOMBE GARDENS

(3m N of Taunton off A361 near Cheddon Fitzpaine) ☎ *(0823) 87222*

Designed by Edwin Lutyens and Gertrude Jekyll in 1905, it consists of a large sunken plat surrounded by terraces and raised walks with a stone-pillared pergola across its southern boundary. To the east is an orangery which leads to a formal rose garden in the Dutch style. Many fine flower borders. Plants labelled.

Open all year Tue-Thu 12-5 and some Suns in Jun-Aug.

Sun £1 (ch & pen 50p) Tue-Thu donations.
P ♿ *(Sun)*

POUNDISFORD PARK

(Poundisford, 3½m S, signposted off B3170 north of Corfe) ☎ *Blagdon Hill (082342) 244*

The period gardens and deer park at Poundisford provide a beautiful setting for the fine Tudor house. Many interesting and unusual plants are grown and other attractions include the 17th-century brick gazebo and the views of the Quantock and Blackdown Hills. House also open.

Open 4 May-17 Sep Wed & Thu (also Fri Jul & Aug), May, Spring & Aug BH, 11-5. Parties by appointment at other times. Coach parties must be booked.

* Garden only 25p. House and gardens £1.75 (ch 10-16 disabled 80p. accompanied ch 10 free). Prebooked party 15+.
P ♿ ✗ & *(gardens & ground floor only) (wc)*

Temple Sowerby

Cumbria   Map 12 NY62

ACORN BANK GARDEN

This 2½ acre walled garden comprises two orchards with medlar, cherries, mulberry →

and apples. Surrounding these are mixed borders with shrubs, herbaceous plants and climbing roses. Also of interest is the herb garden with a large collection of culinary and medicinal plants. Plants labelled.

Open: Apr–Oct daily 10–5.30.

80p (ch 40p).
⌂ ✖ *(ex guide dogs)* ᴦ *Plants for sale (NT)*

Thoresby

Nottinghamshire   **Map 8 SK67**
THORESBY HALL
☎ *Mansfield (0623) 822301*

The formal terrace gardens at Thoresby include a parterre of Victorian bedding, fountains, pools, gazebos, and a semi-circular sunken lawn. The deer park with its mature trees, avenues and lake, and underplantings of azaleas, rhododendrons and cedars is based on designs by Humphry Repton. House also open.

Open Etr Sun & Mon, then May–Aug, BH & Sun 1–5. Parties by arrangement.

* Garden 50p (ch 20p); house & garden £1.70 (ch 80p).
P ⌂ ⅌ ✖ *wc*

Eryngium
'Sea Holly'

Thornham Magna

Suffolk   **Map 5 TM17**
THORNHAM MAGNA HERB GARDEN
☎ *Mellis (037983) 779*

An 18th-century walled garden, with herb knot garden under reconstruction. Nursery, with comprehensive range of herbs. Plants labelled.

Open daily 9–dusk.

Free.
P ⌂ ⅌ ᴦ *wc Plants for sale*

Tintinhull

Somerset   **Map 3 ST51**
TINTINHULL HOUSE GARDEN
☎ *Martock (0935) 822509*

These 5-acre formal gardens surrounding the 17th-century house were laid out earlier this century. The gardens are divided into a number of smaller gardens, including the walled 'Eagle Court', a fountain garden, a pool garden, an azalea garden. Many unusual plants. House also open.

Open Apr–Sep, Wed, Thu, Sat & BH Mons 2–6 (last admission 5.30). Coaches by prior appointment only.

£1.50.
P ✖ ᴦ *wc (NT)*

Tiverton

Devon   **Map 3 SS91**
KNIGHTSHAYES GARDENS
(2m NE of Tiverton) ☎ *(0884) 254665*

This south-facing garden combines extensive woodland gardens with parkland, sweeping lawns, unique topiary, pools and a fountain. A garden for all seasons with a fine collection of flowering trees, shrubs and bulbs. Attractive displays of rhododendrons and camellias. Plants labelled. House also open.

Open Apr–Oct daily. Garden 11–6; House 1.30–6.

Garden £1.80 (ch 75p); House & garden £2.50 (ch £1.25) Party 15+.
P ⌂ *(licensed)* ✖ ᴦ *wc Plants for sale (NT) (NGS)*

Tolland

Somerset **Map 3 ST13**

GAULDEN MANOR

(1m E of Tolland Church)
☏ Lydeard St Lawrence (09847) 213

A 3-acre garden comprising a secret garden with all white shrubs including roses and lilac, a bog garden with many varieties of moisture loving plants. Also of interest is the fine herb garden. Plants labelled. House also open.

Open Etr Sun & Mon, then 3 May–Jun Sun & Thu, Jul–13 Sep Sun, Wed & Thu also BH 2–5.30.
Garden 75p, House & Garden £1.60 (ch 13 75p).
P ☕ 🐕 *wc Plants for sale*

Torpoint

Cornwall **Map 2 SX45**

ANTONY WOODLAND GARDEN

(2m NW off A38)

A woodland garden bordering the Lynher Estuary containing fine shrubs, magnolias, camellias and rhododendrons set in a Humphrey Repton landscape. Plants labelled.

Open Apr, May, Sep & Oct Tue–Thu, Sun & BH Mon 2–5.30.
£1 (ch 50p).
P 🐕

MOUNT EDGCUMBE COUNTRY PARK

☏ Plymouth (0752) 822236

A Grade I garden on the Rame Peninsula overlooking Plymouth Sound. There are 7 acres of English, French and Italian gardens, and woodland walks.

Open all year 8–dusk.
Free.
P ☕ *(Etr–Sep)* 🛆 ♿ *(wc) wc*

Torquay

Devon **Map 3 SX96**

TORRE ABBEY GARDENS AND PARK

☏ (0803) 23593

An enclosed walled garden with roses, a rockery, maturing shrubs and trial beds of annuals and perennials. Also a large palm house and towards the sea road are ponds and formal gardens containing annuals. House also open.

Open Apr–Oct daily 10–5.

Gardens free. House 50p (ch free, pen 25p).
P *(100yds)* ☕ *(late May–early Sep) wc*

Torrington, Great

Devon **Map 2 SS41**

ROSEMOOR GARDEN TRUST

(1m SE of town on B3220) ☏ (0805) 22256

An 8-acre garden with ornamental trees, shrubs, specie and hybrid rhododendrons planted since 1959. Areas with shrub and trailing roses, a peat garden, a screen garden, dwarf conifer collection and an arboretum. Plants labelled.

Open Apr–Oct daily. Nursery & garden daily 8–5.

£1 (ch 50p, pen 80p) Party.
P *(nearby)* ☕ *(Sun, Wed, BH)* 🛆 ♿ *wc*
Plants for sale

Totnes

Devon **Map 3 SX86**

BOWDEN HOUSE

(1m from town centre) ☏ (0803) 863664

The 12 acres of grounds at Bowden House are particularly attractive in the spring. Trees, shrubs and herbaceous plants are grown, and specialities include bulbs and rhododendrons, and plants suitable for flower arrangements. There are also fine beeches, and a very large plane tree. Tours of gardens for pre-booked parties by prior arrangement. The house, which is also open to the public (guided tours only) dates mainly from Tudor and Queen Anne times. A new attraction is the British Photographic Museum.

Open Apr–Oct, Tue–Thu, & BH Sun & Mon. Grounds 11–6, Museum 11–5.30, house 2–4.30. Coach parties by prior arrangement only.

Grounds only 75p, house, museum and gardens £2.75; house and gardens or museum and gardens £1.75. (Reductions for children).
P ☕ 🐕 ♿ *(ex upper floors of house) (wc) wc*

Truro

Cornwall   **Map 2 SW84**

TRELISSICK GARDEN
(4m S of Truro, on B3289) ☎ *(0872) 862090*

Gardens set in 376 acres of park, farmland and woods with beautiful views over Fal estuary and Falmouth Harbour. Noted for its display of camellias, magnolias, rhododendrons and azaleas and there is a collection of over 100 kinds of hydrangea. Also rare sub-tropical shrubs and woodland walk. Plants labelled.

Open Mar–Oct, Mon–Sat 11–6, Sun 1–6.

£1.60.

P ⵎ ✘ *(in garden)* ♿ *(wc) Plants for sale* *(NT)*

Uckfield

East Sussex   **Map 5 TQ41**

BEECHES FARM
Buckham Hill (1½m W of town on Isfield Rd) ☎ *(0825) 2391*

Sixteenth-century tile-hung farmhouse with lawns, yew trees, borders, sunken garden, roses and fine views.

Gardens open all year daily 10–5; House open by appointment only.

Gardens 25p (ch 15p) Conducted tour 75p. Party.
P

Ulverston

Cumbria   **Map 7 SD27**

CONISHEAD PRIORY
Priory Road ☎ *(0229) 54029)*

The 70 acres of grounds of the 19th-century gothic mansion on the shores of Morecambe Bay are mainly woodland. There are also about 2 acres of more formal gardens with lawns, flower beds and shrubs. House also open.

Open Etr–Sep Sat, Sun & BH 2–5; also Wed & Thu, mid Jul–Aug.

Grounds Free. House tours £1 (ch 50p, pen 75p) Party.
P ⵎ ♿ *(ground floor and gardens only) wc Plants for sale*

Upton

Warwickshire   **Map 4 SP34**

UPTON HOUSE
(7m NW of Banbury on A422)
☎ *Edge Hill (029587) 266*

Upton's delightful gardens consist of valleyside terraces, linked by a balustraded stairway, and overlooking a formal lake. Elsewhere in the 31½ acres of grounds, is a water garden in a natural amphitheatre ringed by woods, a classical temple, and a second lake. Herbs, roses, shrubs, low growing perennials, vegetables and flowering cherries are grown. 17th-century house also open.

Open Apr–Sep Mon–Thu 2–6 (last admission to house 5.30). Also some weekends in summer. Coach parties by prior arrangement only.

Grounds £1. House and grounds £2. Party 15+.
P ♿ *wc (NT)*

Garrya elliptica

Waddesdon

Buckinghamshire   Map 4 SP71

WADDESDON MANOR
(6m NW of Aylesbury, gates off A41)
☎ *Aylesbury (0296) 651282*

A French Renaissance-style château with 150 acres of grounds laid out in the 1870's. There are walks and vistas with trees, shrubs, sculpture and fountains. On the South Terrace there is a formal parterre. The aviary, a wrought iron semi-circular structure, with a central grotto, has a formal garden planted with Iceberg roses. Near the aviary is Daffodil Valley. House also open.

Open 25 Mar–29 Oct, Grounds Wed–Sat from 1pm, Sun from 11.30am; House Wed–Sun 2–6 (Wed–Fri 2–5 in Mar, Apr & Oct). House and grounds open Good Fri & BH Mons 11–6 (closed Wed after BH) Ch 10 not admitted to house.

Grounds £1.10 (ch 5 free, 5–17 60p) House & grounds £2.50. Fri from 3 Jul additional rooms £1 extra.
P ⬚ *wc (NT)*

Wadebridge

Cornwall   Map 2 SW97

LONG CROSS VICTORIAN GARDENS
☎ *Bodmin (0208) 880243*

Late Victorian gardens set amidst majestic pines with panoramic sea views.

*Open * Etr–Oct daily 11–dusk.*

Free.
⬚ ᶜ

Walton-in-Gordano

Avon   Map 3 ST47

THE MANOR HOUSE
(2m NE of Clevedon on B3124)
☎ *Clevedon (0272) 872067*

A 4-acre garden with a collection of many rare and unusual plants built-up over the past 10 years. Plants labelled.

Open Apr–17 Sep Mon, Wed & Thu 10–4; also 2nd Sun in each month and 30, 31 Aug 2–6; 20 Apr, 4 & 25 May 10–6.

75p (accompanied ch 14 free).
P ✖ ᶜ *wc*

Wantage

Oxfordshire   Map 4 SU48

KINGSTON LISLE PARK
(4½m W off B4507)
☎ *Uffington (036782) 223*

17th- and early 19th-century house in park and gardens featuring rose gardens, herbaceous borders, lawns and shrubs.

Open Etr–Aug, Thu & BH Sat–Mon 2–5.

£2 (ch 80p) Party.
P ⬚ *(BHs & pre booked)* ✖ ᶜ *Plants for sale*

Warrington

Cheshire   Map 7 SJ68

WALTON HALL GARDENS
High Walton ☎ *(0925) 601617*

Formal gardens with roses and bedding plants in the grounds of the Victorian hall. There are guided walks through the parkland. Roses labelled. Hall also open.

Open Park all year daily dawn–dusk; Hall Etr–Sep Thu–Sun 1–5; Oct–Etr, Sun & BH 12.30–4.30.

* Park Free; Hall 50p (ch & pen 25p).
P ᴛᴛ ᶜ*(wc) wc*

Warwick

Warwickshire   Map 4 SP26

WARWICK CASTLE
off Castle Hill ☎ *(0926) 495421*

The castle, which in part dates from the 14th-century, is surrounded by parkland designed by 'Capability' Brown. There are also formal Italian gardens and the grounds include some large cedars of Lebanon. A Rose Garden based on an 1860s design has recently been opened and a special feature is the bed of new roses named 'Warwick Castle'. Roses labelled. Castle and exhibitions also open.

Open daily (ex 25 Dec) Mar–Oct 10–5.30, Nov–Feb 10–4.30.

* £3.50 (ch £2.25, pen £2.75) Family tickets available.
P ⬚ *(licensed)* ᴛᴛ ✖ ᶜ*(garden only; wc) wc*

Washington

Tyne & Wear **Map 12 NZ35**

WASHINGTON OLD HALL

☎ 091-416 6879

Early 17th-century manor house with 6 acres of attractive formal gardens. The lower walled garden has lawns, shrubs, and annual bedding plants. There is also a Sunken Garden and a Rose Garden. House also open.

Open 1–16 Apr & Oct Wed, Sat & Sun 11–5; 17 Apr–Sep daily (ex Fri) 11–5.

Gardens free, House £1 Party.

P *(NT)*

Waterperry

Oxfordshire **Map 4 SP60**

WATERPERRY GARDENS & HORTICULTURAL CENTRE

(2m NE of Wheatley on unclass rd)
☎ Ickford (08447) 226 & 254

Peaceful ornamental gardens and nurseries set in extensive parkland. There is a magnificent herbaceous border, shrub and heather borders, island beds, a rock garden and trained fruit trees including pear and apple avenues. A new herb and knot garden has just been planted. Interesting herbaceous, shrub and alpine nurseries. Riverside walks. Plants labelled. Garden Centre. Advisory service.

Open all year (ex Xmas, New Year & during 'Art in Action' preparation and event 16–19 July); Apr–Sep Mon–Fri 10–5.30, Sat & Sun 10–6; Oct–Mar daily 10–4.30.

Mar–Oct £1 (ch 10 free, 10–16 50p, pen 75p), Nov–Feb free. Party.

P ☕ ♿ *wc*

Watford

Hertfordshire **Map 4 TQ19**

CHESLYN GARDENS

Nascot Wood Rd ☎ (0923) 26400 ext 384

Small woodland and formal gardens with lawns, herbaceous borders, bedding and rock plants. Plants labelled.

Open all year daily (ex Thu and Xmas) Apr–Sep 10–8, Oct–Mar 10–4.

Free.

P ♿

Welshpool

Powys **Map 7 SJ20**

POWIS CASTLE

(1m S of Welshpool, pedestrians' access from High St (A490). Cars turn right 1m along A483 Newtown Rd. Enter by 2nd drive gate on right). ☎ (0938) 4336 (Administrator) or 2952 (Head Gardener).

The castle is perched high above the 30 acres of formal and informal gardens and woodlands. The magnificent 17th-century terraces, dominated by large clipped yews, are planted with colourful herbaceous borders and many rare and tender shrubs. Below the terraces are lawns, roses and peaceful woodland gardens with conifers, oaks and rhododendrons. Plants labelled. Castle also open.

Open 18 Apr–Jun, Sep & Oct Wed–Sun & BH Mon 12–5; Jul & Aug Tue–Sun & BH Mon 11–6.

Garden £1.50 (ch 60p); Castle & Garden £2.10 (ch £1). Family ticket £5.60. Party 20+.

P ☕ 🚫🐕 *(ex guide dogs)* ♿ *wc Plants for sale (NT)*

West Bromwich

West Midlands Map 7 SP09

OAK HOUSE
Oak Rd ☎ 021-553 0759

At the front of the half-timbered 16th-century house is an Elizabethan garden. Flowering plants and shrubs, including old-fashioned roses, daffodils, tulips and poppies are grown, and there are also some herb plants. A path bordered by flower (mainly rose) beds leads round the side and back of the house and overlooks the bowling green (also open to the public, but bowls not supplied). House also open.

* Open Apr–Sep Mon–Sat 10–8 (ex Thu 10–1 & Sun 2.30–8) Oct–Mar Mon–Sat 10–4.

Free.
P *(50yds)* ✻ & *(ground floor & gardens only) wc*

Westbury-on-Severn

Gloucestershire Map 3 SO71

WESTBURY COURT GARDEN

A formal Dutch water garden dating from 1696–1705 with canals and yew hedges; the earliest of its kind remaining in England. A small walled garden has been planted with 100 species of plants grown in England before 1700. Rose garden with 40 different varieties of old roses.

Open Apr–Oct Wed–Sun & BH Mons 11–6 (closed Good Fri).

£1 (ch 50p).
✻ *(NT)*

West Clandon

Surrey Map 4 TQ05

CLANDON PARK
(on A247) ☎ *Guildford (0483) 222482*

An 18th-century house with 7 acres of lawns, herbaceous plants, spring bulbs, shrubs and mature trees. There is a formal Dutch Garden and a parterre. A Grotto and a Maori House are sited in the main gardens. House also open.

Open Apr–mid Oct incl BH Mon 2–6 (closed Mon & Fri, also Tue following BH Mon).

Garden free; House £2.
P ✻ & *(NT)*

West Dean

West Sussex Map 4 SU81

WEST DEAN GARDENS
☎ *Singleton (024363) 301*

Extensive informal gardens situated in a valley at the foot of the South Downs. The main feature of the gardens is the fine collection of specimen trees which includes cedars of Lebanon, planted in 1746, Ginkgos, and Fern Leaf beeches. There are also rustic summerhouses, a 300ft pergola, a wild garden and a walled garden with Victorian glasshouses. Some plants labelled. Nursery.

Open Apr–Sep daily 11–6.
£1.10 (ch 50p, pen 95p) Party.
P ♫ ⊞ ✻ & *(wc) wc*

Westerham

Kent Map 5 TQ45

CHARTWELL
(2m SE) ☎ *Edenbridge (0732) 866368*

Home of Sir Winston Churchill from 1922 until his death in 1964. Lawns, terraces, rose gardens, trees, a lake and ornamental pools are all included in the simple design of the garden. The famous wall which Churchill built can also be seen and the garden also contains his studio where a number of his paintings are on display. House also open.

Open Garden, studio & House Apr–Oct Tue–Thu 12–5, Sat, Sun & BH Mon 11–5. House also open Mar & Nov Wed, Sat & Sun 11–4.
Gardens £1 (ch 50p); House & garden £2.50 (ch £1.30) studio 40p.
P ♫ *(May–Nov) (NT)*

SQUERREYS COURT
☎ *(0959) 62345 or 63118*

The manor house, dating from 1680, is situated in 20 acres of attractive landscaped gardens with a lake and many fine trees including an old lime avenue. Spring brings colourful displays of snowdrops, daffodils, rhododendrons and azaleas, whilst in the summer the formal gardens are ablaze with roses and herbaceous plants. House also open.

Open Mar–Sep; Mar Sun only, Apr–Sep Wed, Sat, Sun & BH Mon 2–6.
Gardens 80p (ch 40p); House & gardens £1.50 (ch 80p) Party.
P ♫ *(weekends)* ⊞ & *(gardens only) wc*

Westonbirt

Gloucestershire Map 3 ST88
WESTONBIRT ARBORETUM
☎ (066688) 220

A comprehensive collection of temperate trees and shrubs dating from 1829. The network of paths includes several signposted trails. Attractive spring flowering shrubs and autumn foliage.

Open daily 10–8 or sunset.

* £1 (ch & pen 50p).
P ♨ (from 11.30 daily from spring to autumn) ♻ ᕙ (wc) wc

Lonicera periclymenum
'Honeysuckle'

Weston-under-Lizard

Staffordshire Map 7 SJ81
WESTON PARK
(7m W of junc 12 on M6 & 3m N of junc 3 on M54) ☎ (095276) 207

A 17th-century mansion with 4 acres of formal terraced gardens, lawns and an orangery. The vast parkland, landscaped by 'Capability' Brown, includes 3 lakes and plantings of rhododendrons and azaleas in Temple Wood. Special exhibitions and events throughout the year. House also open.

Open Apr, May & Sep wknds & BHs; Jun & Jul daily ex Mon & Fri; daily in Aug. Grounds 11–5; House 1–5.

Grounds £1.80 (ch & pen £1.30); House 75p (ch & pen 50p).
P ♨ (licensed) ♻ ✗ (in house) ᕙ

Westwood

Wiltshire Map 3 ST85
WESTWOOD MANOR

This beautiful 15th-century to 17th-century manor house has formal gardens. These include modern topiary and a particular attraction is the 'tree cottage' which has a doorway through which visitors can walk. House also open.

Open Apr–Sep Sun & Mon 2–6.

£1.50.
P (NT)

West Wycombe

Buckinghamshire Map 4 SU89
WEST WYCOMBE PARK
☎ High Wycombe (0494) 24411

The house, which was re-built for Sir Francis Dashwood in the 18th-century, is situated in a large park with a lake, temples and many fine trees. Both 'Capability' Brown and Humphrey Repton influences are obvious, and new planting is currently being undertaken.

Grounds only Etr (ex Good Fri), May Day & Spring BH Sun & Mon 2–6; House and grounds Jun Mon–Fri, Jul & Aug Sun–Fri 2–6. Coaches by prior appointment only.

Grounds £1.40. House and grounds £2.20.
P ✗ ᕙ (gardens) wc (NT) (NGS)

Weymouth

Dorset Map 3 SY67
BENNETTS WATER LILY FARM
Putton Lane, Chickerell ☎ (0305) 785150

Water-lilies, pond plants and fish can be viewed in a unique natural setting in these 7 acres of gardens, which are at their best in July and August. Plants labelled.

Open May–Sep Tue–Sat 9.30–12.30 & 2–4.30.

60p (ch 20p).
P ✗ 🚌 ᕙ wc Plants for sale

Whalley
Lancashire   **Map 7 SD73**
WHALLEY ABBEY
☎ (025482) 2268

The abbey ruins are in delightful gardens reaching down to the river. Fifteen acres of lawns, roses, heathers and formal bedding plants.

Open all year daily, 10–dusk.

* 60p (ch 4 free, ch 13 & pen 30p) Party.
P ⌂ *(parties only)* 🌐 &

Whickham
Tyne & Wear   **Map 12 NZ26**
CHASE PARK
☎ 091-488 7141

Twenty five acre park with extensive ornamental area of rose beds and flower-beds, and wide variety of trees. Something in flower at all times of the year.

Open all year, daily 7.30–dusk (winter 9–dusk).

Free.
&

Wight, Isle of
Arreton   **Map 4 SZ58**
HASELEY MANOR
☎ (0983) 865420

Attractive water gardens with waterfalls, stream and a small lake. Herb garden.

Open all year daily 10–6 (ex Xmas Day).

£1.60 (ch £1.10, pen £1.50).
P ⌂ *(licensed)* 🌐

Brading   **Map 4 SZ68**
MORTON MANOR
☎ (0983) 406168

Manor, built in 1680 set in 8 acres of magnificently landscaped gardens. There are rose and terraced gardens, an Elizabethan sunken garden and parkland with fine specimen trees. In spring countless bulbs, rhododendrons and magnolias are followed by roses and herbaceous plants which provide colour throughout the summer. Some plants labelled. Vineyard and winery. House also open.

* Open Etr–Oct daily 10–5.30 (closed Sat).

* £1.35 (ch 60p, pen £1.20) Party 15+.
P ⌂ *(licensed)* & *Plants for sale*

NUNWELL HOUSE
☎ (0983) 407240

The peaceful setting with views over parkland and across the Solent to Sussex are part of the attraction of the gardens at 15th century Nunwell House. Good collections of trees, shrubs, roses and perennials include tender species which appreciate the milder climate. Some plants labelled. House also open.

Open 24 May–24 Sep, Sun–Thu 1.30–5.

House & gardens £1.20 (ch 60p).
P ⌂ *(Jul–Sep)* 🌐 ✖ wc

East Cowes   **Map 4 SZ59**
BARTON MANOR VINEYARD AND GARDENS
☎ (0983) 292835

Gardens of 20 acres originally laid out by Prince Albert and Queen Victoria. Beautiful woodland and lakeside walk with about ¼ million daffodils in spring. Azaleas, rhododendrons, roses and herbaceous borders. Water garden, scented secret garden and cork and Ilex plantation. Garden houses national collection of Kniphofia (red-hot pokers) and Watsonia. Entrance price also includes 15-acre vineyard and winery.

Open daily May–11 Oct (plus Etr & Sat & Sun in Apr), 10–30–5.30.

* £1.50 (ch free, pen £1.25) Season tickets also available.
P ⌂ *(licensed)* ✖ & wc Plants for sale

Ventnor   **Map 4 SZ57**
BOTANIC GARDENS
☎ (0983) 852501

These gardens, set in a valley specialise in plants tender in the British Isles. A diverse collection of trees and shrubs from New Zealand, Australia and South Africa are grown. The gardens also contain a smuggling museum. Guided tours by prior arrangement. Plants labelled. →

Gardens open daily throughout year.
Smuggling Museum Etr–Sep daily 10–5.30.

Gardens Free; Smuggling Museum 80p,
accompanied ch 7 free, ch 7–14 & pen 50p.
P *(30p)* 🍴 *(licensed)* 🎌 ♿ *(wc) wc*

Wroxall — Map 4 SZ57
APPULDURCOMBE HOUSE
(½m W off B3327) 📞 *(0983) 852484*

The ornamental grounds of Appuldurcombe
House include a park landscaped by
'Capability' Brown. Other plantings and the
shrubbery date from Victorian times. The
roofless shell of a mansion dating from the
early 18th-century can also be seen.

* *Open mid Oct–mid Mar weekdays 9.30–4,*
Sun 2–4; mid Mar–mid Oct weekdays 9.30–
6.30, Sun 2–6.30.

* *75p (ch 16 & pen 25p).*
P *wc (AM)*

Willoughbridge
Staffordshire — Map 7 SJ73
THE DOROTHY CLIVE GARDEN
📞 *Pipe Gate (063081) 237*

These 7 acres of gardens feature rhododendron, azalea and woodland plantings, a
scree garden and a wealth of unusual plants.
Daffodils, water and rock gardens can also
be seen. There are fine views of the Staffordshire and Shropshire countryside. Guided
tours for parties by prior arrangement.
Plants labelled.

Open Mar–Nov 11–7.30 or dusk.

£1 *(ch 25p) Party 20+.*
P 🎌 ♿ *(wc) wc*

Wilton (Nr Salisbury)
Wiltshire — Map 4 SU03
WILTON HOUSE
📞 *Salisbury (0722) 743115*

The grounds at Wilton House are mainly
parkland lawns with giant cedars of Lebanon
and other trees. There is also an old-fashioned rose garden. Some plants labelled.
South of England Flower Show 25–26 Jul.
House also open.

Open 7 Apr–11 Oct Tue–Sat & BH Mon 11–
6, Sun 1–6 (last admission 5.15).

* *Grounds 95p (ch 16 65p); house, grounds,*
exhibitions and railway £3.35 (ch 16 £1.90,
pen & students £2.50) Party 20+.
P 🍴 *(licensed)* 🎌 ♿ *(wc) wc*

Wimpole
Cambridgeshire — Map 4 TL35
WIMPOLE HALL
(8m SW of Cambridge at junc of A14 and
A603) 📞 *Cambridge (0223) 207257*

The garden enclosed by railings and a ha-ha
has fine views across a landscaped park
which is attributed to landscape gardeners
such as Charles Bridgeman, 'Capability'
Brown and Humphrey Repton. The 19th-cen-
tury shrubbery or pleasure grounds east of
the house contain large specimen conifers
and a large Cornelian Cherry. In the spring
the whole area is covered with narcissus and
daffodils, as well as many wild flowers.

Open 11 Apr–25 Oct, Tue–Thu, Sat & Sun
1–5 BH Mon 11–6.

£2 *(ch £1) Party 15+.*
🍴 ♿ *(wheelchairs available) wc (NT)*

Forsythia intermedia

RIVER CAM FARM HOUSE
(Cambridge Road A603)
☎ *Cambridge (0223) 207750*

This garden is described by its owners as a 'Gardeners' Garden'. It has shrub and long herbaceous borders with unusual plants. There is also a natural pond and lovely views. A knot garden, collar garden, herb garden, bog garden and rose garden are being developed. The owners are often available to show visitors round gardens. Some plants labelled. Also fine art studio and gallery.

Open daily (ex Fri and Mon) 15 Jun–15 Oct. Other times by appointment only. Children must be accompanied.

* £1 (accompanied ch free, pen 50p). Fine art studio and gallery free.
P ✖ 🚌 *(but minibuses accepted)* ♿ *Plants for sale*

Winchcombe
Gloucestershire **Map 4 SP02**
SUDELEY CASTLE AND GARDENS
☎ *(0242) 602308*

The formal Elizabethan herb garden is one of the most popular attractions at Sudeley. Other features include yew hedges and clipped yews, shrub borders, cedars and limes, lawns and spring bulbs. There is also a waterfowl collection. Falconry displays Tue–Thu May–Aug. Castle also open.

Open daily Apr–Oct. Grounds 11–5.30, castle and museum 12–5. Parties at other times by prior arrangement.

£2.95 (ch £1.80, pen £2.50) Party.
P ☕ *(licensed)* 🛝 ✖ ♿ *(gardens only) wc garden centre*

Windsor
Berkshire **Map 4 SU97**
SAVILL GARDEN (WINDSOR GREAT PARK)
(reached via Wick lane, Englefield Green, near Egham) ☎ *(07535) 60222*

Thirty-five acres of grounds and gardens. The formal part of the gardens has roses, alpines and herbaceous plants, providing a wealth of summer colour. Rhododendrons, azaleas, magnolias and camellias create a superb display of colour from March–June. Plants labelled. Plants for sale.

Open daily (ex 25 & 26 Dec) 10–6 (or sunset if earlier).

£1.50 (ch 16 accompanied free, pen £1.30), half-price Nov–Feb Party.
P ☕ *(licensed) Mar–Oct,* ✖ ♿ *wc & garden centre*

VALLEY GARDENS (WINDSOR GREAT PARK)
near Virginia Water ☎ *(07535) 60222*

The gardens cover some 400 acres of fine woodland with a superb collection of rhododendrons, azaleas, camellias, magnolias and other spring-flowering trees and shrubs. A 10-acre heather garden provides colour and interest during summer and winter. Fifty acres contain the largest planting of rhododendron specimens in the world and a dwarf and slow-growing conifer collection. Autumn is particularly colourful with numerous Japanese maples, red oaks, and cherry trees. Plants labelled.

Open all year daily 8–7.

Free to pedestrians.
P *(£1)* ☕ *(licensed) Mar–Oct;* 🚌 ♿ *wc*

Windermere
Cumbria **Map 7 SD49**
LAKE DISTRICT NATIONAL PARK VISITOR CENTRE
Brockhole (on A591) ☎ *(09662) 6601*

Designed in 1899 by Thomas Mawson, the well-known northern landscape architect, the gardens have a fine lake and mountain setting with neat terraces, yew borders, clipped box and seasonal bedding schemes. A feature of the garden is a superb wall-trained magnolia. Herbaceous borders alternate with terraces of roses and hydrangeas. National Park Visitor Centre also open. Plants labelled. Guided walks.

Open Late Mar–early Nov daily from 10am (closing times vary with the season). Winter opening for parties by arrangement.

£1.20 (ch 5–18 60p) Party.
P ☕ 🛝 ♿ *(ground floor & gardens only; wc) wc*

LAKELAND HORTICULTURAL SOCIETY GARDENS
(Holehird) ☎ *Lazonby (076883) 742 (Hon Sec of Society)*

These 3½-acre gardens include an attractive and well-stocked alpine garden. Heathers, roses, azaleas and rhododendrons are also grown and there is a walled herbaceous garden and a winter garden. Displays of daffodils in springtime. There are superb views of the lakeland mountains from the gardens. Guided tours for gardening clubs, etc. by prior arrangement. Plants labelled. Lectures and talks given at the gardens.

Open daily throughout year. Children must be accompanied. Coach parties by prior arrangement only.

Free (but donations welcome).
P ✱

Wing
Buckinghamshire   Map 4 SP82
ASCOTT
☎ *Aylesbury (0296) 688242*

The 30-acre gardens around the house contain specimen trees and shrubs. A series of grass terraces lie below the house and one has an evergreen sundial, the roman figures of the clock are made from box. A central feature of the terrace is a pond from which rises a group of bronze figures by the American sculptor, Thomas Waldo Story. West of the terrace is a formal flower garden with a marble fountain. House also open.

Gardens Apr–mid Jul, Thu, last Sun in each month & 24 & 27 Sep 2–6. House and gardens 21 Jul–20 Sep; Tue–Sun 2–6, also Aug BH Mon (closed 1 Sep). Garden only last Sun in each month.

Garden £1.40, House & garden £2.20.
wc (NT) (NGS)

Wisbech
Cambridgeshire   Map 5 TF40
PECKOVER HOUSE
North Brink ☎ *(0945) 583463*

The garden is essentially Victorian in style and has many interesting and rare plants. There are several fine trees, among them maidenhair and tulip. In the conservatory

are fruiting orange trees reputed to be over 300 years old. House also open.

Open 11 Apr–18 Oct, May–Sep daily ex Thu & Fri, Apr & Oct wknds & BH only.

£1.25 (ch 60p & pen £1).
✱ *wc (NT) (NGS)*

Wisley
Surrey   Map 4 TQ05
WISLEY GARDEN (ROYAL HORTICULTURAL SOCIETY)
☎ *Guildford (0483) 224163*

This is the famous and extensive garden of the Royal Horticultural Society and its purpose is to show every aspect of gardening at its best. It offers wooded slopes with massed rhododendrons and azaleas, wild daffodils in the alpine meadow, a pinetum, banked mounds of heathers, a rock garden and an alpine house. Also of interest are the fruit and vegetable gardens and the range of greenhouses. There is an advisory service. Our special colour feature on Decorative Vegetables was written by Peter Harlington of Wisley's Vegetable Department, See page 147.

* *Open all year Mon–Sat 10–7 or dusk (4.30 Jan, Nov & Dec), Sun 2–7 or dusk. Members only on Sunday mornings.*

* *£1.80 (ch 6 90p) Party.*
P 🍴 *(licensed)* 🎋 ✱ &

Witney
Oxfordshire   Map 4 SP31
COGGES FARM MUSEUM
(½m SE off A4022) ☎ *(0993) 72602*

The walled garden around this Edwardian farmhouse, now a museum, is laid out in the same period. A feature of the central pathway running through the garden is a lavender border and espalier apple trees with a rose bower in the centre. Flower borders and beds. Herb plot. Museum also open. Plants labelled.

* *Open 29 Apr–26 Oct, Tue–Sun & BH Mon 10.30–5.30 daily.*

* *£1.50 (ch, pen & students 80p) Party 10 +.*
P 🍴 *(licensed)* 🎋 & *(ground floor & gardens only) wc Plants for sale*

Wolverhampton

West Midlands   Map 7 SO99

WIGHTWICK MANOR
(3m W off A454) ☎ *(0902) 761108*

Both the gardens and house of Wightwick show strong pre-Raphaelite influence. The gardens were laid out by Alfred Parsons with shrubs and plants supplied by Morris. There are also yew hedges and topiary, terraces, two pools, trees planted by notable people, and a rose garden. House also open.

Open Thu, Sat & BH Sun & Mon 2.30–5.30 (closed 25 & 26 Dec, 1 & 2 Jan and Feb). Coach parties by prior arrangement. Children must be accompanied, ch 10 not admitted.

Gardens £1; house and gardens £2 (ch £1); £2.50 on Sat, when extra rooms are shown.
P & wc (NT)

Woodstock

Oxfordshire   Map 4 SP41

BLENHEIM PALACE
☎ *(0993) 811325*

These large and spectacular gardens have both formal and informal features. Much of the formal garden designed by Henry Wise was swept away by 'Capability' Brown landscaping, but a formal Italian garden and terraces were added in the 1920s. As well as these grand design features, other attractions include the mature trees, topiary, shrubs and lawns. House and Butterfly house also open.

Open Palace and gardens mid Mar–Oct daily, 11–6 (last admission 5pm) Park open all year 9–5.

* £3.60 (ch 16 & pen £2.70, ch 5–15 £1.70, ch 5 free).
P ⬚ & wc Shop & garden centre

Woolton Hill

Berkshire   Map 4 SU46

HOLLINGTON NURSERIES
(4m SW of Newbury off A434)
☎ *Highclere (0635) 253908*

A carefully laid-out herb nursery with display gardens showing formal and informal plantings using a large range of herbs. Twice Gold Medal winners at the Chelsea Flower Show, the 1986 exhibit is being re-built at Hollington for 1987. Plants labelled. Advisory service. Guided tours by arrangement. The proprietor, Simon Hopkinson, is the author of our special colour feature 'Creating a Culinary Herb Garden' see page 11.

Open all year, 14 Mar–Sep Mon–Sat 10–5.30, Sun & BH's 11–5; Oct–13 Mar Mon–Fri 10–dusk.

Free.
P & wc

Worksop

Nottinghamshire   Map 8 SK57

CLUMBER PARK KITCHEN GARDENS
☎ *(0909) 476592*

About 2 acres in extent, the present garden is contained within the old walled garden which used to supply Clumber House, the former seat of the Dukes of Newcastle. In recent years the Fig House, Vineries and Palm house have recently been replanted as have the orchard and fruit and vegetable borders.

Open Apr–Sep, Sat, Sun & BH 10–4. Prebooked parties on Tue & Wed.

50p (ch 25p–must be accompanied by an adult) Admission charge includes entry to Kitchen garden tools exhibition.
P ⬚ & (wc) wc

Lathyrus odoratus
'Sweet Pea'

Wrexham

Clwyd **Map 7 SJ35**

ERDDIG

(off the A525, 2m S)

The gardens at Erddig have been restored to their 18th-century formal design as shown in an 1738 engraving. Features include fruit trees with old varieties of fruit and methods of training, pleached limes, a long straight canal and walks. There is also a Victorian flower garden with yew hedges. House also open.

Open (ex Fri) 17 Apr–18 Oct, 12–5.30 (last admission 4.30). School and youth groups mornings only by prior arrangement. Coach parties by prior arrangement only. (Tapestry and Chinese rooms open Wed & Sat only).

Garden £1 (ch 50p). House and garden £2.10 (ch 80p) Family ticket, Party 20+.
P ⊡ ✖ ᕕ *(gardens and parts of outbuildings) wc (NT)*

Wroxton

Oxfordshire **Map 4 SP44**

WROXTON ABBEY

☎ *Wroxton St Mary (029573) 551*

Recently restored 18th-century gardens of the 17th-century manor house, with large lawns, specimen trees and woodlands. There are various buildings and stone features in the gardens including a Gothic-styled dovecot and a Doric temple.

Open all year daily.

Free, 50p BH's.
P ᕕ

Yealand Conyers

Lancashire **Map 7 SD47**

LEIGHTON HALL

(3m N of Carnforth off A6) ☎ *Carnforth (0524) 701353 or 734474*

Set against a backdrop of beautiful fell country, this 2-acre garden surrounds the home of the Gillow family. There are lawns with herbaceous borders, and a walled garden enclosing herbs, vegetables, many colourful blooms and flowering cherries. House also open. Birds of prey regularly flown.

Open May–Sep 2–5 (Closed Sat & Mon ex BH Mons).

* *House & grounds £1.50 (ch 15 90p) Party.*
P ⊡ ✚ ᕕ *wc*

Yelverton

Devon **Map 2 SX56**

THE GARDEN HOUSE

Eight-acre garden of all-year-round interest, including a fine 2-acre walled garden. Colourful collections of herbaceous and woody plants. Great attention is paid to the grouping of plants with regard to both colour and form. Nursery.

* *Open Apr–Sep daily (ex BH) 2–5.*

* *£1 (ch 20p) Party.*
P ✖ *Plants for sale*

*Hibbertia scandens
'Snake vine'*

York

North Yorkshire   Map 8 SE65

BOTANICAL GARDENS

Museum St ☎ (0904) 29745

Gardens founded in 1822 and including interesting specimen trees such as a large monkey puzzle. They are the grounds of the Yorkshire Museum which also includes the ruins of St Mary's Abbey and an observatory.

*Open gardens daily: museum open Mon–Sat 10–5, Sun 1–5; observatory Wed–Sun Summer only (closed 25 & 26 Dec).

* Gardens free; observatory 15p (ch 10p), museum 80p (ch & pen 40p).
P 🅟 &

MUSEUM GARDENS

St Mary's Abbey, Museum St ☎ (0904) 29745

The 10 acres of grounds surrounding the ruins of St Mary's Abbey were laid out between the 1820s and 1850s in gardenesque style. The lawns slope towards the River Ouse and are planted with picturesque groups of trees and individual specimen trees. Within the gardens are labelled collections of shrubs and herbaceous plants, and there is also a limestock rock garden with plants including alpines and dwarf conifers. Guided tours for parties by prior arrangement. Museum, tours, observatory and city walls can also be seen.

Gardens open daily (ex 25 & 26 Dec) Mon–Fri 7.30–dusk, Sat 8–dusk, Sun 10–dusk; Museum Mon–Sat 10–5, Sun 1–5; Observatory Wed–Sun Apr–Sep.

Gardens free. Museum £1.50 (ch & pen 75p), observatory 15p (ch 10p).
P *(public car park at Marygate)* & *(wc)* wc

Y Rhiw

Gwynedd   Map 6 SH22

PLAS-YN-RHIW

(8m SW of Llanbedrog off B4413)
☎ *Rhiw (075888) 219*

Small manor house with gardens and woodland leading down to the shore of Porth Neigwl (Hell's Mouth Bay). There are flowering trees and shrubs, sub-tropical plants, a snowdrop wood, stream and waterfall.

Open 17 Apr–Sep daily (ex Sat) 11–5 (last admission 4.45).

£1 (ch 50p) Party 20+.
P 🅟 *(ex guide dogs)* 🚌 *(NT)*

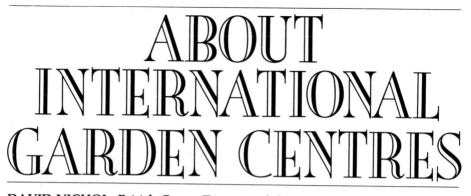

ABOUT INTERNATIONAL GARDEN CENTRES

DAVID NICHOL, British Group Director of the International Garden Centre Association pinpoints the differences between the good garden centres and the rest.

Visiting garden centres is a bit different from shopping anywhere else, combining as they do something of the atmosphere of a botanical garden, a garden fete and a superior DIY store. The reason for all this stems quite simply from two main aims of a garden centre. The first is to provide true one-stop shopping for the gardener backed by expert advice and second, arising from their usual out of town location, is to ensure that the visit is an enjoyable day out for the whole family — frequently at the week-end.

Garden centres are not all alike — and this is part of their attraction. Most of them did not just spring up in a few short weeks like a modern superstore. They developed slowly, often from nursery origins sometimes going back several generations. Names like Notcutts and Webbs, Waterers and Caldwell, Wheatcroft and Russell, Haskins and Jackmans reveal their background. The result is that while today they aim to meet all gardener's needs they do sometimes have their specialities, be it roses or seed potatoes, rhododendrons or onions, that reflect their past.

So having said all that how do you go about finding a good one for your own needs?

Unfortunately, but not surprisingly, the words 'garden centre' mean very little. Anyone can call themselves a garden centre and if you look them up in Yellow Pages, there are dozens listed — some being small high street shops with a few plants on the forecourt, others perhaps run to several acres of plant and garden sundries. It was largely because of the need to distinguish the true garden centre from the rest that the British Group of the International Garden Centre Association was formed.

Membership of the Association really does mean something because the Association (called IGC for short) is tough on who it accepts as members and who it allows to remain as members. These centres are inspected regularly to ensure that high standards are being maintained. You may have seen them in your area flying the pale blue flag of the Association.

All Association members have to provide a very wide range of trees, shrubs, fruit, roses and other plants in top quality condition and they have to provide all the composts, fertilisers, chemicals and tools which are needed to look after them properly. Adequate free parking is always provided although naturally limited in town centres.

But perhaps the two most important requirements from the customer's point of view are first that members must employ a reasonable proportion of skilled horticulturalists and second that all hardy nursery stock sold is guaranteed for 12 months. This means that everyone from a complete beginner wrestling with a new garden that closely resembles a builder's yard to the dedicated expert concerned about pollination of his skimmia can get essential advice, and everyone can buy with confidence protected by the renowned IGC guarantee.

Perhaps the larger garden centres could be better described as garden and leisure centres because as well as offering you every sort of garden plant, insecticide, fungicide and fertiliser, many help you to enjoy your garden with a wide selection of garden furniture, ornaments, pools, fish, garden games, barbecues and if the site is big enough they may have garden sheds and summer houses, greenhouses and swimming pools as well. Plus, just to ensure that you can really enjoy your visit, you may be able to buy an ice cream, have a cup of tea or even a light meal and let your children loose in a protected play area.

As you walk around an IGC garden centre you should expect to find all these facilities:-

☐ Good signs and attractive planting to give you a feeling of welcome. The car park should be easy to find and not too much underwater even after heavy rain!

☐ A good supply of trolleys on which you can load and carry your purchases.

☐ Good quality plants looking clean and strong.

☐ Wide paths that can take at least two trolleys passing each other.

☐ Some raised beds giving easy access to the small plants.

☐ A clearly defined spot where you can get expert advice.

☐ Some area under cover where you can shop in bad weather.

☐ Planted beds clearly labelled to help you choose.

☐ Mature garden settings full of ideas for improving your own garden.

☐ Plenty of pictorial labels to show what to expect from fruit or flowers.

☐ A place, if space allows, just to enjoy plants, lawns and water in a garden setting.

☐ A shop where you can easily find the tools, composts, fertiliser, trellis, chemicals, watering equipment and so on that you will need to look after the plants you have selected.

☐ Perhaps a cup of coffee or an ice cream if you have time!

☐ Plenty of friendly assistants to 'cash up' and allow you to pay without too much queueing even at weekends.

☐ Help available to get your purchases to your car.

☐ Someone to say thank you for coming and please visit us again.

We hope you will find what you are looking for.

In the pages that follow is a directory of garden centres, all of whom are members of the Association. Further information is available from the Head Office at 19 High Street, Theale, Reading, Berks, RG7 5AH.

Aberdeen

Grampian *Aberdeenshire* Map 15 NJ90

HAZELHEAD GARDEN CENTRE
Hazeldean Rd ☎ *(0224) 318658*

Wide selection of indoor and outdoor plants, many of which can be seen in demonstration beds. Specialists in home-grown shrubs and plants suited to northern gardens. There is also a full range of garden sundries, furniture, giftware and water gardening. Calendar of weekend events include planting and pruning demonstrations. Garden buildings; children's play area; landscaping service; advisory service; mail order; delivery; gift vouchers; discounts.

Open all year daily (ex Xmas & New Year) 9-5.30 (8 Thu & Fri).

P ⚲ ♿ *(wheelchairs available; special parking area) wc*

Ambleside

Cumbria Map 7 NY30

HAYES GARDEN WORLD
Lake District Nurseries ☎ *(0966) 33434/5*

A good selection of plants for the house and garden including shrubs, conifers and bonsai trees, also water garden equipment and garden furniture. Children's playground, landscaping service; advisory service; delivery; gift vouchers.

Open all year daily (ex Xmas & BH) Mon-Sat 9-6 (dusk in winter) Sun 10-dusk.

Angmering

West Sussex Map 4 TQ00

ROUNDSTONE GARDEN CENTRE
Roundstone By-Pass
☎ *Worthing (0903) 776481/2/3*

A large part of the garden centre is under cover and offers an extensive range of plants, including pot plants, shrubs and container grown perennials displayed in attractive surroundings. A good selection of sundries and accessories. Landscaping service; advisory service; delivery; gift vouchers; discounts.

Open all year daily Mon-Fri 8.30-5.30 (9.30am, Tue), Sat, Sun & BH 9-5.30, closes 5pm Mon, Wed, Thu & Fri in winter.

P ⚲ *wc*

Ardleigh

Essex Map 5 TM02

NOTCUTTS GARDEN CENTRE
Station Road ☎ *Colchester (0206) 230271*

Over 2,000 varieties of plants listed in a catalogue including nursery-grown shrubs and hardy plants. 'Garden Design' and 'Plant-a-Plan' schemes to help with garden planning. Demonstration gardens include a rhododendron walk and well-planted mature grounds. Water garden and landscape materials, and a good selection of garden furniture, sundries and pot plants. Advisory service; delivery; gift vouchers.

Open all year Mon-Sat 8.30-5.30, Sun & BH 10-5.30.

P ⚲ *wc*

See advertisement on p.168.

Ashford

Devon Map 2 SS53

THE NORTH DEVON GARDEN CENTER
☎ *Barnstaple (0271) 42880*

A 3-acre site with scenic views over river Taw estuary offering a complete range of shrubs, plants and garden equipment. House plants; advisory service; delivery; gift vouchers.

Open all year Mon-Sat 9-5.30, Sun & BH 10-5.30.

P ⚲ *wc*

Bagshot

Surrey Map 4 SU96

NOTCUTTS GARDEN CENTRE
Waterers' Nurseries, London Rd
☎ *(0276) 72288*

A wide selection of plants including seasonal bedding, shrubs, trees, fruit, roses, herbaceous, heathers, alpines and bonsai. Pot Plant House with specimen plants. Garden furniture showroom and shop carrying a full range of sundries. Swimming pools, garden machinery and aquarium. Advisory service; mail order service; delivery; gift vouchers.

Open all year Mon-Sat 9-5.30, Sun & BH 10.30-5.30 (closes 6pm Mar-23 Jun).

P ⚲ *wc*

See advertisement on p.168.

Banbury
Oxfordshire   **Map 4 SP44**

CLOWS GARDEN CENTRE
Compton Road (off Castle Street)
☎ *(0295) 66300*

A modern garden centre offering a wide range of container-grown plants including alpines, heathers, herbs, shrubs, roses, trees and fruit. Large cold water fish department open throughout the summer. Comprehensive selection of houseplants with specimen plants for commercial premises. Garden sundries; seasonal bulbs; advisory service; delivery; gift vouchers.

Open all year daily 8.30–5.30 (5pm in winter).

P ⏚ wc

Barton
Lancashire   **Map 7 SD53**

BARTON GRANGE GARDEN CENTRE
☎ *Preston (0772) 862551*

Stocks of trees, shrubs, roses, perennials, alpines and houseplants with many unusual varieties. Large specimen conifers and shrubs are a speciality. Water-garden department with fish, water-plants, pools and ornaments. Leisure furniture. Landscaping service; advisory service; delivery; gift vouchers.

Open all year daily Mon–Fri 9–5.30, Sat & Sun 10–5.30.

P ⏚ wc

Basildon
Essex   **Map 5 TQ78**

BASILDON ROSE GARDENS
Burnt Mills Road ☎ *(0268) 726320*

Vast range of plants, some displayed in rockery and demonstration beds. The main shop includes homebrew equipment, fireplaces, fabric flowers and plants and all the usual garden related products. Tool hire and repair; DIY shop; pet centre; landscaping service; advisory service; mail order; delivery; gift vouchers; discounts.

Open all year daily 9–5.30.

P ⏚ wc

Bath
Avon   **Map 3 ST76**

POINTINGS GARDEN CENTRE
Monmouth Street and Sawclose
☎ *(0225) 64281*

Roof top garden centre, in the centre of Bath alongside the Theatre Royal, comprising a large outdoor planteria and an architecturally unique curved steel and glass building. Collection of trees, shrubs, outdoor and indoor plants, including some unusual varieties. Wide range of garden furniture and sundries. Advisory service; delivery; gift vouchers; discounts.

Open all year daily (ex Xmas) Mon–Sat 9–5.30, Sun 10–5.

P ⏚ (wc) wc

Beaconsfield
Buckinghamshire   **Map 4 SU99**

BEACONSFIELD GARDEN CENTRE
London Road ☎ *(04946) 2522 & 5339*

A good selection of indoor and outdoor plants. Children's play area. Delivery service; gift vouchers.

Open all year daily (ex Xmas) 9–6.

P wc

Papaver rhoeas
'Poppy'

Beaulieu

Hampshire   Map 4 SU30

FAIRWEATHERS' GARDEN CENTRE
High Street ☎ *(0590) 612307*

Garden centre in a country village setting specialising in rhododendrons and azaleas. A wide range of shrubs, heathers, alpines, herbaceous, trees, water plants, and indoor plants. Demonstration areas of hedging and shrubs. Show site of greenhouses, sheds and conservatories. Children's play area; advisory service; delivery; gift vouchers.

Open all year daily 9–5.

P *wc*

Birmingham

West Midlands   Map 7 SP08

BOURNEVILLE GARDEN CENTRE
Maple Road
☎ *021-472 8812 & 021-472 0303*

Delightfully situated in the centre of Stocks Wood just a few miles SW of the city centre. The garden centre has been recently modernised and has a new showroom, and planteria with an information and advice centre. Seasonal displays, large demonstration gardens including a large rockery, also a small Japanese feature garden. Aquatic department due to open spring 1987. Landscaping service; delivery; gift vouchers.

Open all year Mon–Sat 9–6.

P ⬚ *wc*

Bishopsteignton

Devon   Map 3 SX97

JACK'S PATCH GARDEN CENTRE
Newton Road ☎ *Teignmouth (06267) 6996*

A large plant-orientated garden centre offering a good range of interesting and unusual plants, gardening sundries and equipment. There are three 30ft × 30ft demonstration gardens in front of false house fronts to help with garden planning, also extensive rockeries and other display areas. Children's play park; houseplants; landscaping service; advisory service; delivery; gift vouchers.

Open all year daily Mon–Sat 9–5 Sun 11–5.

P ⬚ *wc*

Blackpool

Lancashire   Map 7 SD33

TREBARON GARDEN CENTRE
350 Common Edge Road, South Shore
☎ *(0253) 691368*

This garden centre stocks a wide range of plants for both large and small gardens including many plants which are suitable for coastal gardens. Houseplant showroom with top quality indoor plants. Garden furniture department. Landscaping service; advisory service; delivery; gift vouchers.

Open all year daily 9.30–5.30.

P ⬚ *wc*

Boothstown

Gt Manchester   Map 7 SD70

WORSLEY HALL GARDEN CENTRE
Leigh Rd ☎ *061-790 8792*

A large garden centre with a walled garden which was once part of Worsley New Hall, now demolished. The 2½-acre plant area is filled with container grown plants, shrubs, trees and herbs. Paving, peat, gravels, rustic poles, garden seats and planters on show outside. Houseplant greenhouse. Two beds demonstrating ground cover and other mature plants. Playground; picnic area; advisory service; delivery; gift vouchers.

Open all year daily 8.30–5.30, limited Sun opening.

P ⬚ *wc*

Brampton

Cambridgeshire   Map 4 TL27

BRAMPTON GARDEN CENTRE
Buckden Rd
☎ *Huntingdon (0480) 53048 and 51075*

A well laid-out garden centre with a wide range of nursery-grown stock including alpines, climbers, trees, fruit, perennials and roses. There are three gardens demonstrating what can be achieved in a small garden. Children's play area; houseplants; advisory service; delivery; gift vouchers.

Open all year daily Mon–Sat 9–5.30 (late closing Thu & Fri early Apr–late Jun) Sun & BH 10–5.30.

P ⬚ *wc*

Bromsgrove

Hereford and Worcester   Map 7 SO97

BARNS GARDEN CENTRE

Alcester Road, Burcot ☎ (0527) 73470

Well-stocked plant area with alpines, heathers, conifers, fruit trees and shrubs. Many common and rare plants in the large pot plant house. Aquaria with tropical and cold water fish. Play area; landscaping service; advisory service; delivery; gift vouchers.

Open all year daily (ex Xmas) Mon–Sat 9–6, Sun 9.30–6.

P ♻ ♿ (wc) wc

Broom Hill

Dorset   Map 4 SU00

STEWARTS GARDEN-LANDS

God's Blessing Lane (2½m NE of Wimborne Minster on unclass rd off B3078) ☎ Wimborne (0202) 882462

A small but neat garden centre with a good range of plants grown in the adjoining nursery including conifers and roses. Visitors are welcome to walk round the nursery. Garden shop; houseplants; landscaping service; advisory service; delivery; gift vouchers; discounts.

Open all year daily (ex Xmas) Mon–Sat 9–5, Sun 10–5.

P ♻ wc

Burton

Cheshire   Map 7 SJ37

GORDALE NURSERIES

Chester High Road (A540) ☎ 051-336 2116

One of the largest garden centres in the NW, in an attractive wooded setting. The wide range of plants includes shrubs, trees, fruit, roses, herbaceous and perennials. Garden sundries, pottery, furniture, barbecues, water garden equipment and books are also available. Petrol station; houseplants advisory service; delivery; gift vouchers; discounts.

Open all year daily Mon–Fri 9–5.30, Sat & Sun 9–6.

P ♻ ♿ (wc) wc

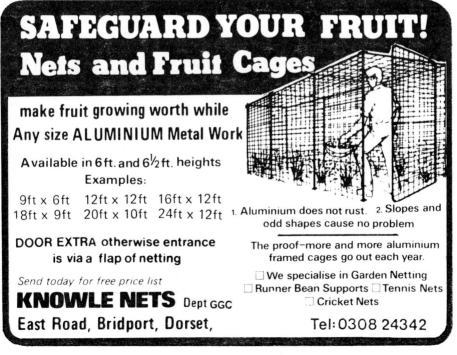

Bury St Edmunds

Suffolk   Map 5 TL86

MARLOWS DIY & GARDEN CENTRE
Hollow Road ☎ *(0284) 63155*

There is a wide range of plants, trees, shrubs, conifers, heathers and roses. Water garden equipment with plants, pools, fountains and pumps. Display of conservatories and greenhouses. Paving, walling and fencing, and a full range of sundries. Children's play area. Houseplants; landscaping service; advisory service; delivery; gift vouchers; discounts.

Open all year daily Mon–Fri 8.30–8, Sat 8.30–6, Sun 10–5.30.
P *wc*

Caddington

Bedfordshire   Map 4 TL01

FARR'S GARDEN CENTRE
Dunstable Road ☎ *Dunstable (0582) 20551*

A wide selection of indoor and outdoor plants including alpines, heathers, trees, shrubs and conifers. Specialists in paving and fencing. There is also a full range of garden sundries, greenhouses, sheds, swimming pool and sauna equipment. Tropical and cold water aquatic area. Houseplants; landscaping; advisory service; delivery; gift vouchers.

Open all year daily Mon–Sat 9.30–6 (5 in winter), Sun 10–5. Closed Xmas & New Year.
P ⏹ *(hot meals all day)* ⅋ *(wc) wc*

Capel St Mary

Suffolk   Map 5 TM03

BY-PASS NURSERIES
A12 Rd ☎ *Ipswich (0473) 310604*

This garden centre has a full range of outdoor and indoor plants. Also thousands of plants are grown in its nursery area and visitors can walk round and choose their plants. Specialists in flowering houseplants, primulas, geraniums and fuchsias. Swimming pool display. Cotswold Garden. Children's play area; houseplants; advisory service; delivery; gift vouchers; discounts.

Open all year daily, 10–5.
P ⏹ ⅋ *(wc) wc*

Channel Islands, Guernsey

St Andrews   Map 16

MARTEL'S GARDEN WORLD
☎ *(0481) 36888*

Garden centre in a rural setting offering a range of bedding plants, perennials, bulbs, alpines, fuchsias, trees and shrubs. Garden furniture; houseplants; mail order; delivery; gift vouchers.

Open all year daily (ex Xmas & New Year) Mon–Sat 8–6, Sun 9.30–6.
P *wc*

Chatsworth

Derbyshire   Map 8 SK27

CHATSWORTH GARDEN CENTRE
Chatsworth Park ☎ *Matlock (0629) 734004*

Situated in Chatsworth Park the garden centre offers a wide range of plants and sundries. Demonstration gardens. Houseplants; delivery service; gift vouchers.

Open all year daily 10–5 (6 pm Mar–Sep) Closed 25 Dec–2 Jan.
P ⏹ ⅋ *(wc) wc*

Chenies

Buckinghamshire   Map 4 TQ09

CHENIES GARDEN CENTRE
☎ *Little Chalfont (02404) 4545*

A selection of indoor and outdoor plants. A full range of garden sundries, furniture, sheds, fencing and paving. Swimming pools; pot plants; advisory service; delivery; gift vouchers.

Open daily throughout year 9–5.30.

Chester

Cheshire   Map 7 SJ46

GROSVENOR GARDEN LEISURE
Wrexham Rd, Belgrave (3m SW of Chester on the A483) ☎ *(0244) 672856*

Pleasantly laid-out on the edge of Grosvenor Estate this garden centre offers a comprehensive range of quality indoor hardy plants, trees and shrubs. There is a range of garden furniture, buildings and machinery; also paving and walling. Pet and Aquatic Centre. Swimming pools; children's play area; house plants; landscaping; advisory service; delivery; gift vouchers.

Open all year daily Mon–Fri & BH 9–5.45; Sat & Sun 10–5.45. (closes 5pm Nov–Mar).

P ⛁ wc

Chesterfield
Derbyshire   Map 8 SK37
GREENLEAVES PLANT CENTRE
Birkin Lane, Wingerworth ☎ (0246) 20214

This small plant centre caters for the specialist gardener and stocks rare and unusual plants. Houseplants are also available, and there are demonstration gardens. Advisory service; delivery; gift vouchers.

Open all year daily (ex 25 Dec–2 Jan) Oct–Feb 10–5, Mar–Sep 10–6.

P ⛁ wc

Chester-le-Street
Durham   Map 12 NZ25
LAMBTON PARK GARDEN CENTRE
Lambton Park ☎ Durham (0385) 855154

A 5-acre site with a large covered area for the sale of houseplants and garden sundries. A wide range of outdoor plants from alpines to trees. Specialist areas include water gardening, greenhouses and garden machinery. Demonstration cottage garden, heather and conifer beds, shrub beds. Pet Centre; children's play area; advisory service; delivery; gift vouchers.

Open all year daily (ex Xmas & New Year) 9–6 (5 pm winter).

P ⛁ ♿ (wc) wc

Chichester
West Sussex   Map 4 SU80
CHICHESTER GARDEN CENTRE
Bognor Road, Merston (2m SE of A259)
☎(0243) 789276

The range of outdoor plants includes bedding plants, shrubs, conifers, soft fruit and

specimen trees. Garden sundries, lawn mowers, swimming pools. Children's play area; houseplants; delivery; gift vouchers.

Open all year daily (ex Xmas) 9–6.

P ⛁

Chilton
Oxfordshire   Map 4 SU48
CHILTON GARDEN CENTRE
Newbury Rd ☎ Abingdon (0235) 833900

A well-designed garden centre complex on the A34 between Oxford and Newbury. It offers a comprehensive range of trees, shrubs, conifers, climbers, alpines, heathers, herbs, houseplants, perennials, fruit trees and annuals. There is also a wide selection of items for the home, conservatory and garden including furniture and furnishings, barbecues, books, gifts and leisure goods. Exhibition Hall with interesting seasonal displays. Landscaping; advisory service; delivery; gift vouchers.

Open all year daily 9.30–6 (7pm Thu & Fri).

P ⛁ ♿ (wc) wc

Chislehurst
Kent   Map 5 TQ47
COOLINGS NURSERIES & GARDEN CENTRE
Willow Grove ☎ 01-467 5064

Plant orientated garden centre specialising in high quality bedding plants which are grown in the nursery. Great emphasis on trained staff who are able to advise. Houseplants; delivery; gift vouchers.

Open all year daily (ex Sun) Mon–Sat 8.30–5.30 also Etr & Spring BH.

P wc

Christchurch
Dorset   Map 4 SZ19
STEWARTS GARDEN-LANDS
Lyndhurst Rd ☎ Highcliffe (04252) 72244

Built over 23 years ago, this was the first purpose-built garden centre in the country. The Planteria stocks a comprehensive range of high quality outdoor plants. Large shop →

with garden sundries. Three small demonstration gardens to spark the imagination. Display of garden buildings. Houseplants; landscaping; advisory service; delivery; gift vouchers.

Open all year daily (ex Xmas) Mon–Sat 9–6, Sun 10–6.

P ⊟ wc

Churchdown

Gloucestershire   Map 3 SO81

HURRANS GARDEN CENTRE
Cheltenham Road East ☎ (0452) 712232

Developed nearly 20 years ago this garden centre offers a wide range of quality products to suit most gardening needs. There is a comprehensive range of trees and shrubs including azaleas, rhododendrons, heathers, alpines, roses and dwarf conifers, also summer and autumn bedding. Garden sheds and conservatories. Houseplants; advisory service; delivery; gift vouchers.

Open all year daily (ex Xmas) Mon–Fri 9–8, Sat & Sun 9–6 (closes 5 pm Oct–Feb) BH's 9–6.

P ⊟ wc

Cirencester

Gloucestershire   Map 4 SP00

CIRENCESTER GARDEN CENTRE
Kingsmeadow, Cricklade Road
☎ (0285) 67036

Situated on the outskirts of Cirencester on the A419 Swindon Road. The centre was formerly owned by the Jeffries family, renowned nurserymen for over 200 years, who remain actively involved. There is a full range of trees, shrubs, conifers, climbers, alpines, heathers, herbs, perennials, fruit trees and seasonal annuals. A wide selection of items for the home, conservatory and garden including furniture, furnishings, barbecues, books, gifts and leisure goods. Permanent displays of conservatories, sheds, greenhouses and swimming pools. Houseplants; landscaping; advisory service; delivery; gift vouchers.

Open daily throughout year Mon–Sat 9–6, Sun 10–6.

P wc

Clacton-on-Sea

Essex   Map 5 TM11

CLACTON GARDEN CENTRE
St Johns Road ☎ (0255) 425711

Located just outside town on the B1027, this garden centre offers a large range of trees, shrubs, conifers and roses (mostly container-grown), also heathers, alpines and houseplants. Also available are garden sundries, furniture, machinery, and buildings; fencing, paving and walling bricks. Delivery; gift vouchers.

Open daily throughout year, Mon–Sat 9–5.30, Sun 9.30–5.30.

P wc

Cleethorpes

Humberside   Map 8 TA30

PENNELLS GARDEN CENTRE
Humberston Rd ☎ (0472) 694272

A modern garden centre offering an extensive range of plants for both house and garden. Also sundries including compost, fertilizer and garden furniture. Clematis is the speciality here and the nursery stock also includes climbers, roses, shrubs, perennials and trees. There is an interesting hedge demonstration garden. Advisory service; delivery; gift vouchers.

Open all year daily, Mon–Sat 8.30–5.30, Sun & BH 10–5.30.

P ⊟ wc

Codicote

Hertfordshire   Map 4 TL21

JACKMANS GARDEN CENTRE
High St ☎ Stevenage (0438) 820433

A very attractive garden centre offering a good range of indoor and outdoor plants and specialising in clematis. Garden furniture; swimming pools; cold water fish; adventure play area; houseplants; landscaping service; advisory service; delivery; gift vouchers; discounts.

Open all year daily (ex Xmas and New Year) 9–5.

P ⊟ ᵫ (wc) wc

Colchester

Essex   **Map 5 TM02**

BY-PASS NURSERIES
Ipswich Rd Roundabout ☎ (0206) 865500

Flowering houseplants, primroses, geraniums, fuchsias and F1 hybrid bedding plants are amongst the plants available here. Demonstration gardens include a large detached house garden, a cottage garden, a patio garden, a conifer garden, a vegetable garden and a wild garden. There is also a large selection of conservatories on sale and other attractions include an aquatic, tropical fish and pet centre. Advisory service; delivery; gift vouchers; discounts.

Open all year daily Mon–Sat 8.30–5.30, Sun 10–5.

P 🚽 *wc*

W & G GARDEN CENTRE
Cowdray Av ☎ (0206) 571212

This large centre occupies a 4½-acre site, part of which is devoted to display gardens with water features and a wide range of trees and shrubs. The main building has large display areas for garden sundries, machinery and furniture and there is a 100′ × 30′ greenhouse for houseplants, specimen and unusual plants, silk flowers and ceramics. Children's play area. Advisory service; delivery; gift vouchers.

Open daily weekdays 9–5.30, Sun 10–5.

P 🚽 ♿ *wc*

Congleton

Cheshire   **Map 7 SJ86**

ASTBURY MEADOW GARDEN CENTRE
Newcastle Rd, Astbury ☎ (0260) 276466

A wide range of plants is available here including trees, shrubs, fuchsias, alpines, roses, heathers, bedding plants and houseplants. Part of the garden centre is planted to provide a spring display. There is a full range of garden supplies including paving, walling, terracotta pots and machinery. →

Bossons display artwork and wildlife figures. Advisory service; mail order; delivery; gift vouchers.

Open daily (ex 25 & 26 Dec & 1 Jan) 9–6 summer; 9–5 winter.

P ᗺ wc

Cotebrook
Cheshire   **Map 7 SJ56**
JARDINERIE
Forest Rd ☎ Little Budworth (0829 21) 433

Large garden centre offering a comprehensive range of shrubs, plants, conifers, trees, garden sundries and buildings. Bulb festivals, flower arranging displays and craft fairs are also held here. Houseplants; landscaping; advisory service; mail order; delivery; gift vouchers; discounts.

Open all year daily Mar–Sep 9–6 (9pm Thu–Sat); Oct–Feb 9–5.

P ᗺ wc

Crawley
West Sussex   **Map 4 TQ23**
CHEALS GARDEN CENTRE
Horsham Rd ☎ (0293) 22101

Medium-sized centre with a compact layout, including demonstration borders of interesting flowering and foliage shrubs. Good range of all types of hardy plants, houseplants and gardening equipment. Tropical and cold water fish; pet shop; advisory service; delivery; gift vouchers.

Open all year daily. Mar–Oct Mon–Sat 9–6, Sun & BH 10–6; Nov–Feb Mon–Sat 9–5, Sun & BH 10–5.

P wc

Croydon
Surrey   **Map 4 TQ36**
ROCKINGHAMS GARDEN CENTRE
Purley Way ☎ 01-688 5117

Good range of outdoor and indoor plants including shrubs and fruit trees. Also artificial flowers, garden equipment, terracotta pots and pet food. There is an aquatic section, paving stones and a lawnmower

department. Camping supplies, pets corner (including snakes) and play area. Landscaping; advisory service; delivery; gift vouchers; discounts.

Open all year Summer Mon–Fri 9–8, Sat & Sun 9–6; winter Mon–Sun 9–5.30. Closed BH & Xmas.

P ᗺ wc

Darlington
Co Durham   **Map 8 NZ21**
STRIKES GARDEN CENTRE
299 Woodlands Rd, Cockerton
☎ (0325) 468474

A town garden centre offering a wide range of plants including trees, shrubs, climbers, roses, bedding plants, heathers and indoor plants, as well as gardening equipment and gift products. Advisory service; delivery; gift vouchers.

Open all year daily, Mon–Sat 9–6 (7 in spring), Sun 10–6 (5 in winter).

P ᗺ

Dronfield
Derbyshire   **Map 8 SK37**
FERNDALE NURSERY AND GARDEN CENTRE
Dyche Lane, Coal Aston ☎ (0246) 412763

Good range of plants available including conifers, heathers, roses, shrubs, bedding plants, alpines and houseplants. Also greenhouses, garden tools and furniture. Tropical and cold-water fish. Advisory service; mail order; delivery; discounts.

Open all year (ex 1 Jan) 9–6.

P wc

Eaglescliffe
Cleveland   **Map 8 NZ41**
STRIKES GARDEN CENTRE
Urlay Nook Rd (on A67, Teeside Airport Rd, ½m from Yarm High St)
☎ (0642) 780481

Garden centre has comprehensive range of gardening and gift products while the plants available include trees, shrubs, climbers, roses, bedding plants, heathers and indoor plants. Visitors can also see the glasshouse nursery unit where the indoor and bedding plants are raised. Advisory service; delivery; gift vouchers.

Open all year daily Mon–Sat 9–6 (7 in spring); Sun 10–6 (5 in winter).

P ⌂

Enfield

Gt London   Map 4 TQ39

WOLDEN GARDEN CENTRE
Cattlegate Rd, Crews Hill ☎ 01-363 7003

Compact, family-run garden centre with full range of alpine, perennial and bedding plants; large stocks of conifers, shrubs and trees are set out in nursery display beds, and there are all-year round stocks of container-grown roses. There is a good selection of houseplants, including cacti and air plants. Advisory service; delivery; gift vouchers.

Open all year daily, 8.30–5.30 (closes at 5 Sat & Sun).

P ⌂

Exeter

Devon   Map 3 SX99

CLYST GARDEN CENTRE
(3m from Exeter on Sidmouth Rd)

A branch of St Bridget Nurseries (see next entry) with part of the site franchised to Country Garden Patio Centres, who have good stocks of garden stone, paving, walling

and buildings. There are also pools, aquatic plants and fish for sale. Delivery.

Open all year daily (ex 25 & 26 Dec & 1 Jan) Mon–Sat 8–5, Sun 10–4.30; Patio Centre open Mon–Sat 9–5, Sun 10–4.30 (closed Xmas period).

P wc

ST BRIDGET NURSERIES AND GARDEN CENTRE
Old Rydon Lane
☎ Topsham (039 287) 3672/3/4

Very large nursery producing nearly 90% of the plants, trees and shrubs for sale. At various times of the year parts of the nursery are open to visitors, otherwise it is the garden centre only which is open, offering a comprehensive array of plants and equipment. Demonstration gardens include a pond and borders and there is a children's playground. Houseplants; landscaping; advisory service; mail order; delivery; gift vouchers; discounts.

Open all year daily (ex 25 & 26 Dec and 1 Jan). Mon–Sat 8–5, Sun 10–4.30.

P wc

Failsworth

Lancashire   Map 7 SD90

DAISY NOOK GARDEN CENTRE
Daisy Nook ☎ 061-681 4245

This garden centre specialises in dwarf conifers and herbaceous plants. Landscaping; advisory service; delivery; gift vouchers.

Open all year daily, Mon–Fri 9–8, Sat & Sun 9–5.

P ♿ *(wc) wc*

Farnham

Surrey   Map 4 SU84

BADSHOT LEA GARDEN CENTRE
(on A324) ☎ *Aldershot (0252) 333666*

An extensive showpiece garden centre, renowned for the variety and quantity of gardening goods. Large outdoor plant area includes demonstration beds and there are lots of indoor plants to choose from. Garden and floral sundries, paving, machinery (including workshop with spare parts), furniture and barbecues are all available as well as cold-water and tropical fish. Advisory service; delivery; gift vouchers; discounts.

Open all year daily Mon–Fri 9–5.30, Sat & Sun 9.30–5.30.

P ⊟ ㅊ *(wc) wc*

FOREST LODGE GARDEN CENTRE
Holt Pound ☎ *Bentley (0420) 23275*

This extensive family-run garden centre occupies 6½ acres of beautifully landscaped grounds including demonstration gardens, a large pool and a rockery. A comprehensive range of plants is available as well as house plants, garden furniture and ornaments, tools and sundries, barbecues, water gardening, dried flowers, paving, fencing etc. Advisory service; delivery; gift vouchers; discounts.

Open all year daily Mon–Sat 8.30–5.30, Sun & BH 9–5.30.

P ⊟ *(licensed)* ㅊ *(wc) wc*

Ferndown

Dorset   Map 4 SU00

HASKINS GARDEN CENTRE
Ringwood Rd, Tricketts Cross
☎ *(0202) 872282*

Large garden centre with a wide range of products including gardening accessories, furniture, barbecues, tubs, urns and gift items. The selection of plants include a number of unusual species and water gardening is another speciality (including cold-water fish). Advisory service; delivery; gift vouchers.

Open all year daily until 6; open until 8 on Wed from Apr–Sep.

P ⊟ ㅊ *(wc) wc*

Frilford

Oxfordshire   Map 4 SU49

MILLETS FARM GARDEN CENTRE
Kingston Rd ☎ *(0865) 391923*

This garden centre is arranged around a rustic-style barn and includes a selection of hardy shrubs, trees, alpines, conifers and heathers. Also indoor plants, furniture, a wide range of sundries and a book shop. 'Pick-your-own' fruit and vegetables when available. Advisory service; mail order; delivery.

Open all year daily (ex 25 & 26 Dec); Summer 9–6; winter 9–5.

P ⊟ *wc*

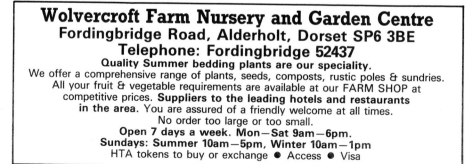

Gaerwen

Anglesey, Gwynedd   Map 6 SH47

HOLLAND ARMS GARDEN CENTRE

☎ (024 877) 655

Large stocks of a variety of plants are always available here and there are a number of special seasonal displays, demonstrations (including barbecues), and a bulb festival. Houseplants are also available. Advisory service; delivery; gift vouchers.

Open all year daily (ex 25 & 26 Dec), Mon–Sat 9–5.30, Sun & BH 10–5.

P ⏛ wc

Glasgow

Strathclyde *Lanarkshire*   Map 11 NS56

ROUKEN GLEN GARDEN CENTRE

Rouken Glen Rd, Giffnock ☎ 041-620 0566

A large garden centre catering for all gardener's requirements and specialising in houseplants. There is a comprehensive range of both indoor and outdoor plants as well as gardening equipment. Also Eastwood Butterfly Kingdom with free flying butterflies in tropical gardens. Advisory service; delivery; gift vouchers; discounts.

Open all year daily 9–7.30.

P ⏛ ḁ (wc) wc

Hibiscus syriacus

Glazebury

Cheshire   Map 7 SJ69

BENTS NURSERIES AND GARDEN CENTRE

Warrington Rd ☎ (0942) 671028

Specialising in trees, shrubs and herbs, this garden centre also has a good range of other plants, including perennials, annuals, rock plants and houseplants. Demonstration gardens include a rockery and water garden. There is also an aquarium, and an aviary, 3-acre lake with ducks and geese, steam railway and a play area.

Open all year daily (ex 25 & 26 Dec) Mon–Sat 9–5; Sun 9.30–5.

P ⏛ wc

Godstone

Surrey   Map 5 TQ35

KNIGHTS GARDEN CENTRE

Naggs Hall Nursery, Oxted Rd
☎ (0883) 842275

Family-run garden centre which has been landscaped with lawns and various planted borders to give ideas for customer's gardens. Wide range of hardy plants, arranged according to the position or soil they prefer. I.G.C.A. award for best Houseplant House in the south-east. Range of sundries includes dried and silk flowers, garden furniture, barbecues and fencing. Advisory service; delivery; gift vouchers.

Open all year daily, Mon–Sat 8–5.30, Sun & BH 9–5. During winter closes at 5 on Sat.

P wc

Grays

Essex   Map 5 TQ67

ORCHARD GARDEN CENTRE

Chadwell Rd
☎ Grays Thurrock (0375) 372195

Long-established garden centre/nursery in pleasant residential area. There is a comprehensive range of houseplants and large displays of conifers, climbers, trees and shrubs. Also show areas for greenhouses and conservatories. Landscaping; advisory service; delivery; gift vouchers.

Open all year daily, Mon–Sat 9–5.30, Sun & BH 9.30–5.30.

P ⏛ wc

Great Shelford
Cambridgeshire   Map 5 TL45
SCOTSDALE NURSERY AND GARDEN CENTRE
120 Cambridge Rd
☎ Cambridge (0223) 842777

A very comprehensive garden centre with many years of experience, having previously been a nursery for wholesale cut flowers. Trees, shrubs and houseplants are available as well as garden sundries, paving, rockery stone, walling, furniture and sheds etc. Aquatic department includes pools, fish and aquariums and there is a pet shop. Garden Design Service; advisory service; delivery; gift vouchers.

Open all year daily summer 9–6, winter 9–5.30.

P ⏻ wc

Great Warley
Essex   Map 5 TQ59
WARLEY GARDEN CENTRE
Warley St
☎ Brentwood (0277) 221966 or 219344

These rose specialists, who celebrated their Silver Jubilee in 1986, stock an extensive range of roses and the rose fields are open to visitors during the flowering season. There are also demonstration borders of mature plants and hedges. Among the other plants offered for sale are herbs, herbaceous plants, alpines, house plants, bulbs, bedding plants etc. There is an aquatic section with plants and cold water fish. Garden design. Landscaping; advisory service; mail order; delivery; gift vouchers.

Open all year daily (ex Sun) Mon–Sat 9–5.30 (late opening Tue, Fri & Sat–closing time varies according to season).

P ⏻ wc

Philadelphus

Hagley
Hereford and Worcester   Map 7 5098
HURRANS GARDEN CENTRE
Kidderminster Rd South
☎ Kidderminster (0562) 700511

Approximately 200 species of shrubs, in addition to trees, conifers, fruit bushes, etc. are stocked, and there is also a wide range of house plants available at this 7-acre garden centre. Conifer, water, patio, 'front' and flower demonstration gardens. Also falconry centre, swimming pools and barbecue centre. Landscaping; advisory service; delivery; gift vouchers; discounts.

Open all year daily Mar–Sep Mon–Fri 9–8, Sat & Sun 9–6; Oct–Feb 9–5.

P ⏻ wc

Handcross
West Sussex   Map 4 TQ23
HANDCROSS GARDEN CENTRE
London Rd ☎ (0444) 400725

This large garden centre stocks a wide selection of plants, some displayed in demonstration gardens. They include shrubs, conifers, hardy plants and, for particularly sheltered gardens, palms. The 'Aquapet' department has an extensive range of small pets, birds and accessories as well as tropical and cold water fish and pond plants. Advisory service; delivery; gift vouchers.

Open all year daily 9–6 (5.30 in winter).

P wc

Harden
West Yorkshire   Map 7 SE03
STEPHEN H SMITH GARDEN CENTRE
Wilsden Road
☎ Cullingworth (0535) 274653

A 4¼-acre all-weather centre with wide range of plants, shrubs, herbs, roses and silk plants. There is also an extensive selection of garden furniture, pottery, lawnmowers and giftware. Pets corner; play area; advisory service; delivery; gift vouchers; discounts.

Open daily (ex 25 & 26 Dec) summer 9–6 (9–8 Apr–Jun); winter 9–5.30 (9–8 Fri in Dec).

P ⏻ wc

Haresfield

Gloucestershire   Map 3 SO81

JARDINERIE
Bath Road ☎ Gloucester (0452) 721081

A compact garden centre offering a wide range of shrubs, alpines, heathers, seasonal plants, bulbs and a good variety of house-plants. Also available is a high quality range of garden sheds, conservatories and green-houses. Flower arranging and Craft Fayres. Landscaping; advisory service; mail order; delivery; gift vouchers; discounts.

Open all year daily Mar–Sep 8.30–6 (Thu–Sat 8.30–9); Oct–Feb 9–5.

P ⌷ wc

Harmondsworth

Middlesex   Map 4 TQ07

HURRANS GARDEN CENTRE
Holloway Ln ☎ 01-897 6075

Large centre with full range of shrubs laid out on a ten-bed system i.e. according to their uses and planting sites, such as seasons, tubs, difficult places, labour saving and year-round interest. Extensive range of house-plants including air-plants, carnivorous plants and flowering varieties. Full range of garden sundries, furniture, barbecues and tools. Aquatic section. Advisory service; mail order; delivery; gift vouchers; discounts.

Open all year (ex 25 & 26 Dec) Mar–Sep Mon–Fri 9–8, Sat & Sun 9–6; Oct–Feb daily 9–5.

P wc

Hermitage

Berkshire   Map 4 SU57

FAIRFIELD NURSERIES
☎ Newbury (0635) 200442

A ten-acre, nursery, garden centre and show gardens with comprehensive range of top quality trees, shrubs, roses, conifers, herba-ceous, alpine and herb plants and fruit trees. Large undercover display of garden sundries, furniture and ornaments. Patio centre, green-house and garden buildings. Advisory service; delivery; gift vouchers; discounts.

Open all year daily (ex Xmas & New Year).

P ⌷ wc

Hersham

Surrey   Map 4 TQ16

SQUIRE'S GARDEN CENTRE
Burwood Rd
☎ Walton-on-Thames (0932) 247579

Unique garden centre created in Victorian farm complex. The coach house is used for seasonal displays of garden furniture. Old stables house the garden sundries department with bulbs, fertilizers and tools. The yard has a large display of trees and shrubs. There are landscaped gardens and a houseplant shop. Landscaping; advisory service; delivery; gift vouchers. Lectures and demonstrations throughout year.

Open all year daily summer 9–6; winter 8.30–5.30.

P wc

High Wycombe

Buckinghamshire   Map 4 SU89

BOOKER GARDEN CENTRE
Clay Ln, Booker ☎ (0494) 33945

Garden centre with wide range of plants, trees and shrubs including fuchsias, conifers, roses, heathers, annuals and perennials. Aquatic centre with ponds and fish. House plants; advisory service; delivery; gift vouchers; discounts.

Open all year daily (ex 25–26 Dec & 1 Jan) 8.30–6 (5.30 winter).

P ⌷ wc

Horncastle

Lincolnshire   Map 8 TF26

CROWDERS GARDEN CENTRE
Lincoln Rd ☎ (06582) 7686

Interesting centre with large tree and shrub area offering a wide range of container grown stock, the majority of which is from their own nursery. Extensive selection of al-pines, heathers and herbaceous plants as well as garden ornaments, furniture and bar-becues. Houseplants; landscaping; advisory service; delivery; gift vouchers.

Open all year daily (ex Xmas & New Year) 8.30–5.30.

P ⌷ wc

Huddersfield

West Yorkshire   Map 7 SE11

HAMPSONS GARDEN CENTRE
Long Ln, Moldgreen
☎ *(0484) 23519 or 29159*

Award-winning garden centre with 10,000 sq ft of indoor houseplants, Silks Floral Art and Garden Furniture showrooms and garden equipment displays. Large outdoor demonstration area displays conservatories and garden-room extensions. There is a wide range of both indoor and outdoor plants including alpine rockery plants, roses and dwarf conifers. 'Garden Centre of the Year' 1983, 1984, 1986. Advisory service; delivery; gift vouchers.

Open all year daily 9–8 (5.30 autumn & winter).

P ☕ wc

Ivybridge

Devon   Map 2 SX65

ENDSLEIGH GARDEN CENTRE
☎ *Plymouth (0752) 892254*

An eight-acre site with a large outdoor plant sales area with a comprehensive range of all plants. Specialist departments include garden construction; machinery; aquatics and swimming pools. Landscaping; advisory service; delivery; gift vouchers.

Open all year daily Mon–Sat 9–5 (6 in summer), Sun 10–5.

P ☕ ♿ (wc)

Kelso

Borders *Roxburghshire*   Map 12 NT73

MAYFIELD GARDEN CENTRE
☎ *(0573) 24124*

Situated beside the River Tweed, the garden centre stocks a very comprehensive range of all garden plants and sundries including lawnmowers and powered garden equipment. Specialists in exhibition onions. Houseplants; advisory service; mail order; delivery; gift vouchers.

Open all year daily Mon–Fri 8.30–5, Sat, Sun & BH 9–5.

P ☕ wc

Kendal

Cumbria   Map 7 SD59

WEBBS GARDEN CENTRE
Burnside Rd ☎ *(0539) 20068*

Home of the 'original Webbs wonder lettuce', the centre has a large verandah area showing garden plants. Specialises in trees and shrubs, with fine shrub and tree borders on show. Silk flowers and plants; patio furniture. House plants; landscaping; delivery; gift vouchers; discounts.

Open all year daily Mon–Sat 8.30–5.15, Sun 11–5.

P ☕ wc

Kessingland

Suffolk   Map 5 TM58

ASHLEY NURSERIES GARDEN CENTRE
London Rd ☎ *Lowestoft (0502) 740264*

Centre with a large selection of shrubs, conifers, climbers, heathers, alpines and aquatics. Specialises in home-grown shrubs and conifers. Wide range of greenhouses, conservatories, summerhouses and sheds on show. Demonstration rock, alpine and pool gardens. Houseplants; advisory service; delivery; gift vouchers; discounts.

Open all year daily summer Mon–Sat 9–5.30 (5 winter) Sun 10–5.30 (5 winter).

P ☕ wc

Keynsham

Avon   Map 3 ST66

HURRANS GARDEN CENTRE
Hicks Gate ☎ *Bristol (0272) 778945*

Centre with three styled and landscaped gardens displaying a comprehensive range of shrubs, bedding plants, conifers and lawns. Also on show are roses, fuchsias, geraniums, garden furniture, tools and aquatic section. On site there are also a potter, an artist and a glass engraver. Houseplants; landscaping; advisory service; delivery; gift vouchers; discounts.

Open all year daily Mar–Sep 9–8 (5 winter) Sun 9–6 (5 winter).

P ☕ wc

Kirby Cross
Essex   Map 5 TM22

FRINTON ROAD NURSERIES
☎ *Frinton-on-Sea (02556) 4838*

Nursery and garden centre, offering a wide range of plants and shrubs.

Open all year Mon–Sat 8.30–5.30.

Knaresborough
North Yorkshire   Map 8 SE35

STRIKES GARDEN CENTRE
York Rd ☎ *Harrogate (0423) 865351*

A small garden centre whose stock includes trees, conifers, shrubs, climbers, roses, bedding plants, heathers and indoor plants. Houseplants; advisory service; delivery; gift vouchers.

Open all year daily Mon–Sat 9–6 (7 in spring) Sun 10–6 (5 in winter).

P ⌂

See advertisement on p.137.

Knutsford
Cheshire   Map 7 SJ77

THE NURSERIES & GARDEN CENTRE
Chelford Rd ☎ *(0565) 4281*

A well-established centre which offers a wide range of trees, shrubs, conifers, herbaceous and alpine plants, bedding and houseplants. Also available are garden sundries such as furniture, ornaments and statuary. Landscaping; advisory service; mail order; delivery; gift vouchers; discounts.

Open all year daily (ex Xmas) Mon–Sat 8.30–5, Sun & BH's 10–5.

P ⌂ *wc*

Lacock
Wiltshire   Map 3 ST96

WHITEHALL GARDEN CENTRE
☎ *(024973) 204*

This garden centre offers a wide range of quality plants for the garden, plus a specialist area for houseplants. Two acres of landscaped garden, aquatic section and large selection of stoneware. Children's play area; landscaping; advisory service; delivery; gift vouchers.

Open all year daily (ex Xmas) Mon–Sat 9–5, Sun 10–5.

P ⌂ *wc*

Leamington Spa
Warwickshire   Map 4 SP36

CLOWS GARDEN CENTRE
Myton Rd (on A425 midway between Leamington Spa and Warwick)
☎ *(0926) 881122*

A modern garden centre offering a wide range of container-grown plants including alpines, heathers, herbs, shrubs, roses, trees and fruit. Large cold water fish department open throughout the summer. Comprehensive selection of houseplants with specimen plants for commercial premises. Garden sundries; seasonal bulbs; advisory service; delivery; gift vouchers.

Open all year daily (ex 25 & 26 Dec & 1 Jan) Mon–Sat 8.30–5.30 Sun 9–5.30 (5pm in winter).

P ⌂ *wc*

Directory continues on page 153.

At Cramphorns you'll find everything you need for the garden. After all, we're Britain's biggest chain of specialist garden centres—and a whole lot more.

CRAMPHORNS
We're full of bright ideas

Bring the family and pick up some bright ideas at the Cramphorns Garden Centre near you.

Bromley, Oakley Road, Keston Mark
Bury St Edmunds, Rougham Road
Chelmsford, Cuton Flyover, Springfield
East Grinstead, Copthorne Road, Felbridge

Enfield, Cattlegate Road, Crews Hill
Kettering, Northfield Avenue
Letchworth, Icknield Way West
Milton Keynes, Secklow Gate

Rayleigh, Eastwood Road
Sudbury, Newton Road
Wheatley, Old London Road
Witham, Maldon Road

Mini Garden Centres: **Brentwood, Colchester** (Fiveways), **Southend** (at Keddies).
We've many high street shops too.

Frost Garden Centre at Woburn Sands.

LET'S VISIT A GARDEN CENTRE

By Jim Wilson

Garden centre visiting is enjoyed by keen gardeners and hesitant garden-owners hoping to improve, and by many who merely want to browse and relax.

Ever since the first garden centres evolved from traditional nurseries in the mid '50s car parks have been as important as selling areas, and virtually every reputable centre today offers free parking adjacent to the entrance.

Weekends are the busiest times with Sunday the day of leisurely family browsing, except in the few cases where Sunday trading laws prevent centres from opening or restrict sales to plants only. It is wise to make a phone call to unfamiliar centres on your itinerary and check their trading hours.

If you have a choice, avoid weekends if you want personal attention and serious discussion about garden planning and plants. Staff on duty will help but they cannot give all the time they'd like when hundreds of visitors are milling around seeking the experts. Mid-week is a good time to visit, and specialists will be able to help with your problems.

Monday during the spring rush often reflects the frantic buying at the weekend. Plant beds are depleted and shelves are half-empty, but replenishing is usually swift. If you want maximum choice of plants, leave your visit to later in the week.

Many garden centres are situated in tourist areas and have geared their product range to appeal to visitors. Gifts, honeys and jams, games and crafts are often as prevalent as alpines, roses and busy lizzies, and the best centres have tearoom facilities and toilets. Nearer large towns, garden centres offer a more serious selection of gardening and leisure products and services and often you will find greenhouses and sheds, aquatics and construction materials with a delivery service.

There are probably 900 garden centres, of sorts, in the U.K. of which around 150 are members of International Garden Centre (British Group) Ltd., IGC — the cream of the industry offering service, guaranteed plants, and launching seasonal promotions to highlight gardening activities. These IGC members, all independent firms, aim to maintain quality standards by annual inspections. Most IGC centres and many others have catering or refreshment facilities. Some have picnic areas where you can relax in pleasant surroundings. The trend is towards increasing leisure pursuits and a number of centres have aviaries, pets and small animals, butterfly houses and elaborate aquariums to amuse and educate the children.

For the more serious gardener, display gardens provide plenty of ideas on design, materials for landscaping, plant associations and cost. Indoor plants for different room environments are highlighted in practical displays or via labels and illustrations. Remember that with container-grown plants you can plant at any time of the year, but autumn is the best time for many plants — and spring the most comfortable for the planters.

Of course some centres are more interesting than others, according to personal choice. Visit a number of centres in your area or call on others when on holiday or travelling around, and find for yourself where the best service and friendliest welcome awaits.

Jim Wilson is a horticultural journalist. As well as contributing to journals such as *Nurserymen and Garden Centres*, he also tutors trainee garden centre employees. He has been closely involved with garden centres since the beginning of their development and is a regular judge for IGC awards.

Geranium and Fuchsia display at Bridgmere Garden World.

146

DECORATIVE VEGETABLES
By Peter Harlington

Vegetable gardens have been cultivated since earliest times, but until the 18th century they were maintained for food production. In the 19th century, as new vegetables were introduced and the eating of these became fashionable, a more varied diet ensued. With this, competition became rife between the country houses for the earliest and largest range of produce. Generally vegetable gardens were square, laid out very formally and surrounded by walls clad in trained fruit. A central feature, such as a well or statue, was approached by a pathway flanked by large herbaceous borders. Parsley, lavender and alpine strawberries were used as added decoration to edge other pathways.

Modern gardens tend to be small, easily managed units and there is little room for the traditional vegetable garden to fit into the design, but this need not be the case. There is nothing more dynamic in shape and form than many of the most common vegetable plants — the unique shape of brussels sprouts, the feathery leaves of carrots or the large elephant ears of rhubarb leaves. More unusual vegetables include ornamental kales, the silver-grey foliage of globe artichokes and the edible flowers, such as nasturtiums, hemercocallis and hollyhocks.

Few gardens have one or two acres to spare, but in most there is room for a border or an island bed. Vegetables are not difficult to grow, but require full sun, ideally facing south to south-east with an easily accessible water supply.

Brassica Oleracea — a decorative cabbage.

Once the site is decided, you must plan the vegetables to grow, considering your soil type and personal taste. If you have clay soil, avoid carrots, parsnips and peas, but grow brassicas. On sandy soils carrots and parsnips respond well, but as these soils tend to dry out, celery, cauliflowers and calabrese might not be as successful. In peaty or organic soils grow celery, celeriac, peas or parsnips, but avoid brussels sprouts. Early crops may be a problem in silty soils due to surface capping. For ideas on vegetables that will do well on your soil, ascertain what vegetables grow well locally.

The Globe artichoke.

A circular island bed makes the best use of a small area, a bed 10′ (3.06m) in diameter, accommodates a simple hexagon: the area in the middle is ideal for taller subjects, the points of the hexagon for mid-height items, the remaining circumferal plots for low-growing crops. By following these rules a mound of colour is created and the vegetables are shown off to their best advantage.

Variegated Nasturums
— not only attractive but also edible.

If the bed is to be grown for more than one year, a rotational system must be followed to make full use of the soil, thus reducing the risks of a possible build-up of pest and diseases. A three-year system is best, so consider your hexagon as two overlapping triangles. In the first year grow brassicas (*cabbage, Kohl Rabi*) in the triangle points I, the roots (*carrots, parsnips, scorzonera etc*) in triangle II. Peas, beans, walking stick kale, fennel, globe artichokes or cardoons may be grown successfully as they do not require rotating and make good central feature plants.

Swap triangles in the second year, growing brassicas where the roots were and vice versa. In the third year either grow root crops on the old brassica plot and legumes where the roots were, giving the whole plot a rest from brassicas for that year OR change the orientation of the hexagon.

An easier method is to have three island beds growing one type of vegetable on each, ie ROOTS, LEGUMES and BRASSICAS, then following a straightforward crop rotation system.

Remember when making your plans the times of year the vegetables reach maturity for their best effect.

Peter Harlington is assistant to the Vegetable Trials Supervisor at the Royal Horticultural Society's Gardens at Wisley.

HOME & GARDEN

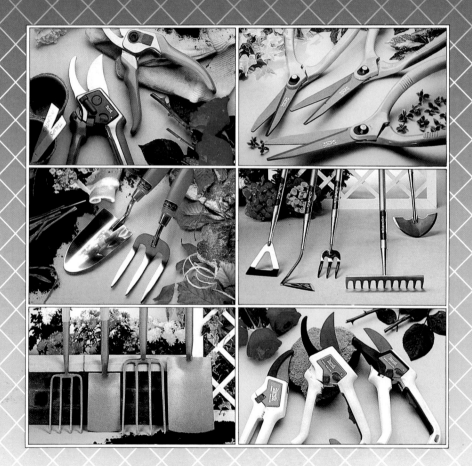

A range of garden tools
worthy of our name

→ From page 143.

Lechlade

Gloucestershire   **Map 4 SU29**

LECHLADE GARDEN AND FUCHSIA CENTRE

Fairford Rd ☎ Faringdon (0367) 52372

Specialising mainly in fuchsias with the indoor garden open between May and Dec. There is also a display of annuals, perennials, bedding plants, potted plants and houseplants, garden furniture, tools and sheds. Sheepskin and woollen shop. Landscaping; advisory service; mail order; delivery; gift vouchers.

Open all year daily (ex 25-26 Dec & 1 Jan), Mon–Sat 9-5.30, Sun 10-5.

P wc

Leeds

West Yorkshire   **Map 8 SE33**

STRIKES GARDEN CENTRE

Red Hall Ln, Wellington Hill
☎ (0532) 657839

Recently modernized to a high standard with large greenhouses containing the stock for sale. Comprehensive range including trees, conifers, shrubs, climbers, roses, bedding plants, heathers and indoor plants. Advisory service; delivery; gift vouchers.

Open all year daily Mon–Sat 9-6 (7 in spring) Sun 10-6 (5 in winter).

P

See advertisement on p.137.

STRIKES GARDEN CENTRE

Selby Rd (on A63 near Garforth)
☎ (0532) 862981

This garden centre has a wide range of gardening and gift products. Plants include trees, shrubs, climbers, roses, bedding plants, heathers and houseplants. Advisory service; delivery; gift vouchers.

Open all year daily Mon–Sat 9-6 (7 in spring), Sun 10-6 (5 in winter).

P

See advertisement on p.137.

Lincoln

Lincolnshire   **Map 8 SK97**

PENNEL & SONS LTD

Newark Rd, South Hykeham
☎ (0522) 682088

An extensive range of bedding plants, shrubs, trees, conifers and perennials. A demonstration bed, laid out to look like a town garden, gives ideas on plants etc. Children's play area; houseplants; advisory service; mail order; delivery.

Open all year daily (ex Xmas & New Year) 8.30-5.30 (opens at 9 Sun & BH).

wc

Liss

Hampshire   **Map 4 SU72**

HILLIER GARDEN CENTRE

Bowyers Nursery, Farnham Rd
☎ (0730) 892196

Landscaped garden centre specialising in hardy shrubs and bonsai. Also on sale are trees, bedding plants, houseplants, garden furniture, stoneware, fencing, paving and greenhouses. There is a pet shop which includes fish and general pet requirements. Advisory service; mail order; delivery.

Open all year daily Mon–Sat 9-5.30, Sun 10-5.30.

P wc

Liverpool

Merseyside   **Map 7 SJ39**

GATEACRE GARDEN CENTRE

(Near Woolton) ☎ 051-428 6556

Demonstration gardens include bedding layouts and seasonal plunge bed displays, while items for sale include a very large range of shrubs, trees, fruit, roses, perennials, alpines, heathers and bulbs. Comprehensive range of houseplants, pottery and giftware. Silk and dried flowers are made into arrangements by a resident florist, who will plant mixed bowls of houseplants to order. Delivery; gift vouchers.

Open all year daily Mon–Sat 9-5.30 (5 in winter; 7pm Mon–Fri Apr–Jun) Sun & BH 10-4.30.

P wc

London

Gt London   Map 4 TQ37

THE GARDEN CENTRE AT ALEXANDRA PALACE
N22 ☎ 01-444 2555

This extensive and very interesting garden centre has display gardens including a Wildlife Conservation Garden, planted and maintained by the British Trust for Conservation volunteers. A very wide range of hardy plants is offered, some of which are very rare varieties. The centre specialises in plants for the town gardener including climbers, plants for shade, plants for instant effect and old-fashioned shrub roses — all of which are displayed in garden-like settings. Houseplants; landscaping; advisory service; delivery; gift vouchers; discounts.

Open all year daily Mon-Fri 9.30-5.30, Sat 9.30-6, Sun & BH 10-6.

P 🛒 wc

THE CHELSEA GARDENER
125 Sydney St, Kings Rd, SW3
☎ 01-352 5656

Demonstration gardens include two typical London town gardens and three roof gardens. The centre specialises in large specimen indoor and outdoor plants and unusual plants. A range of high quality garden furniture is available and there are good stocks of garden books. Landscaping; advisory service; delivery; gift vouchers; discounts.

Open all year daily 10.30-6 (5 Sun & BH).

P 🛒 ♿ (wc) wc

MILL HILL GARDEN CENTRE
Daws Lane NW7

Well-designed garden centre with a comprehensive range of trees, shrubs, conifers, climbers, herbs, perennials, fruit trees and bedding plants. Also a wide selection of items for the home and garden including furniture, barbecues, books and giftware. A new conservatory houses a collection of houseplants imported from Italy and an international range of conservatory furniture, whilst the exhibition hall has interesting seasonal displays. Landscaping; advisory service; delivery; gift vouchers.

Open all year daily.

P 🛒 ♿ (wc) wc

London Colney

Hertfordshire   Map 4 TL10

AYLETT NURSERIES
North Orbital Road (A405)
☎ Bowmansgreen (0727) 22255

Ayletts nurseries have been awarded many gold medals over the years for their dahlias. They also specialise in houseplants. There is a wide range of fuchsias, a comprehensive garden centre and a floristry department. Advisory service; delivery; gift vouchers.

Open all year daily (ex Xmas) 9-5.

P wc

Maidstone

Kent   Map 5 TQ75

NOTCUTTS GARDEN CENTRE
Newnham Court Farm, Bearsted Rd
☎ (0622) 39944

This garden centre has over 1500 plant varieties on show at any one time. Large areas, some covered, some open, are devoted to the culture of trees, shrubs and plants for sale. Garden sundries, furniture, buildings and machinery are also sold. Other attractions at the site include a pet centre, a floral centre, a farm shop and, in season, pick-your-own fruit. Houseplants; landscaping; advisory service; mail order; delivery; gift vouchers.

Open all year daily Mon-Sat 9-5.45, Sun 10-5.30.

P 🛒 wc
See advertisement on p. 168.

Mark Cross

East Sussex   Map 5 TQ53

HUGH PAGE (BEECHGLADE)
☎ Rotherfield (089 2851) 2828

In an attractive setting with views over the Sussex Downs, this centre offers a full range of plants, including many specimens. Specialists in conifers and heathers, there are also garden sheds, greenhouses and general garden sundries, garden furniture, barbecues, fencing and paving. Houseplants; advisory service; delivery; gift vouchers; discounts.

Open all year daily 9-5.

P wc

Marldon

Devon   Map 3 SX86

STYLE PARK GARDENS
Moles Ln ☎ (08047) 3056

A large range of trees and shrubs, most plants grown at the garden centre itself. There are demonstration beds, indoor pot plants, an aquatic section, greenhouse and conservatory display centres, sheds and summerhouses. Advisory service; delivery; gift vouchers.

Open all year daily Mon–Sat 9–5, (Sun 10–5).

P ⏏ & *(wc) wc*

Matlock

Derbyshire   Map 8 SK38

MATLOCK GARDEN WATERLIFE & PET CENTRE
Nottingham Rd ☎ (0629) 4221

A wide selection of plants with speciality departments of bonsai trees and water gardens. Demonstration beds all permanently planted with gardens and lawns, and there is a full range of garden sundries. Waterlife Centre and Tropical Aquarium. House plants; delivery; gift vouchers.

Open all year daily (ex 25 Dec–2 Jan), 10–5, (6 Mar–Sep).

P ⏏ *wc*

Menston

West Yorkshire   Map 7 SE14

WARDS GARDEN CENTRE
Burley Rd ☎ (0943) 74330

This garden centre offers a wide range of products to suit all your gardening needs. There is a comprehensive selection of trees, shrubs, bedding plants and bulbs. Rustic garden furniture. Bird tables and pottery. Houseplants; advisory service; delivery; gift vouchers.

Open all year daily, 8.30–5.30; Sat 8.30–5; Sun 10–5.

P *wc*

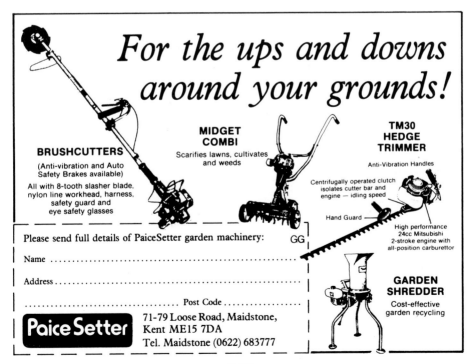

Middleton

Gt Manchester   Map 7 SD80

ALL-IN-ONE GARDEN CENTRE
Slattocks ☎ *Rochdale (0706) 32793*

Offers a wide range of houseplants, cacti, airplants, bonsai etc, plus an extensive nursery area with show gardens, conifers, and trees including fruit trees. Also the 'Adrian Bloom' all-year-round garden. Garden furniture, garden sundries, building products, fencing etc all also available here. Advisory service; delivery; gift vouchers.

Open all year daily Mon–Fri 8.30–8; Sat 8.30–6; Sun 10–6 (or dusk in winter).

P *wc*

Milford

Surrey   Map 4 SU94

THE SECRETT GARDEN CENTRE
Portsmouth Rd ☎ *Godalming (04868) 4553*

An 8-acre site, 3 acres of which is a show garden with lawns, shrub areas, trees, bulbs and a water garden. The garden centre specialises in houseplants and hardy outdoor plants. One of the main attractions is a Connoisseurs Corner. A complete range of garden sundries, furniture, pots, urns etc. A large 'pick your own', 30 acres in extent, and a farm shop. Children's play area; advisory service; delivery; gift vouchers; discounts.

Open all year daily (ex 25 & 26 Dec), Mon–Sat 9–5.30, Sun 10–5.

P ☐ *wc*

Milngavie

Strathclyde *Lanarkshire*   Map 11 NS57

DUNCANS OF MILNGAVIE
☎ *041-956 2377*

A wide selection of indoor and outdoor plants. Rock garden feature. There is also a full range of garden sundries. Large floristry department. Garden furniture; Xmas display from mid-Oct. Houseplants; advisory service; delivery; gift vouchers.

Open all year daily, 8.30–5.30 (10–5 Sun) ex Christmas & New Year.

P   *wc*

FINDLAY CLARK GARDEN CENTRE
Boclair Rd ☎ *Balmore (0360) 20721*

A large garden centre, with 6,000 sq.ft of covered outdoor plant areas and ½ acre of shrubs uncovered. An extensive greenhouse area contains pot plants and accessories. There is also an alpine rock garden, a water garden having three pools stocked with Koi carp and incorporating a number of waterfalls. Specialises in indoor and hardy plants. Garden buildings and greenhouses. Landscaping; advisory service; delivery; gift vouchers.

Open all year daily summer 9–9, Oct–Mar 9–6.

P ☐ ♿ *(wc) wc*

Morpeth

Northumberland   Map 12 NZ18

HEIGHLEY GATE NURSERY GARDEN CENTRE
☎ *(0670) 513416*

Large garden centre in attractive surroundings. A comprehensive range of plants, trees, shrubs, roses etc., water garden plants and equipment including pools. Greenhouses and conservatories, herbaceous plants laid out in demonstration beds with walling and pergola. Garden equipment and sundries. Floral art requisites and pottery. Produce for sale includes fruit and vegetables, eggs, goats milk and honey. Garden furniture and bird tables. Houseplants; children's play area; picnic area; advisory service; delivery; gift vouchers.

Open all year daily summer Mon–Fri 9–6 Sat & Sun 9.30–5; winter Mon–Fri 9–5 Sat & Sun 9.30–5.

P ☐ *wc*

Newcastle-upon-Tyne

Tyne and Wear   Map 12 NZ26

PETER BARRATT'S GARDEN CENTRE
Gosforth Park ☎ *Tyneside (091) 2365614*

A large garden centre stocking everything that the gardener needs to buy. Wide choice of pot plants, shrubs, alpines etc. Landscaped areas with paving and walling. Large display of conservatories. Tropical and cold water fish. Children's playground; advisory service; delivery; gift vouchers.

Open all year daily (ex 25 & 26 Dec & 1 Jan) 9–5.30.

P ⚘ wc

Newport

Gwent   Map 3 ST38

HURRANS GARDEN CENTRE
Catsash Road, Langstone
☎ *Llanwern (0633) 413355*

This recently opened garden centre has bedding plants, houseplants, trees, shrubs, roses, fuchsias, alpines, heathers, bulbs and seeds. Garden furniture and sheds are also sold. Advisory service; delivery; gift vouchers; discounts.

Open all year daily (ex 25 & 26 Dec) Mar–Sep Mon–Fri 9–8, Sat & Sun 9–6; Oct–Feb 9–5.

P ⚘ wc

Northallerton

North Yorkshire   Map 8 SE39

STRIKES GARDEN CENTRE
Boroughbridge Rd (A167) ☎ *(0609) 3694*

Plants stocked at this small garden centre include trees, conifers, shrubs, climbers, roses, bedding plants, heathers and indoor and foliage plants. A good range of gardening products and some giftware is also available. Advisory service; delivery; gift vouchers.

Open all year daily Mon–Sat 9–6 (7 in spring), Sun 10–6 (5 in winter).

P ⚘

See advertisement on p. 137.

Norwich

Norfolk   Map 5 TG20

NOTCUTTS GARDEN CENTRE
Daniels Rd ☎ *(0603) 53155*

A large selection of plants are on offer here and several demonstration beds are →

permanently planted. Extensive range of garden sundries and furniture. Aquatic area; pet shop; children's play area; houseplants; landscaping; advisory service; delivery; gift vouchers.

Open all year daily, Mon–Sat 8.30–5.30, Sun & BH 10–5.

P ☕ *wc*
See advertisement on p. 168.

SPROWSTON GARDEN CENTRE
Blue Boar Lane (off A1151) ☎ (0603) 412239

Set in a beautiful woodland setting, this centre has a large selection of trees, shrubs, fruit trees, conifers, heathers, roses, perennials, hedging plants, bulbs and seeds. Demonstration heather garden. Greenhouses, lawnmowers, aquatic supplies and gifts are also available. The centre has won the Ruxley Rose Trophy for the best houseplant department in a garden centre in the British Isles. Landscaping; advisory service; delivery; gift vouchers; discounts.

Open daily throughout year, Mon–Sat 8.30–5.30, Sun & BH 10.30–5.

P ☕ *wc*

Nottingham

Nottinghamshire **Map 8 SK53**

NOTTINGHAM GARDEN CENTRE
Clifton Ln, Wilford ☎ 815656

Occupying a 2–3 acre site, this garden centre has a full range of plants which include alpines, heathers and shrubs. There is a demonstration bed featuring a variety of conifers. Garden furniture and house plants are also on sale. Advisory service; delivery; gift vouchers.

Open all year daily (ex 25 & 26 Dec) 9–5.30 (6 summer; 8 Fri).

P ☕ *wc*

Orton Waterville

Cambridgeshire **Map 4 TL19**

NOTCUTTS GARDEN CENTRE
Oundle Rd ☎ (0733) 234600

A medium-sized garden centre at the entrance to Nene Park. The garden centre offers a wide choice of plants with a rock garden and water garden, as well as the usual range of garden sundries. Cold-water and tropical fish. There are also garden buildings, sheds, garages, swimming pools and a pet shop. Play area; houseplants; advisory service; delivery; gift vouchers.

Open all year daily, 8.30–5.30 (from 10 Sun & BH).

P ☕ *wc*
See advertisement on p. 168.

Otley

West Yorkshire **Map 8 SE24**

STEPHEN H SMITH GARDEN CENTRE AND NURSERIES
Pool Rd ☎ (0943) 462195

A large centre with an extensive range of garden sundries, including flowering/foliage houseplants and a good selection of plants for the garden. Also available are flags, fencing and garden buildings. Advisory service; delivery; gift vouchers.

Open all year daily 9–6.

P *wc*

Ottery St Mary

Devon **Map 3 SY19**

OTTER NURSERIES
Gosford Rd ☎ (040481) 3341

Winners of the IGC Garden Plant area 1986 it has an attractive indoor and covered sales area and large display beds with ideas for both the amateur and professional gardener. Also available are greenhouses, conservatories, rock and water features and walling and patio sales areas. Houseplants; landscaping; advisory service; delivery; gift vouchers.

Open all year daily (ex 25–26 Dec) Mon–Sat 8–5 Sun 9–5.

P ☕ *wc*

Owermoigne

Dorset **Map 3 SY78**

GALTON GARDEN CENTRE
☎ Warmwell (0305) 852324

A large garden centre with a wide range of attractions for all the family. Extensive choice of plants, pet shop, wholefood shop.

Play area; houseplants; delivery; gift vouchers; discounts.

Open all year daily Mar–Oct Mon–Sat 9–6 Sun 10–6; Nov–Feb Mon–Sat 9–5, Sun 10–5.

P ⊟ *wc*

Perivale
Gt London   Map 4 TQ18
BARRALETS GARDEN CENTRE
Western Ave, Perivale Ln ☎ *01-998 3905*

A large surburban centre with a comprehensive range of trees, shrubs, roses and bedding plants. Sundries include fencing, paving, walling and all the usual horticultural requisites. Houseplants; landscaping; advisory service; mail order; delivery; gift vouchers; discounts.

Open all year daily Mon–Sat 8.30–5.30 Sun 10–5.

P *wc*

Plymouth
Devon   Map 2 SX45
PLYMOUTH GARDEN CENTRE
Bowden Battery, Fort Austin Ave, Crownhill ☎ *(0752) 771820 or 703684*

Garden centre housed in an old fort and displaying many landscaped rockeries. It specialises in conifers and heathers and also available are greenhouses, sheds, fencing, ornaments and conservatories. Play area; houseplants, advisory service; delivery; gift vouchers; discounts.

Open all year daily Mon–Sat 8.30–5.30, Sun 10.30–5.

P ⊟ *wc*

Podington
Bedfordshire   Map 4 SP96
PODINGTON NURSERIES GARDEN CENTRE
High St ☎ *Wellingborough (0933) 53656*

Centre offering a wide range of plants, shrubs, conifers, alpines, and herbaceous plants. Garden sundries are also available, including furniture and pots. Dried and silk

flowers. Houseplants; advisory service; delivery; gift vouchers; discounts.

Open all year daily (ex Xmas) 9–6.30 (5.30 winter).

P ⊟ *wc*

Poppleton
North Yorkshire   Map 8 SE55
CHALLIS GARDEN CENTRE
(A59 Boroughbridge Rd)
☎*York (0904) 796161*

Large garden centre with full selection of trees, shrubs, pot plants, herbaceous and alpine plants. Garden furniture and barbecue displays and shop with all gardening accessories, tools and gift area. Water garden; play area; house plants; landscaping; advisory service; delivery; gift vouchers; discounts.

Open all year daily 9–6.

P ⊟ *wc*

Pulborough
West Sussex   Map 4 TQ01
CHEALS GARDEN AND LEISURE CENTRE
Stopham Road ☎ *(07982) 2981 or 2982*

Close to the River Arun, the centre offers a full range of plants, sundries, furniture, garden buildings, machinery, swimming pools and water gardening. Also available are fish, crafts, gifts and pet supplies. Play area; houseplants; landscaping; advisory service; delivery; gift vouchers.

Open all year daily Mon–Fri 8.30–5.30 Sat 9–5.30, Sun 10–5.30.

P ⊟ *wc*

Radyr
South Glamorgan   Map 3 ST18
TYNANT NURSERY
Morganstown ☎ *Cardiff (0222) 842017*

Fully stocked garden centre with shrubs, conifers, trees, alpines and herbaceous plants. Complete range of garden sundries including stoneware, garden sheds, greenhouses and fencing products. Houseplants; →

landscaping; advisory service; delivery; gift vouchers.

Open all year daily Mon–Sat 9–6 Sun 10–5.30.

P ⊟ wc

Rangemore
Staffordshire   **Map 7 SK12**

BYRKLEY PARK CENTRE
☎ *Barton-under-Needwood (028371) 6467*

Garden centre with wide range of facilities. Extensive collection of shrubs, trees, conifers, heathers and alpines arranged in a 'plants for a purpose' layout. Also available paving, fencing and stoneware. Craft workshops, farm animals, play area. Houseplants; landscaping; advisory service; delivery; gift vouchers.

Open all year daily, Apr–Aug 9–6 (9 pm Thu–Sat) Sep–Mar 9–5.

P ⊟ ♿ (wc)

Romsey
Hampshire   **Map 4 SU32**

HILLIER GARDEN CENTRE
Botley Road ☎ (0794) 513459

Offers a very wide range of hardy garden plants as well as a good selection of indoor and outdoor sundries. Houseplants; landscaping; advisory service; mail order; delivery; gift vouchers; discounts.

Open all year daily Mon–Sat & BH's 9–5.30, Sun 10–5.30.

P wc

Rugby
Warwickshire   **Map 4 SP57**

BERNHARD'S RUGBY GARDEN AND LEISURE CENTRE
Bilton Rd ☎ (0788) 811500

Fine centre with large selection of trees, shrubs, alpines and heathers — many grown in their own nurseries. Extensive range of pools, fountains, garden furniture, barbecues, greenhouses, conservatories and sheds. Gifts and books. Houseplants; landscaping; advisory service; mail order; delivery; gift vouchers; discounts.

Open all year daily Mon–Sat 9–6.30 Sun 9.30–6.

P ⊟ wc

St Albans
Hertfordshire   **Map 4 TL10**

NOTCUTTS GARDEN CENTRE
605 Hatfield Rd, Smallford
☎ *(0727) 64922 or 53224*

A good range of trees, shrubs, perennials, roses, climbing plants, conifers and heathers. Indoor plants, florist sundries and cut flowers. Shop with selection of sundries, chemicals, peats, landscape materials and garden furniture. Also available greenhouses, conservatories and sheds. Play area, advisory service; delivery; gift vouchers.

Open all year daily, Nov–Feb Mon–Sat 8.30–5, Sun & BH 10–5; Mar–Jun Mon–Sat 8.30–6, Sun & BH 10–5.30, Jul–Oct Mon–Sat 8.30–5.30, Sun & BH 10–5.30.

P wc

See advertisement on p. 168.

St Leonards-on-Sea
East Sussex   Map 5 TQ80

HASTINGS GARDEN CENTRE
Bexhill Rd ☎ Hastings (0424) 443414

Bedding plants, bulbs, houseplants, vegetables and a wide range of shrubs are amongst the plants on sale at this smallish garden centre. Garden furniture, fencing, tools, tubs, paving, ponds etc are also available. Demonstration gardens include pond and flower beds. Landscaping; advisory service; mail order; gift vouchers.

Open all year daily 9–6 (7.30 on Fri in summer).

P *wc*

Sandy
Bedfordshire   Map 4 TL14

BICKERDIKES GARDEN CENTRE
London Rd ☎ (0767) 80559

This 4-acre garden centre stocks all types of plants including houseplants and also has both formal and informal demonstration gardens. Children's play area. Landscaping; advisory service; delivery; gift vouchers.

Open daily throughout year 9–5.30.

P *wc*

Shepperton
Surrey   Map 4 TQ06

SQUIRE'S GARDEN CENTRE
Halliford Rd, Upper Halliford
☎ Sunbury-on-Thames (093 27) 84121

This garden centre is set within a 20-acre rose nursery. As well as roses, clematis, conifers, perennials and bedding plants are particular specialities. However, a full range of trees, shrubs and plants (including bulbs and house plants) is sold. Garden sundries, paving, furniture, fencing, etc., are available. Demonstration gardens include rockeries, lawns and rose beds. Also on the premises are a craft shop, mower shop and a tropical cold-water fish franchise. Landscaping; advisory service; delivery; gift vouchers. Squire's Annual Rose Show in June.

Open daily throughout year, summer 9–6, winter 8.30–5.30.

P *wc*

Sherfield-on-Loddon
Hampshire   Map 4 SU65

BAILEYS GARDEN CENTRE
Wildmoor Lane (A33)
☎ Basingstoke (0256) 882776

This centre offers a comprehensive range of trees and shrubs, specialising particularly in azaleas, rhododendrons and conifers. Houseplants are also sold and swimming pools, and there is a franchise for stone and paving. Landscaping; advisory service; delivery; gift vouchers.

Open all year daily 9–5.30.

P *wc*

Sidcup
Kent   Map 5 TQ47

RUXLEY MANOR GARDEN CENTRE
Maidstone Rd ☎ 01-300 0084/0900

This very large garden centre specialises in houseplants, though it also sells a full range of plants. Sheds, greenhouses, garden sundries, tropical and cold-water fish and swimming pools are also sold. Advisory service; delivery; gift vouchers.

Open all year daily (ex Aug BH) Mon–Sat 9–5.30 Sun 9–12.

P & *(wc) wc*

Helleborus argutifolius

Sittingbourne

Kent   Map 5 TQ96

EDEN PARK GARDEN CENTRE
Grove End, Tunstall
☎ *(0795) 71583/78108*

Shrubs, trees, roses, houseplants, bulbs and seeds are sold at this garden centre, where garden furniture, composts, sundries and pet and aquatic supplies are also available. Landscaping; advisory service; delivery; gift vouchers; discounts. Other attractions include a bird aviary and displays of leisure rooms, greenhouses, etc.

Open all year daily (ex 25 Dec) 9–5.30.

P ⊟ wc

Solihull

West Midlands   Map 7 SP17

NOTCUTTS GARDEN CENTRE
Stratford Rd, Shirley ☎ *021-744 4501*

This is the largest of the Notcutts garden centres and has an extensive range of plants, accessories and services. The plants stocked are based on the 2000 varieties listed in the Notcutts catalogue and include trees, shrubs, climbers, perennials, fruit trees and houseplants. Demonstration gardens include displays of water and climbing plants. Children's play area. Garages, conservatories and extensions are also on show. During 1987 the site is being redeveloped to improve facilities further, but the existing garden centre will continue trading throughout. Landscaping; advisory service; mail order; delivery; gift vouchers.

Open all year daily (ex 25–28 Dec) Mon–Sat 9–6 (5.30 winter), Sun & BH 10.30–6 (5.30 winter).

P ⊟ wc
See advertisement on p. 168.

Southampton

Hampshire   Map 4 SU41

SWAN GARDEN CENTRE
Gaters Hill ☎ *(0703) 472324*

Offering a wide selection of plants including conifers, bedding plants, fruit trees, heathers and shrubs. Full range of garden sundries and furniture. Farm shop. Houseplants; landscaping; advisory service; delivery; gift vouchers.

Open all year daily 9–5.30 (9.30 am Thur) (ex Xmas and New Year).

P ⊟ wc

South Ockenden

Essex   Map 5 TQ58

SOUTH OCKENDEN GARDEN CENTRE
South Rd ☎ *(0708) 853714*

This small, family-run garden centre sells a wide range of plants including many varieties of houseplants. There are two seasonal demonstration areas. Also available are lawn-mower sales and servicing, fish and pond plants, garden buildings and paving. Landscaping; advisory service; delivery; gift vouchers; discounts.

Open all year daily Mon–Sat 9–5, Sun & BH 10–5.

P ⊟ wc

Stevenage

Hertfordshire   **Map 4 TL22**

ROGER HARVEY GARDEN CENTRE

Bragbury Lane (A602 Stevenage to Hertford Road) ☎ *(0438) 811777*

A full range of hardy garden plants including trees, heathers, rockery plants and bulbs are sold at this garden centre. Houseplants are also stocked. Also available in and around the historic farm buildings at the site are garden sundries, machinery and buildings. A Pet's Corner, children's corner and underwater world are other attractions, and the centre has Saturday gardening demonstrations as well as other special events during the year. Landscaping; advisory service; gift vouchers.

Open all year daily 9-5.30 (9.30-5.30 Fri); Apr-Jun open until 8 on Thu & Fri.

P ⚲ *wc*

Stokesley

North Yorkshire   **Map 8 NZ50**

STRIKES GARDEN CENTRE

Meadowfields (at junction of A172 and B1365) ☎ *(0642) 710419*

The stock at this garden centre includes trees, conifers, shrubs, climbers, roses, bedding plants, heathers and indoor flowering and foliage plants. There is a large covered area for wet-weather shopping, and a wide range of gardening products and giftware. Advisory service; delivery; gift vouchers.

Open all year daily, Mon-Sat 9-6 (7 in spring) Sun 10-6 (5 in winter).

P ⚲
See advertisement on p. 137.

Stowmarket

Suffolk   **Map 5 TM05**

NAREY'S GARDEN CENTRE

Bury Rd (on A45 dual carriageway) ☎ *(0449) 612559*

A full range of bedding plants and geraniums grown in the Nursery which is also part of the garden centre. Brick built showrooms containing garden equipment and a large display of garden furniture. Stockist and supplier of above ground pools. Houseplants; landscaping; advisory service; delivery; gift vouchers.

Open all year daily, 8.30-5.30 (9.30 am Sun & BH).

P *wc*

Studley

Warwickshire   **Map 4 SP06**

MIKE DAVIES NURSERIES

Mappleborough Green ☎ *(052785) 3288*

An interesting range of plants for every corner of the garden. Established pool and rockery, new borders of interesting and unusual plants can be seen in demonstration beds. Specialises in conifers and unusual plants. Full range of garden sundries, tools etc. Houseplants; landscaping; advisory service; delivery; gift vouchers; discounts.

Open all year daily (ex Xmas & Boxing Day) 10-6.

P ⚲ *wc*

PEETS GARDEN CENTRE
Birmingham Rd, Mappleborough Green
☎ *(052785) 2631*

A wide choice of plants is available here. Specialises in heathers, shrubs, conifers and trees. Plants are grouped together for special effect; low-growing, shade-loving etc. New and unusual varieties of shrubs and conifers are always being added. Houseplants, silk and dried flowers are also sold. Demonstration gardens showing rockery plants. Children's play area; advisory service; delivery; gift vouchers.

Open all year daily 9–6, Sun & BH 10–6; closes at 5 in the winter

P *wc*

Torquay
Devon   **Map 3 SX96**

OTTER NURSERIES LTD
250 Babbacombe Rd ☎ *(0803) 214294*

A small but well-stocked garden centre, with a comprehensive range of plants and shrubs. Some of the shrubs stocked are quite rare. Houseplants; advisory service; delivery; gift vouchers.

Open all year daily Mon–Fri 9–8 Sat 9–5.30, Sun 10–5.

P

Tunbridge Wells
Kent   **Map 5 TQ53**

COBLANDS GARDENS
Eridge Rd ☎ *(0892) 26326*

A large, comprehensive range of shrubs, trees, rhododendrons, roses, fruit, aquatic and alpine plants. Specialists in shrubs, rhododendrons and trees. They offer a full range of garden sundries, furniture etc. Landscaping service; delivery; gift vouchers; discounts.

Open all year daily 8.30–6 (10–4.30 Sun & BH).

P *wc*

Twickenham
Middlesex   **Map 4 TQ17**

SQUIRE'S GARDEN CENTRE
Sixth Cross Rd ☎ *01-977 9241*

A large garden centre with an extremely wide range of trees, shrubs and bedding plants on sale, including a good range of unusual plants and larger specimens. Rock garden plants and general shrubs can be seen in demonstration beds. Specialists in a number of plants including roses, conifers, perennials and unusual conservatory plants. House plants, floristry, general garden sundries, stone paving, fencing. Displays of conservatories, sheds, greenhouses and garages, as well as garden furniture. Health food shop, pets and aquatic section. Calendar of events: The Thames Valley Fuchsia and Pelargonium Society hold their shows here during the summer months and the Hampton Hill Floral Art Club give lectures and demonstrations throughout the year. Landscaping service; advisory service; delivery; gift vouchers.

Open all year daily, 9–6 summer, 8.30–5.30 winter.

P 🏠 *wc*

Ware
Hertfordshire   Map 5 TL31
VAN HAGE'S GARDEN CENTRE
Amwell Hill, Great Amwell ☎ (0920) 870811

This huge garden centre has a very wide selection of indoor and outdoor plants including bulbs. The recently constructed demonstration gardens include a town garden, oriental garden, patio garden, kitchen garden, suburban garden and urban garden. Recent winner of best garden centre in North Thames area for houseplants. Large ranges of garden hardware including fencing, paving, pots, pools, composts, etc. and garden sundries. Also mini farm attraction. Customer information points; mail order (seeds only); delivery; gift vouchers; discounts.

Open all year daily winter, 9–5.30, summer 9–6. Open until 8 on Thur & Fri for most of Apr–Jul.

P ⊡ & *(wc) wc*

Warrington
Cheshire   Map 7 SJ68
CANTILEVER GARDEN CENTRE
Station Rd, Latchford ☎ (0925) 35799

A full range of container-grown shrubs, conifers, trees, heathers, rockery plants and border plants are available. Also many seasonal bedding plants for tubs, hanging baskets and gardens, foliage and flowering houseplants. Banbury Buildings showcentre. Advisory service; delivery; gift vouchers.

Open all year daily, winter 9–5 (10–5 Sun), summer 9–6 (10–6 Sun)

P ⊡ *wc*

West Monkton
Somerset   Map 3 ST22
MONKTON ELM GARDEN CENTRE
AND NURSERIES
3½m from Taunton at junction of A38 and A361 ☎ (0823) 412381

A full range of plants, trees and shrubs is stocked, with most being container-grown. Houseplants, garden sundries, garden pools and water garden accessories, garden ornaments, paving and sheds are also sold. Demonstration gardens under construction. Advisory service; delivery; gift vouchers; discounts.

Open all year daily 9.30–5.30.

P ⊡ & *(special parking area) wc*

Weston
Lincolnshire   Map 8 TF22
BAYTREE NURSERIES GARDEN
CENTRE
High Road ☎ Holbeach (0406) 370242

These nurseries sell pot plants, bedding plants, and everything for the garden. There is a 2½-acre display garden which is planted with approximately ½ million bulbs for spring, followed by bedding plants in the summer. Also children's play area and pet corner. Houseplants; landscaping; advisory service; delivery: gift vouchers.

Open all year daily, summer 9–6, winter 9–5.

P ⊡ & *(wc) wc*

165

Wickford

Essex Map 5 TQ79

ALTON GARDEN CENTRE
Arterial Rd ☎ Basildon (0268) 726421

This garden centre is known particularly for its garden furniture and machinery. There is 25,000 sq ft of undercover sales area and a large display of conservatories and greenhouses. Another attraction is the large landscaped water garden section. Houseplants; landscaping; advisory service; delivery; gift vouchers; discounts.

Open all year daily 9–6.

P *wc*

Widnes

Cheshire Map 7 SJ58

PILKINGTON GARDEN CENTRE
Bold Heath (on A57) ☎ 051-424 6264

This large garden centre has a very wide range of plants including, herbaceous perennials, fruit trees and bushes, rhododendrons, azaleas, herbs, climbing and wall plants, and roses. Also conifers and a large selection of houseplants. Plants are displayed in raised beds, and both beds and plants are well labelled. There are demonstration gardens for alpines, heathers, shrubs and trees, bedding plants and bulbs, and regular demonstrations are held. The centre specialises in plants for difficult positions and for special purposes. Garden buildings, camping, fish, and floristry departments. Landscaping; advisory service; delivery; gift vouchers; discounts.

Open all year daily, spring and summer Thu 9–8, Sun & BH 10–6, other days 9–6; autumn and winter Mon–Sat 9–5, Sun & BH 10–5.

P ☐ *wc*

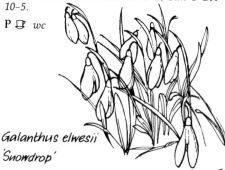

Galanthus elwesii
'Snowdrop'

Willington

Bedfordshire Map 4 TL15

WILLINGTON GARDEN CENTRE
Sandy Road ☎ Cardington (02303) 777

This large garden centre is set in 14 acres of Bedfordshire countryside. It offers a comprehensive range of indoor and outdoor plants and there are extensive display gardens with labelled specimen plants. Also camping centre, children's play area and picnic area, and grapefruit tree featured in *Guiness Book of Records*. Landscaping service; advisory service; delivery; gift vouchers; discounts.

Open all year daily Mon–Sat 9–5.30, Sun & BH 10–5.30.

P ☐ *wc*

Wilmslow

Cheshire Map 7 SJ88

THE WILMSLOW GARDEN CENTRE
Manchester Road ☎ (0625) 525700

Shrubs, pot plants and house plants, bedding plants, trees, bulbs, alpines, fencing and garden furniture are amongst the items on sale here. Also large pet franchise. Landscaping; advisory service; delivery; discounts.

Open all year daily (ex 25 & 26 Dec and New Year) 9–5.

P ☐ *wc*

Winchester

Hampshire Map 4 SU42

HILLIER GARDEN CENTRE
Romsey Road ☎ (0962) 67471

This well-stocked nursery sells trees, shrubs, heathers, alpines, fuchsias, bulbs and houseplants, as well as a selection of garden furniture and machinery, ponds, paving, terracotta, stoneware and other garden sundries. Seeds are also available. Many of the trees and shrubs available can be seen at the nearby arboretum (see under Ampfield in gardens section). Landscaping; advisory service; mail order; delivery; gift vouchers.

Open all year daily (ex 25 & 26 Dec), Mon–Fri 9–5, Sat & Sun 10–5.30.

P *wc*

Windlesham

Surrey   **Map 4 SU96**

L R RUSSELL NURSERY GARDEN CENTRE
London Road ☏ *Ascot (0990) 21411*

This old-established nursery and garden centre stocks a wide range of hardy plants including azaleas, rhododendrons, camellias, hydrangeas and roses. House plants are also available, as are fertilizers, garden equipment, mowers, greenhouses and garden furniture. Demonstration mixed shrub and tree borders show plant associations. The garden centre also has one of the largest ranges of Italian statuary and garden ornaments in the country. Landscaping; advisory service; delivery; gift vouchers.

Open all year daily, Mon–Sat 8.30–5.30, Sun & BH 10–5.

P ⏚ wc

Woburn Sands

Buckinghamshire   **Map 4 SP93**

FROSTS GARDEN CENTRE
☏ *Milton Keynes (0908) 583511*

A wide range of plants for both indoors and the garden is available, and the emphasis is on shrubs and houseplants from the garden centre's own nursery. Demonstration planted areas. Garden furniture. Substantial covered sales area. Landscaping; advisory service; delivery; gift vouchers.

Open all year daily, Mon–Sat 9–5, Sun 10–5.

P ⏚ wc

Woking

Surrey   **Map 4 TQ05**

JACKMANS THE GARDEN CENTRE
Egley Road, Mayford ☏ *(04862) 4861*

As well as a wide variety of garden and houseplants, this garden centre also sells garden sundries, furniture, barbecues, pots, ornaments, pools and water garden accessories. Franchises on-site add sheds, greenhouses, lawnmowers, chainsaws, swimming pools and bottled gas to the range of items that can be bought. There are demonstration gardens with planted beds, a rockery and a pond and also displays of paving, walling and fencing. Advisory service; delivery; gift vouchers.

Open all year daily, Jul–Mar, Mon–Sat & BH 9–5, Sun 10–5; Apr–Jun open until 6pm.

P wc

Woldingham

Surrey   **Map 5 TQ35**

KNIGHTS GARDEN CENTRE
Rosedene Nursery, Woldingham Road ☏ *(088 385) 3142*

This garden centre specialises in aquatic plants, but also has extensive ranges of pot plants, houseplants, shrubs and garden accessories. Demonstration gardens. Advisory service; gift vouchers.

Open all year daily (ex 25 & 26 Dec & 1 Jan), Mon–Sat 8–5.30. Sun 9–5.

P wc

Ivy leafed Pelargonium

Woodbridge

Suffolk   **Map 5 TM24**

NOTCUTTS GARDEN CENTRE

☎ *(03943) 3344*

Over 2,000 varieties of plants listed in the Notcutts catalogue are available at the garden centre which is set in landscaped grounds on a well-established site on the outskirts of the town. Shrubs and hardy nursery stock, roses, azaleas and rhododendrons are particular specialities. Demonstration gardens include climbing and patio gardens. Children's play area; houseplants; landscaping; advisory service; mail order; delivery; gift vouchers.

Open all year daily, Mon–Sat 8.30–5.30 (5.45 in summer), Sun & BH 10–5.

P   *wc*

Woore
Shropshire   Map 7 SJ74
BRIDGEMERE GARDEN WORLD
(2m N off A51)
☎ *Bridgemere (09365) 239 or 381*

This garden centre claims to be one of the largest retailers of outdoor and houseplants in the UK. There are large display gardens. A wide selection of garden care products, garden furniture, greenhouses and garden machinery is also on sale. Landscaping; advisory service; delivery; gift vouchers.

Open all year daily Mon–Sat 9–dusk, Sun 10–dusk (latest closing summer 8,30pm, winter 5pm).

P ⛬ ⅙ *(wc) wc*

Wordsley
West Midlands   Map 7 SO88
WEBBS GARDEN CENTRE
High Street (A491)
☎ *Brierley Hill (0384) 78834*

On the site previously occupied by Webbs Seeds, this medium-sized garden centre specialises in the sale of houseplants, seeds and bulbs, and also carries a large range of shrubs, trees, roses and heathers grown in the nurseries at Wychbold. Landscaping; advisory service; delivery; gift vouchers;

Open all year daily summer weekdays (ex Wed) 9–5.45, Sun BH 10–5; winter weekdays (ex Wed) 9–5, Sun 10–5; Wed throughout year open from 9.30.

P ⛬ *wc*

Wychbold
Hereford and Worcester   Map 7 SO96
WEBBS GARDEN CENTRE
Adjacent to A38 between Droitwich and Bromsgrove ☎ *(052786) 245*

This 30-acre site, formerly the trial grounds for Webbs Seeds, now grows over half a million plants from azaleas to yuccas. A large selection of houseplants, trees, shrubs, roses, conifers, seeds, bulbs, garden furniture and sundries are available. Covered walkways for wet-weather browsing. Midland Area winners of 1986 International Garden Centre Houseplant competition. Other attractions include camping and garden building retailers, children's play area, pick-your-own fruit and national forsythia collection. Landscaping; advisory service; delivery; gift vouchers.

Open all year daily summer week days (ex Wed) 9–5.45, Sun & BH 10–5.45; winter weekdays (ex Wed) 9–5, Sun 10–5, Wed throughout year open from 9.30.

P ⛬ ⅙ *(wc) wc*

Yarnton
Oxfordshire   Map 4 SP41
YARNTON NURSERIES GARDEN CENTRE
Sandy Lane ☎ *Kidlington (08675) 2124*

This large garden centre sells a wide selection of house and pot plants, shrubs, bedding plants, geraniums, etc. Garden accessories are also sold and include furniture, barbecues, books, composts, fertilisers and peat. Landscaping; advisory service; delivery; gift vouchers.

Open all year daily 9–5.30.

P ⛬ *wc*

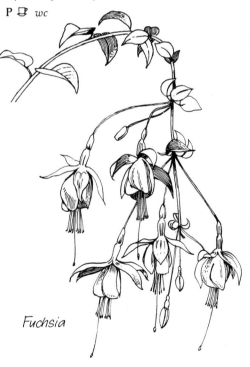

Fuchsia

INDEX

† Indicates that the establishment is a garden centre

Index

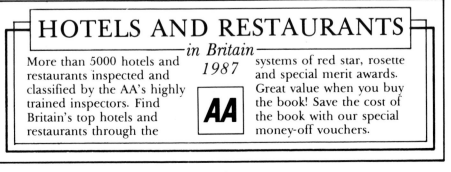

Index

The National Grid

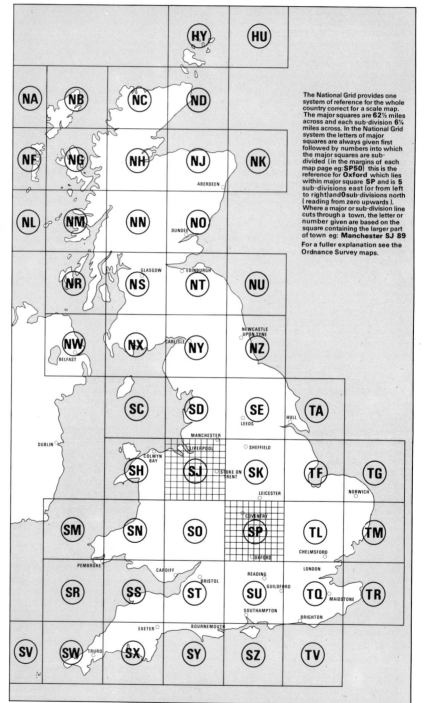

The National Grid provides one system of reference for the whole country correct for a scale map. The major squares are 62½ miles across and each sub-division 6¼ miles across. In the National Grid system the letters of major squares are always given first followed by numbers into which the major squares are sub-divided (in the margins of each map page eg: **SP50**) this is the reference for **Oxford** which lies within major square **SP** and is 5 sub-divisions east (or from left to right) and 0 sub-divisions north (reading from zero upwards). Where a major or sub-division line cuts through a town, the letter or number given are based on the square containing the larger part of town eg: **Manchester SJ 89**

For a fuller explanation see the Ordnance Survey maps.

Key to Atlas

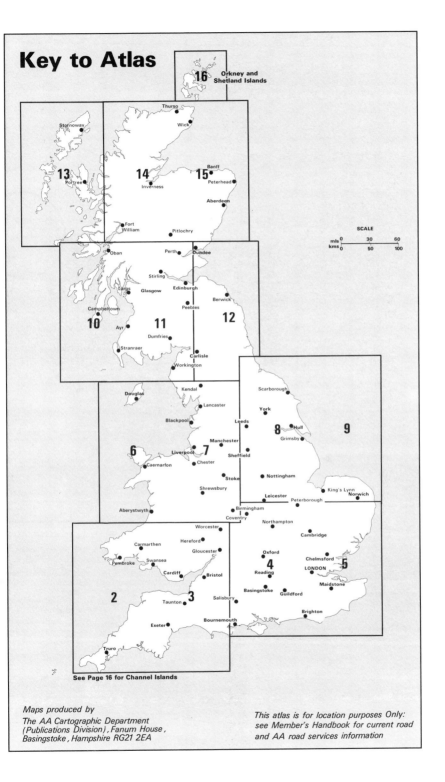

16 Orkney and Shetland Islands

Thurso

Stornoway

Wick

Banff

13 Portree **14** Inverness **15** Peterhead

Aberdeen

SCALE

mls 0   30   60
kms 0   50   100

Fort William

Pitlochry

Oban   Perth   Dundee

Stirling

Largs   Glasgow   Edinburgh

Campbeltown   Berwick

Peebles

10   **11**   **12**

Ayr

Dumfries

Stranraer

Carlisle

Workington

Douglas   Kendal   Scarborough

Lancaster   York

Blackpool   Leeds

Manchester   **8** Hull   **9**

Grimsby

6   Liverpool   **7**   Sheffield

Caernarfon   Chester

Stoke   Nottingham

Shrewsbury

Leicester   King's Lynn   Norwich

Peterborough

Aberystwyth   Birmingham

Coventry

Worcester   Northampton   Cambridge

Hereford

Carmarthen   Gloucester   Oxford   Chelmsford   **5**

Pembroke   Swansea   LONDON

Cardiff   Bristol   Reading   Basingstoke   Guildford   Maidstone

2   **3**   Salisbury

Taunton   Brighton

Exeter   Bournemouth

Truro

See Page 16 for Channel Islands

Maps produced by
The AA Cartographic Department
(Publications Division), Fanum House,
Basingstoke, Hampshire RG21 2EA

This atlas is for location purposes Only:
see Member's Handbook for current road
and AA road services information

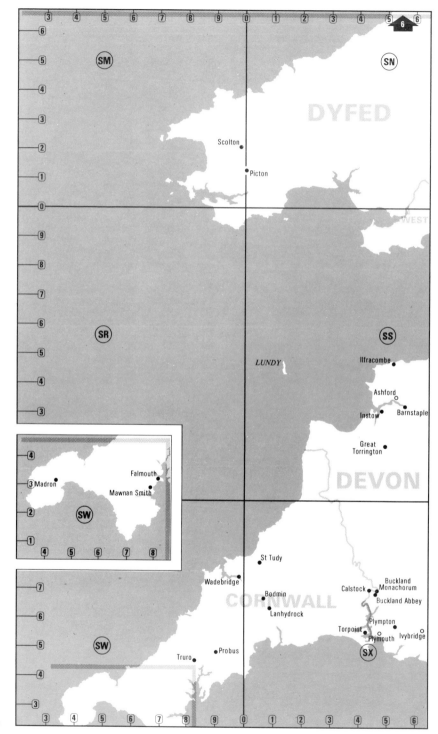

SM   SN

DYFED

Scolton

Picton

WEST

SR   SS

LUNDY   Ilfracombe

Ashford

Instow   Barnstaple

Great
Torrington

DEVON

Falmouth

Madron   Mawnan Smith

SW

St Tudy

Wadebridge

Buckland
Monachorum

Calstock

Buckland Abbey

Bodmin

CORNWALL

Lanhydrock

Plympton

Torpoint

Plymouth   Ivybridge

SW

Truro   Probus

SX

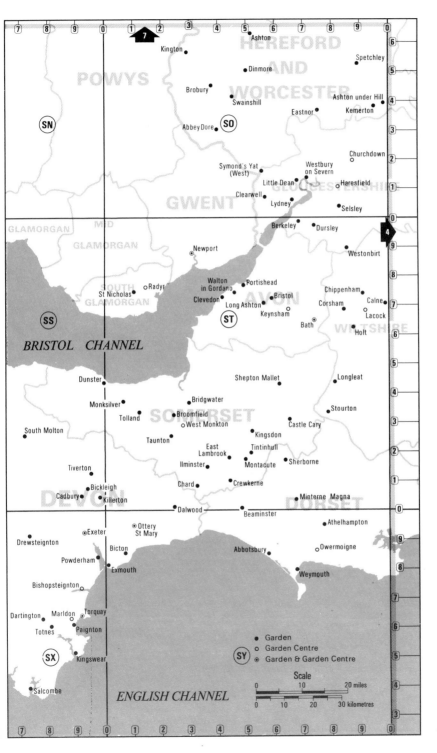

Map legend:
- ● Garden
- ○ Garden Centre
- ◉ Garden & Garden Centre

Scale
0 — 10 — 20 miles
0 — 10 — 20 — 30 kilometres

BRISTOL CHANNEL

ENGLISH CHANNEL

Places shown on the map:

Ashton, Kington, HEREFORD, Spetchley, Dinmore, AND, POWYS, Brobury, WORCESTER, Ashton under Hill, Swainshill, Eastnor, Kemerton, SN, AbbeyDore, SO, Churchdown, Symond's Yat (West), Westbury on Severn, Little Dean, Haresfield, Clearwell, GLOUCESTERSHIRE, Lydney, Selsley, GWENT, Berkeley, Dursley, GLAMORGAN, MID, Newport, Westonbirt, GLAMORGAN, SS, Walton in Gordano, Portishead, Chippenham, Radyr, SOUTH, St Nicholas, Clevedon, Bristol, Corsham, Calne, GLAMORGAN, AVON, Long Ashton, Keynsham, Lacock, Bath, WILTSHIRE, Holt, Dunster, Shepton Mallet, Longleat, Monksilver, Bridgwater, Stourton, Tolland, Broomfield, SOMERSET, West Monkton, Castle Cary, South Molton, Taunton, Kingsdon, East Lambrook, Tintinhull, Ilminster, Montacute, Sherborne, Tiverton, Chard, Crewkerne, Cadbury, Bickleigh, Killerton, Minterne Magna, DEVON, Dalwood, Beaminster, DORSET, Athelhampton, Ottery St Mary, Exeter, Drewsteignton, Bicton, Abbotsbury, Owermoigne, Powderham, Exmouth, Weymouth, Bishopsteignton, Dartington, Marldon, Torquay, Totnes, Paignton, SX, Kingswear, SY, Salcombe

3

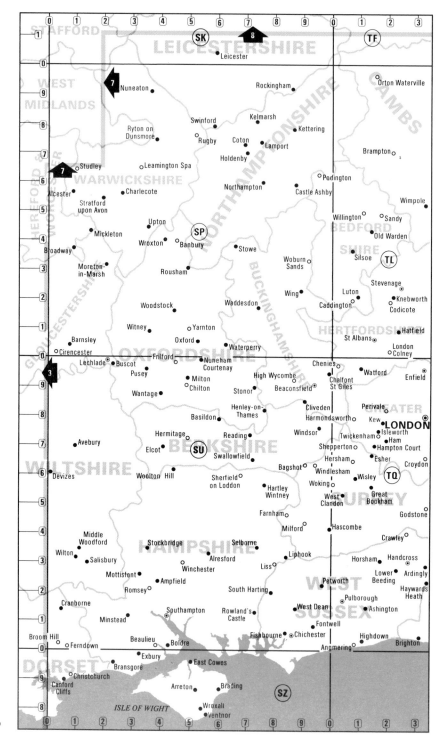

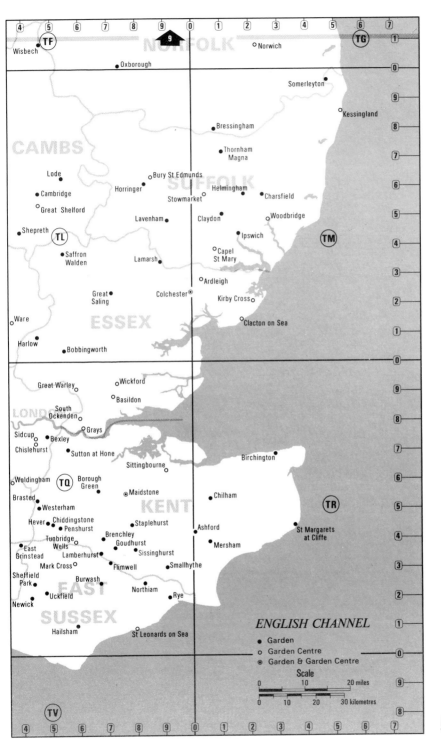

NORFOLK
SUFFOLK
CAMBS
ESSEX
LONDON
KENT
EAST SUSSEX

ENGLISH CHANNEL

- Garden
- Garden Centre
- Garden & Garden Centre

Scale

0   10   20 miles

0   10   20   30 kilometres

TF · TG · TL · TM · TQ · TR · TV

Wisbech
Oxborough
Norwich
Somerleyton
Kessingland
Bressingham
Thornham Magna
Lode
Bury St Edmunds
Horringer
Helmingham
Charsfield
Stowmarket
Cambridge
Great Shelford
Lavenham
Claydon
Woodbridge
Shepreth
Ipswich
Saffron Walden
Lamarsh
Capel St Mary
Ardleigh
Great Saling
Colchester
Kirby Cross
Ware
Clacton on Sea
Harlow
Bobbingworth
Great Warley
Wickford
Basildon
South Ockenden
Grays
Sidcup
Bexley
Chislehurst
Sutton at Hone
Sittingbourne
Birchington
Woldingham
Borough Green
Maidstone
Chilham
Brasted
Westerham
Hever
Chiddingstone
Penshurst
Staplehurst
Ashford
St Margarets at Cliffe
Tunbridge Wells
Brenchley
Goudhurst
Mersham
East Grinstead
Lamberhurst
Sissinghurst
Mark Cross
Flimwell
Smallhythe
Sheffield Park
Burwash
Northiam
Rye
Newick
Uckfield
Hailsham
St Leonards on Sea

5

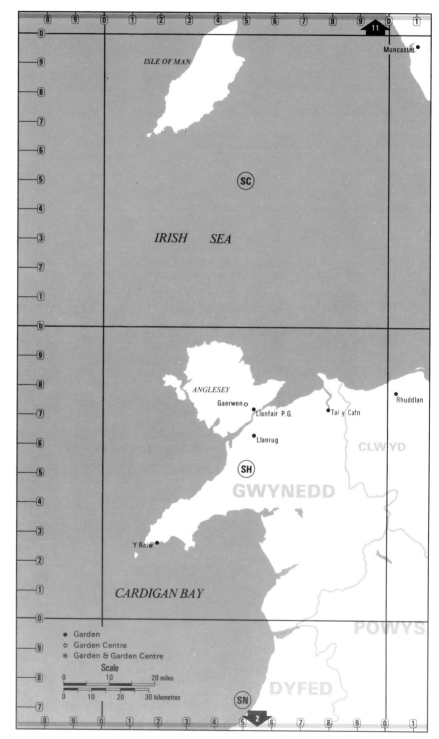

ISLE OF MAN

Muncaster •

SC

IRISH   SEA

ANGLESEY

Gaerwen ○

•Llanfair P.G.

Rhuddlan •

•Tai y Cafn

•Llanrug

CLWYD

SH

GWYNEDD

Y Rhiw •

CARDIGAN BAY

POWYS

● Garden
○ Garden Centre
◉ Garden & Garden Centre

Scale

0   10   20 miles

0   10   20   30 kilometres

DYFED

SN

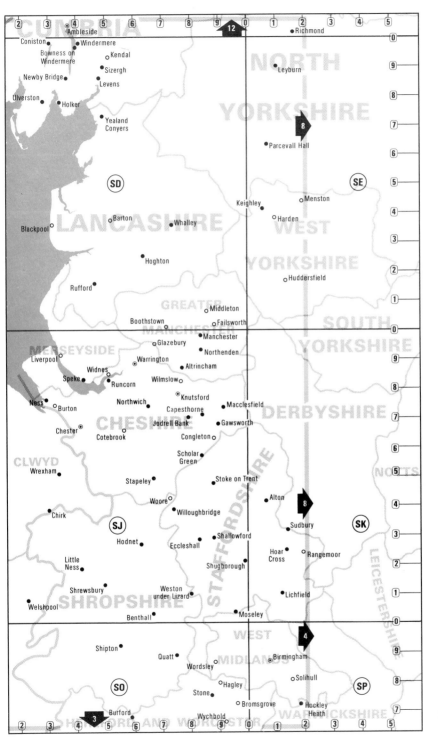

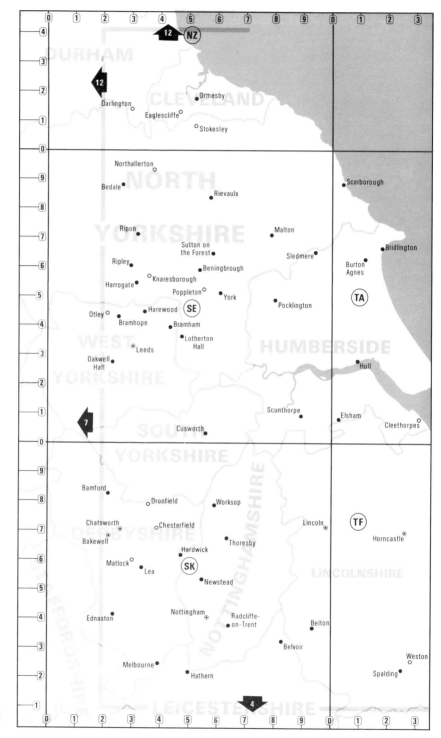

Map grid coordinates (top): 0 1 2 3 4 5 6 7 8 9 0 1 2 3

12 NZ

DURHAM

12

CLEVELAND

Ormesby
Darlington
Eaglescliffe
Stokesley

Northallerton
NORTH
Bedale
Rievaulx
Scarborough

YORKSHIRE
Ripon
Malton
Sutton on
the Forest
Sledmere
Bridlington
Ripley
Beningbrough
Burton
Agnes
Knaresborough
Harrogate
Poppleton
York
TA
Otley
Harewood
SE
Pocklington
Bramhope
Bramham
WEST
Lotherton
Hall
Leeds
HUMBERSIDE
Oakwell
Hall
Hull
YORKSHIRE

7
Scunthorpe
Elsham
Cusworth
Cleethorpes
SOUTH

YORKSHIRE

Bamford
Dronfield
Worksop
NOTTINGHAMSHIRE
Lincoln
TF
Chatsworth
Chesterfield
DERBYSHIRE
Horncastle
Bakewell
Thoresby
Hardwick
LINCOLNSHIRE
Matlock
SK
Lea
Newstead

Ednaston
Nottingham
Radcliffe-
on-Trent
Belton
STAFFORDSHIRE
Belvoir
Weston
Melbourne
Spalding
Hathern

4
LEICESTERSHIRE

Map grid coordinates (bottom): 0 1 2 3 4 5 6 7 8 9 0 1 2 3

8

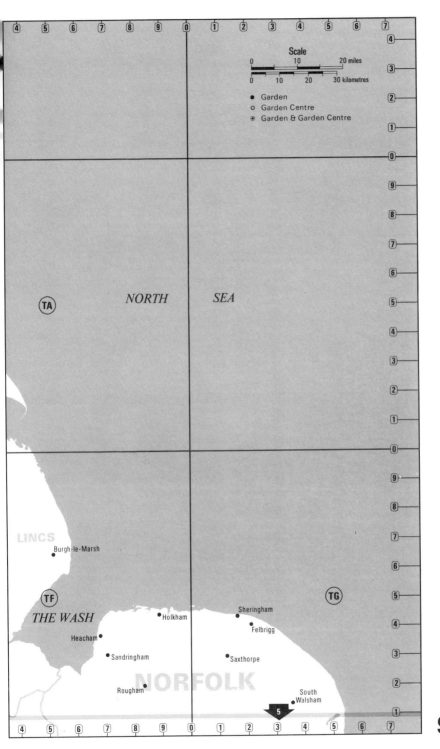

Scale

| 0 | 10 | 20 miles |

| 0 | 10 | 20 | 30 kilometres |

- ● Garden
- ○ Garden Centre
- ◉ Garden & Garden Centre

NORTH   SEA

TA

LINCS

● Burgh-le-Marsh

TF

TG

THE WASH

● Holkham

● Sheringham
● Felbrigg

● Heacham

● Sandringham

● Saxthorpe

NORFOLK

● Rougham

South
● Walsham

5

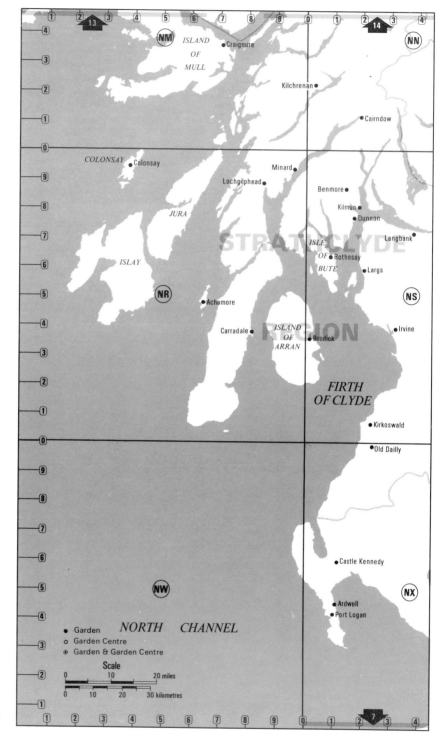

NORTH CHANNEL

- ● Garden
- ○ Garden Centre
- ◉ Garden & Garden Centre

Scale

0   10   20 miles

0   10   20   30 kilometres

10

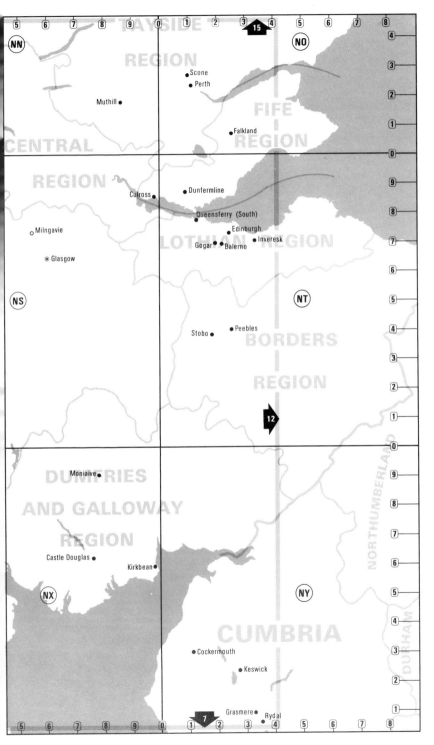

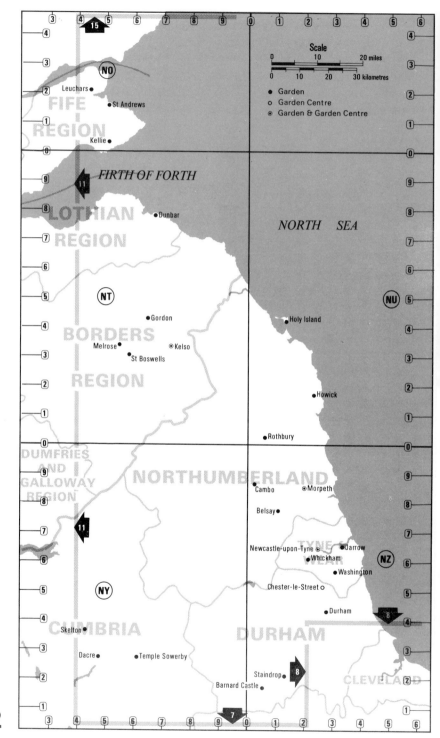

Scale

| 0 | 10 | | 20 miles |
| 0 | 10 | 20 | 30 kilometres |

● Garden
○ Garden Centre
◉ Garden & Garden Centre

FIFE REGION

NO

Leuchars ●
St Andrews ●
Kellie ●

FIRTH OF FORTH

11

LOTHIAN REGION

Dunbar ●

NORTH SEA

NT

Gordon ●

BORDERS REGION

Melrose ●
St Boswells ●
◉ Kelso

NU

Holy Island ●

Howick ●

Rothbury ●

DUMFRIES AND GALLOWAY REGION

NORTHUMBERLAND

Cambo ●
Belsay ●
◉ Morpeth

11

Newcastle-upon-Tyne ◉
Whickham ●
● Jarrow

NZ

Washington ●

Chester-le-Street ○

NY

Durham ●

CUMBRIA

Skelton ●
Dacre ●
Temple Sowerby ●

DURHAM

Staindrop ●
Barnard Castle ●

8

CLEVELAND

7

15

12

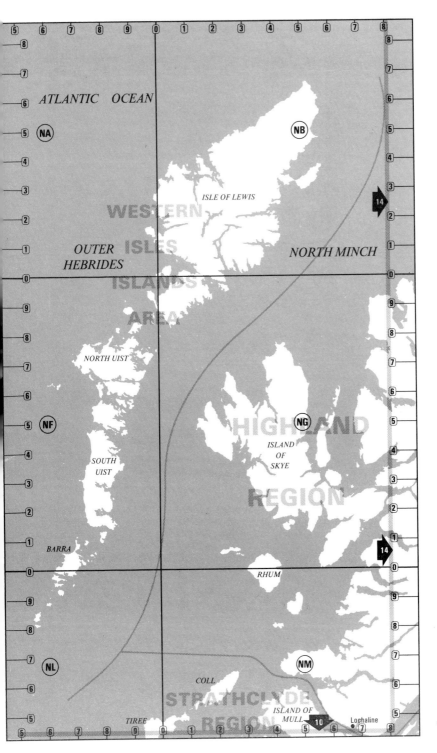

ATLANTIC OCEAN

NA

NB

ISLE OF LEWIS

WESTERN

OUTER ISLES

HEBRIDES

ISLANDS

AREA

NORTH MINCH

14

NORTH UIST

NF

HIGHLAND

NG

ISLAND
OF
SKYE

REGION

SOUTH
UIST

BARRA

14

RHUM

NL

STRATHCLYDE

NM

COLL

REGION

TIREE

ISLAND OF
MULL

10

Lochaline

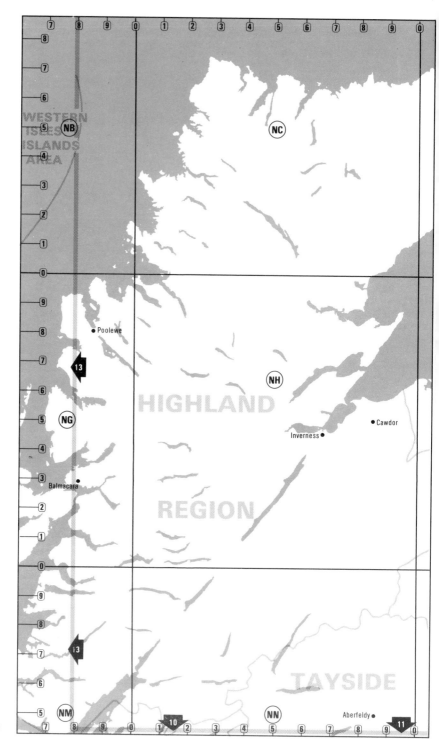

14

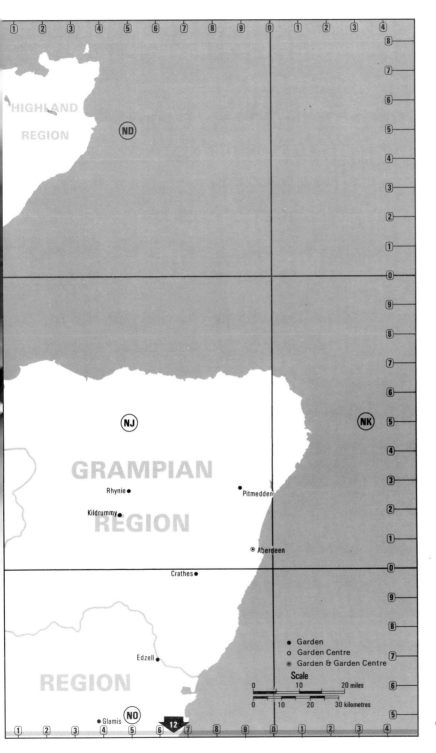

HIGHLAND
REGION

ND

NJ

NK

GRAMPIAN

Rhynie●

●Pitmedden

Kildrummy●
REGION

⊛ Aberdeen

Crathes●

REGION

Edzell●

● Garden
○ Garden Centre
⊛ Garden & Garden Centre

Scale

0   10   20 miles

0   10   20   30 kilometres

●Glamis **NO**

12

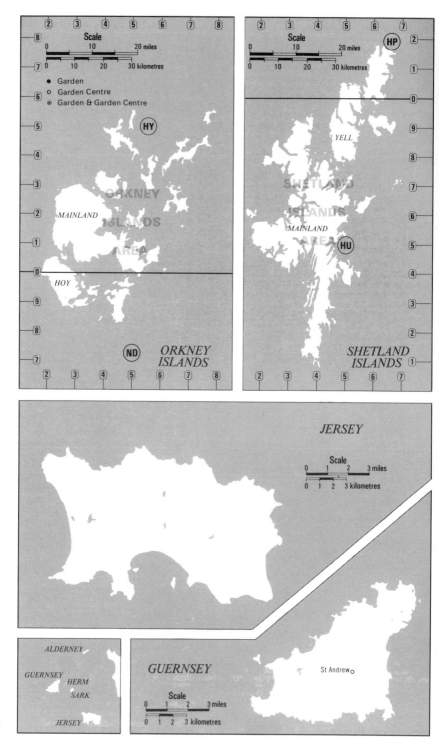

Scale
0   10   20 miles
0   10   20   30 kilometres

● Garden
○ Garden Centre
◉ Garden & Garden Centre

HY

ORKNEY
ISLANDS
AREA

MAINLAND

HOY

ND   *ORKNEY
      ISLANDS*

Scale
0   10   20 miles
0   10   20   30 kilometres

HP

YELL

SHETLAND
ISLANDS
AREA

MAINLAND

HU

*SHETLAND
ISLANDS*

JERSEY

Scale
0   1   2   3 miles
0   1   2   3 kilometres

ALDERNEY

GUERNSEY

HERM

SARK

JERSEY

GUERNSEY

St Andrew○

Scale
0   1   2   3 miles
0   1   2   3 kilometres

16